RECOGNITION AND AMBIVALENCE

NEW DIRECTIONS IN CRITICAL THEORY

NEW DIRECTIONS IN CRITICAL THEORY

AMY ALLEN, GENERAL EDITOR

New Directions in Critical Theory presents outstanding classic and contemporary texts in the tradition of critical social theory, broadly construed. The series aims to renew and advance the program of critical social theory, with a particular focus on theorizing contemporary struggles around gender, race, sexuality, class, and globalization and their complex interconnections.

For a complete list of titles, see page 339

RECOGNITION AND AMBIVALENCE

JUDITH BUTLER,
AXEL HONNETH,
AMY ALLEN,
ROBIN CELIKATES,
JEAN-PHILIPPE DERANTY,
HEIKKI IKÄHEIMO,
KRISTINA LEPOLD,
LOIS McNAY,
DAVID OWEN,
TITUS STAHL

EDITED BY
**HEIKKI IKÄHEIMO,
KRISTINA LEPOLD, AND
TITUS STAHL**

Columbia University Press *New York*

Columbia University Press
Publishers Since 1893
New York Chichester, West Sussex
cup.columbia.edu

Library of Congress Cataloging-in-Publication Data
Names: Ikäheimo, Heikki, editor. | Lepold, Kristina, editor. | Stahl, Titus, 1979– editor.
Title: Recognition and ambivalence / edited by Heikki Ikäheimo, Kristina Lepold, and Titus Stahl.
Description: New York : Columbia University Press, 2021. | Series: New directions in critical theory | Includes bibliographical references and index.
Identifiers: LCCN 2020046693 (print) | LCCN 2020046694 (ebook) | ISBN 9780231177603 (hardback) | ISBN 9780231177610 (trade paperback) | ISBN 9780231544214 (ebook)
Subjects: LCSH: Recognition (Philosophy) | Honneth, Axel, 1949– | Butler, Judith, 1956–
Classification: LCC B105.R23 R39 2021 (print) | LCC B105.R23 (ebook) | DDC 128/.3—dc23
LC record available at https://lccn.loc.gov/2020046693
LC ebook record available at https://lccn.loc.gov/2020046694

Cover design: Chang Jae Lee

CONTENTS

RECOGNITION AND AMBIVALENCE

INTRODUCTION

HEIKKI IKÄHEIMO, KRISTINA LEPOLD,
AND TITUS STAHL

Few concepts in contemporary social and political thought have attracted as widespread an interest as the concept of recognition. Much of its appeal seems to stem from the fact that it builds on an experience with which virtually everyone is familiar, namely the experience of depending on others in one's relation to oneself, for better or for worse. This experience takes many forms. Being ignored by a friend at a party hurts when we find out that she was aware of our presence all along. Receiving praise from a colleague for work we invested time and effort in makes us feel proud and happy. Being subjected to extended background checks at an airport makes us question how welcome we are in the country in question. Examples such as these illustrate that others are involved in shaping our lives and self-perceptions through the way they see and treat us. It is precisely this connection between self and other that the concept of recognition promises to shed light on.

The current interest in recognition—a concept that can be found in the works of a variety of thinkers, but which is, at least in the tradition of European philosophy, most commonly associated with Hegel—is largely thanks to the theoretical interventions of Charles Taylor and Axel Honneth at the beginning of the 1990s.[1] When Taylor coined the phrase "the politics of recognition" in the context of debates on multiculturalism to draw attention to struggles for the recognition or valorization of cultural difference,[2] and when Axel Honneth introduced the idea of the struggle for recognition as a central concept in Frankfurt School critical theory as a tool for making sense of moral motivations for social struggle (a theme he has built on and refined ever since), they struck a nerve.[3] The concept of recognition quickly gained prominence in social and political philosophy, to which an ever-growing body of literature bears witness. Importantly, within these recent discourses, recognition has generally been considered a positive force in people's lives. If others are involved in shaping our lives through the way they see and treat us, recognition designates those forms of this process that are successful. More specifically, recognition in this context is taken to refer to the beliefs, attitudes, and actions of others that *affirm* an individual in an aspect of her self-conception, which is said to allow the individual to realize herself and to live a fulfilling life. When recognition occurs, according to this view, the self and the other are in harmony. The self does not experience friction, alienation, or pain, and is able to see the world that surrounds her as encouraging her to be the person she is or wants to be. Recognition, understood as affirmation, hence contrasts with sets of beliefs, attitudes, and actions of others that *do not affirm* an aspect of an individual's being. As both Taylor and Honneth (as well as those who follow them) highlight, in experiencing this kind of disrespect, the individual finds herself bound to others, often inescapably and to her detriment. In the face of disinterest, neglect, misrecognition, public degradation, or outright hate, she has difficulties relating positively to herself and to her own life goals, and the social world appears as a source of constant frustration and suffering instead of a space of personal expansion. Hence, whereas recognition appears desirable, disrespect signifies trouble. The prevalent framework for thinking about recognition thus relies on a dichotomy between recognition as a relation between self and other that affects individual lives for the better and disrespect as a relation between self and other that affects individual lives for the worse.

While this is in many ways a compelling picture, there are various narratives about recognition in the history of philosophy that are far less sanguine and that portray not only disrespect but recognition itself as a deeply ambivalent phenomenon. This group arguably includes Hegel, who—not only in the more well-known passages of the *Phenomenology* but also in the richer discussion in his Jena lectures—spends far more time on struggles for recognition than on describing an ideal of full and mutual recognition.[4] In the Hegelian story, almost every configuration of recognitive relations may turn out to be unsatisfactory, freedom-undermining, or a vehicle of domination, although Hegel also seems to assume that recognitive relations contain within themselves the resources to motivate participants to struggle for more satisfactory, freer, and equal states of affairs. Nevertheless, recognition is at least ambivalent for Hegel in the sense that the desire for recognition can also lead us into one-sided relationships of dependence.[5] In addition, even if recognition in the fullest sense is clearly a reciprocal relation for Hegel, his account of the social-ontological significance of recognition allows for unequal ascriptions of authority.[6] There is a second, more radical claim regarding recognition's ambivalence that finds its paradigmatic expression in the writings of Jean-Paul Sartre, a claim according to which recognition from others is in itself problematic insofar as it fixes our identity. Recognition, from this perspective, is always *misrecognition* in the sense that it takes away the freedom of those whose autonomy it purports to acknowledge.[7] While this Sartrean argument seems to depend to a large extent on his underlying conception of the freedom of transcendence, which makes it unattractive to many contemporary readers, there have been attempts to reformulate the underlying motif of the freedom-denying character of recognition in the language of other traditions. Most notably, Kelly Oliver and Patchen Markell have questioned the normative desirability of recognition of identities. Both authors attempt to expose what they see as the objectifying character of recognition and the way in which the ideal of recognition stands in the way of other, in their view more just, relations between the self and others, in line with the open-ended and unpredictable character of human social life.[8] Elizabeth Povinelli has explored these very same dynamics with regard to the way in which postcolonial forms of recognition affect Australian indigenous social existence.[9] While the present volume is focused on the debate about recognition that emerged from the post-Hegelian tradition and does not centrally engage with non-European or postcolonial approaches, this critique of recognition provides a natural starting point for engaging with accounts of recognition and its ambivalence.[10] A political claim about the ambivalence of recognition is advanced by a third set of critiques that focus less on the phenomenon of recognition itself than on the language or vocabulary of recognition. According to this critique, understanding social struggles through the language of recognition distorts our perception of what is actually at stake in them. If the agents themselves adopt that language, it can therefore undermine their capacity to defend their interests. While this may seem like a debate that merely concerns the analytic framework offered by recognition theory, it also leads to a substantive argument about the ambivalence of recognition as an empirical phenomenon: if people demand recognition because they mistakenly reformulate their real interests in that language, then others granting them such recognition can reinforce their ideological domination. A critique of recognition-as-analytic category therefore often leads to a critique of recognition-as-social relation. The forms that such critiques take range from the relatively moderate position advanced by scholars such as Nancy Fraser to more radical critiques of recognition such as that offered by Lois McNay. Whereas Fraser mainly wants to resist the use of the category of "recognition" as a monist social-theoretical framework and conceives of recognition as only one aspect of her ideal of participatory parity,[11] McNay argues that the normative ideal of recognition blinds us to the intertwinement of processes of identity formation and larger societal structures of domination.[12] Depending on which version of this critique one accepts, the claim of ambivalence may translate into either a rejection of "recognition" as part of a social theory, or a thoroughgoing skepticism about the extent of the role of the phenomenon of recognition in emancipatory political projects. A fourth claim about the ambivalence of recognition combines, in some sense, many of the strands mentioned thus far. In his famous essay "Ideology and Ideological State Apparatuses,"[13] Louis Althusser placed recognition in a very different context to that of thinking about the conditions for human flourishing, namely the context of the reproduction of the capitalist social order. Althusser surmised that recognition plays a role in the submission of individuals to the dominant order by making them adopt specific roles and shaping their identities. Today's debates contain reverberations of this line of thought, which presents recognition in a much more ambivalent light than optimistic views of its importance to human freedom. Most notably, Judith Butler has accepted parts of Althusser's account, reflecting on what it is in individuals that motivates them to subject themselves to a dominant ideology or system of power.[14] Butler's answer draws on her Kojève-influenced interpretation of Hegel,[15] and consists in the proposal that it is a "desire for recognition" essential to human beings that predetermines individuals' more or less unreflective acceptance of positions within the social order, which subsequently binds them psychologically to their own submission. Among the other questions Butler raises in her work is that of whether recognizing another person is possible without any concomitant destructive tendencies.[16] In other words, she raises doubt about whether harmonious or "pure" recognition is even attainable for beings like us, or whether it is always necessarily accompanied, jeopardized, or thwarted by its negative counterparts. While theorists like Taylor and especially Honneth (whom we may refer to as "optimistic theorists of recognition") often seem to assume that disrespect is something that can be overcome and eventually transformed into stable relations of recognition, Butler worries that it may not be possible to neatly separate recognition and disrespect.

In brief, even though the contemporary philosophical landscape in European and American philosophy is clearly dominated by optimistic accounts of recognition, there are a number of important challenges faced by accounts that picture recognition mainly in positive terms. While there have been attempts to address these challenges,[17] systematic engagement has thus far been lacking. The present volume takes this diagnosis as a point of departure and seeks to systematically think through the potential ambivalence of recognition. Is recognition a positive phenomenon that can function reliably in guiding our normative thinking and practical efforts? Or have the skeptics identified a genuine need to rethink the nature and desirability of recognition?

Optimistic and skeptical accounts seem to disagree about a number of specific questions—questions that any systematic attempt to make progress in clarifying the potential ambivalence of recognition will have to deal with. We will mention only three of these here.

The first question concerns the normative potential of recognition. The "optimistic" tradition is committed to the view that recognition, at least in its reciprocal or full form, constitutes an ideal that can be used to evaluate the given arrangements of ethical life. But what does this mean for dominating or ideological forms of recognition? Are they not, at least prima facie, forms of recognition too? Might it not be risky, then, to use recognition as an ideal insofar as it can blind us to the potential intertwinement of recognition and domination? Or, on an even more pessimistic note, do all forms of recognition in fact lead to constraints on our freedom?

The second question concerns the link between recognition and resistance. Not only denials of recognition but also seemingly positive forms of recognition may give rise to experiences of disrespect and protest, either because they turn out to be insufficient, or because all recognition ultimately poses a limit to human freedom. Both traditions described above acknowledge the inbuilt negativity of recognition. But how exactly should we think about this negativity? Should we take it as an expression of an internal normative demand that is implicit in recognition by definition? Do we have to assume that all forms of recognition equip those who are recognized with the capacities needed to emancipate themselves? Are there also fully ideological forms of recognition that have no liberating potential? Or should we analyze resistance, at least sometimes, as evidence of something which *cannot* be integrated into recognition as a matter of principle?

The third systematic question relates more centrally to the political significance of recognition. Whether one argues from within the "optimist" or the "pessimist" camp, conflicts around recognition will be a central component of our analysis of political struggles. Are struggles against specific forms of recognition futile, or do they have emancipatory potential? To what extent are people's specific claims for recognition *themselves* shaped by politics? Is recognition only one dimension of political emancipation, or are all struggles for liberation also struggles for recognition? How should we understand forms of resistance against either particular forms of recognition, or norms of recognizability in general? Can both of the latter be adequately grasped within the same theoretical framework, or do they call for different approaches?

While the contributions to this volume—in particular those by Robin Celikates and David Owen—consider these questions from the perspective of political theory, and while questions of policy and on-the-ground politics are beyond its scope, it is clear that all three systematic questions have a direct impact on important political debates of our age. While political discourse is often dominated by a rather simplistic confrontation between proponents and opponents of "identity politics" or "multicultural recognition," the analyses offered in this volume make clear not only that there is great diversity in what one might mean by these terms, but also that we can only come to a nuanced and satisfying understanding of related issues once we make clear what normative framework we are employing, and once we acknowledge the ambivalent potential of recognition relations.

The contributions to this volume all take one or several of these three systematic questions as their points of departure, bringing together proponents and critics of theories of recognition to reflect on and clarify the precise problems, stakes, and challenges involved. The goal of the volume as a whole is to explore different routes toward a critical theory that goes beyond a mere affirmation of either the optimistic or the pessimistic view of recognition. In doing so, the contributions shed light on a more general question: How can we rethink recognition, acknowledging its central importance to individual, social, and political life, while at the same time taking seriously the problems and ambivalence it may entail?

THE CONTRIBUTIONS

The volume begins with a debate between Axel Honneth and Judith Butler, the main contemporary proponents of the more optimistic and the more pessimistic perspectives on recognition, respectively. In his opening piece, Honneth argues that there is an ambivalence in Butler's writing between two understandings of recognition: one on which it attributes features to the recognizee while requiring nothing of the recognizer, and another on which recognition requires something of the recognizer, namely the limiting of his "self-love," to use the Kantian expression, or the attribution of moral significance to the recognizee, forcing the recognizer to change his or her attitude toward the recognizee. It is the first understanding of recognition that Honneth identifies as being operative in Butler's early take on recognition as subjugating recognizees into given social roles implied by the attributions. His point, however, is that the full Hegelian concept of recognition is better grasped by the second alternative, and thus that there is more to recognition than Althusserian subjection to social power via the attribution and internalization of features or roles from the repertoire of the given economic, social, and cultural order. Honneth suggests that in her more recent work Butler has been moving toward the latter account, with a Levinasian flavor.

Honneth's opening piece prompts Butler to embark on a fascinating journey through the main elements of her theorizing, and their history. The role of the Hegelian trope of recognition in her work is clarified to a thus far unprecedented extent in her response. One of the points that Butler makes is that her understanding of recognition emphasizes the role of *performativity* in the creation of individual psyches, thus freeing up space for resistance to Althusserian *interpellation* into given social roles. Butler also criticizes the Nietzschean view that all recognition is enslavement, for its ignoring of the necessary mutuality of relations of recognition, and the constitutive interdependence of human beings. According to Butler, this interdependence implies an "ethico-political mandate to live together without destruction." On the whole, Butler's view of recognition turns out to be far from merely pessimistic and better characterized as ambivalent, as it acknowledges both the necessary, constitutive role of recognition in the lives of humans as interdependent, needy beings, and the potential for aggression and destruction in psychic and social life. Toward the end of her piece, Butler challenges Honneth to reflect on the role of "negativity" in his work, proposing that, unlike in her work, "negativity is conceptually separated from recognition" in Honneth's thought. Butler thereby suggests that Honneth's take on recognition may be overly optimistic.

In his second piece, Honneth prompts Butler to further clarify the difference between what he sees as two different conceptualizations of recognition that have not been sufficiently distinguished by Butler: "the institutional ascription of social identities by the public use of identifying categories within social discourses" on the one hand, and "the recognitive granting of a normative authority that requires from the 'recognizer' a limitation of their own space of freedom" on the other. Honneth finds it very important not to run these two phenomena together and proposes that only the latter be called "recognition." Furthermore, he prompts Butler to clarify what he sees as two distinct forms of recognition in the just-specified sense that figure in her work: for Butler, recognition sometimes seems to mean "legal respect," and at other times "love." Honneth is drawing here on the tripartite distinction between forms of recognition—love or care, legal respect, and esteem for contributions—that he reconstructed from the early Hegel and argued for in terms of more contemporary psychological, legal, and social theory in his monograph *The Struggle for Recognition*. Honneth claims that "such distinctions are indispensable for any social analysis" and asks whether Butler agrees, and if not, why.

In her second response, Butler focuses on another distinction that she presents as being crucial to her thought: that between recognition and "recognizability." Deeper than the question of who gets recognized and how, she suggests, is the question of the conditions that determine which particular individuals or groups are "recognizable," or are considered "persons or humans," and thus possible objects of recognition at all. She is referring here to her idea of "frames of recognition" which, in her view, is crucial for thinking about issues of colonial rule, systematic racism, gender inequality, and discrimination of LGBTQ persons—all of which involve normative or discursive orders that have excluded certain groups from recognizability.

The contributions to the second part of the volume add to and deepen the debate launched by Axel Honneth and Judith Butler in the first part by offering different perspectives on the ambivalence of recognition. In her contribution, Lois McNay examines the suitability of Honneth's recognition theory for feminist purposes. Though Honneth's attention to issues of gender inequality and to experiences of injustice more generally connects him with feminist theorists, McNay is skeptical about whether his recognition theory ultimately provides an adequate framework for analyzing gender inequality. Despite what she describes as a recent shift from ontology to history as the foundation of his theory, McNay believes that Honneth is not properly attentive to the ambivalence that still characterizes contemporary recognition relations within families, and to the ways in which families in modern societies are penetrated by larger social and economic forces. According to McNay, this is due to Honneth's reconstruction of the historical development of modern societies as an inevitable progress on the one hand, and to his optimistic normative interpretation of the family more generally on the other.

Amy Allen's contribution deals with the philosophical anthropology that underlies Honneth's recognition theory, and it can be read as picking up a thread from McNay's contribution. While McNay focuses primarily on Honneth's engagement with the history of modern societies, she acknowledges that what she calls ontology is still relevant to his project. This intuition is shared by Allen, who critically engages with Honneth's conception of love as the first and most basic form of recognition, one that she sees as playing a crucial role in Honneth's theory. Allen argues that Honneth's optimistic picture of the parent–infant relationship provides the anthropological basis for his normative conception of recognition, his explanation of struggles for recognition, and even his normative assessment of diverse struggles for recognition. Drawing on Honneth's treatment of same-sex marriage, Allen highlights the problematic consequences of the philosophical anthropology that informs his theory of recognition, and stands alongside Judith Butler in arguing for a more ambivalent conception of recognition.

Kristina Lepold turns to Louis Althusser and Judith Butler, and engages with and finds wanting two prominent interpretations of the link between recognition and subjection in the works of the two thinkers. According to Lepold, it is not the case that—as the first interpretation has it—Althusser and Butler view recognition from others as ontologically constitutive of subjects, and therefore as a form of subjection that harms individuals in their autonomy. Nor is the main point made by Althusser and Butler that recognition can function as a means of subjecting certain individuals to others, as the second interpretation has it. Through a detailed critique of these two interpretations, Lepold develops an alternative interpretation of the link between recognition and subjection in the works of Althusser and Butler, one according to which recognition can make individuals *subject themselves* to norms that belong to problematic social arrangements, therefore making recognition ambivalent.

In his contribution, Titus Stahl contrasts the Hegelian claim that recognition is a precondition of freedom with several ambivalence claims. He argues that the ambivalence of recognition has often been misunderstood as merely referring to the idea that, by making us dependent on normative frameworks controlled by others, recognition actually undermines our freedom. Stahl argues not only that the Hegelian tradition has a response to this objection with its model of immanent critique, but also that actual defenders of the ambivalence claim, such as Althusser and Butler, embrace a more complex version of it according to which recognitive relations can keep us from criticizing their very structure. Stahl argues that, faced with this radical ambivalence claim, defenders of the Hegelian tradition such as Honneth must go beyond the resources of that tradition to safeguard the possibility of emancipation.

The contributions to the third part of the volume extend the debate by thinking about the future of the recognition paradigm in light of the ambivalence of recognition. In his contribution, Heikki Ikäheimo returns to the theme of reification that Honneth elaborated on in his book *Reification*, but which he seems to have subsequently given up. Ikäheimo suggests that Honneth's original model can be improved on by introducing further differentiations and conceptual innovations, thereby developing a usefully differentiated and gradational model of reification as dehumanization or "depersonification." Ikäheimo thereby approaches the question raised by Butler (in her second response to Honneth) about who gets to count as human, or as a person, but from another perspective: not as a separate question of recognizability, but as internal to recognition itself. Ikäheimo also returns to a topic that Butler raised in her response to Honneth's *Reification*: the question of what it means to "take over" the perspective of the other. He suggests that such taking is central to what he calls "purely intersubjective" horizontal recognition, and further distinguishes between two different modes of it: the conditional and the unconditional. Conditional forms of purely intersubjective recognition turn out to be paradigmatic cases of what, in pretheoretical thinking, counts as dehumanizing or depersonifying reification. This suggests that there is a distinct ambivalence within the concept of recognition itself.

Jean-Philippe Deranty's contribution engages more generally with negativity, in recognition, and beyond. Taking the oft-stated criticism that the recognition paradigm downplays the role of negative phenomena as a starting point, Deranty engages in an insightful discussion of how negativity has been conceived of in relation to recognition by different approaches.

Distinguishing between negativity concerning the subject of recognition, social relations of recognition, and recognitional politics, Deranty is able to show that recognition-theoretic approaches—not only in the tradition of French structuralism and poststructuralism but also in post-Habermasian critical theory—assign negativity a crucial role with regard to all three domains. Many lessons can be learned from comparing these approaches, the most interesting of which, according to Deranty, is the fact that these approaches are still limited insofar as they do not see or fully acknowledge the fact that negativity, in the context of recognition, is often inextricably bound up with negativity in the context of the self and the material world. To account for the latter, Deranty advocates what he calls a "generalized object-relations model" on which recognition is only one of the forms that object relations can take.

While Deranty ultimately pushes for an account that is able to address individuals' being in the world in its entirety, Robin Celikates doubts that the development of such foundations will be crucial to the future of the recognition paradigm. In his contribution, Celikates focuses in particular on the prominent idea of a need for recognition, which he believes to be intuitively appealing. Celikates argues that the main problem with the idea that one can ground recognition theory in an account of needs is the difficulty of positively determining how much recognition is needed for the development and maintenance of individual agency. This is itself a matter of political struggle. Furthermore, the assumption of needs as fixed has often had conservative political consequences. While we cannot avoid inscribing a conception of the "power to determine needs" within political institutions, this institutionalization will always again become the object of political resistance by those excluded from such power. In light of difficulties such as these,

Celikates argues that recognition theorists should embrace a negativist and proceduralist approach that focuses on experiences of misrecognition, on struggles over the interpretation of needs, and over who has a say in these struggles. In the context of a negativist and proceduralist approach of this sort, one kind of recognition will turn out to be of special importance, namely recognition as a legitimate party to a struggle.

In the final contribution to this volume, David Owen extends the line of thinking introduced by Robin Celikates. Owen focuses on the work of Jacques Rancière and James Tully, both of whom can be read as proponents of an "agonistic" approach to recognition. The key characteristic of this agonistic approach is that it seeks to enable agents to engage in struggles over recognition, that is, struggles over the norms that currently govern exchanges of recognition, by redescribing social and political practices. Since Tully's work is oriented toward freedom, whereas Rancière's work puts equality first, the interesting question of whether and how these two approaches can be reconciled arises. Owen suggests that the exercise of civic freedom as envisioned by Tully with regard to recognitional orders is just what grounds equality in Rancière's sense. On Owen's view, a properly agonistic approach needs to acknowledge the centrality of recognition to human agency while also taking its ambivalence as a constitutive feature of practices of recognition. Approaches that imagine the possibility of transcending the ambivalence end up obscuring this crucial insight into political life.

NOTES

The editors would like to thank Amy Allen and Wendy Lochner for their patience and unwavering support during this journey, and

Carolyn Benson, Leonie Stibor, and Susanne de Wasch for invaluable help with the manuscript.

1. For a classic account of recognition in Hegel and Fichte, see Ludwig Siep, *Anerkennung als Prinzip der Praktischen Philosophie* (Freiburg: Alber, 1979). Other early recognition theorists include Rousseau (see Frederick Neuhouser, *Rousseau's Theodicy of Self-Love: Evil, Rationality, and the Drive for Recognition* (Oxford: Oxford University Press, 2010)) and Adam Smith (see Axel Honneth, *Recognition: A Chapter in the History of European Ideas* (Cambridge: Cambridge University Press, 2021), 68-84).
2. Charles Taylor, "The Politics of Recognition," in *Multiculturalism: Examining the Politics of Recognition*, ed. Amy Gutmann (Princeton, NJ: Princeton University Press, 1992), 25–73.
3. Axel Honneth, *The Struggle for Recognition: The Moral Grammar of Social Conflicts* (Cambridge: Polity, 1995).
4. Georg Wilhelm Friedrich Hegel, *Phenomenology of Spirit*, trans. A. V. Miller (Oxford: Oxford University Press, 1977), 119–38; Georg Wilhelm Friedrich Hegel, *System of Ethical Life* (1802/3) *and First Philosophy of Spirit* (Part III of the System of Speculative Philosophy 1803/4), ed. and trans. H. S. Harris and T. M. Knox (Albany: State University of New York Press, 1979).
5. This aspect is most famously emphasized by Alexandre Kojève, *Introduction to the Reading of Hegel*, ed. Allan Bloom, trans. James H. Nichols Jr. (Ithaca, NY: Cornell University Press, 1980).
6. This is an important issue that pragmatist readers of Hegel like Robert B. Brandom (*Reason in Philosophy: Animating Ideas* (Cambridge, MA: Belknap, 2009)); Terry Pinkard; and Robert B. Pippin (*Hegel's Practical Philosophy: Rational Agency as Ethical Life* (Cambridge: Cambridge University Press, 2008)) have stressed time and again. See also Cillian McBride, *Recognition* (Cambridge: Polity, 2013).
7. Jean Paul Sartre, *Being and Nothingness: A Phenomenological Essay on Ontology* (New York: Washington Square, 1984), 347–61.
8. Kelly Oliver, *Witnessing: Beyond Recognition* (Minneapolis: University of Minnesota Press, 2001); Patchen Markell, *Bound by Recognition* (Princeton, NJ: Princeton University Press, 2003).
9. Elizabeth A. Povinelli, *The Cunning of Recognition: Indigenous Alterities and the Making of Australian Multiculturalism* (Durham, NC: Duke University Press, 2002).

10. For a discussion of whether current theories of recognition incorporate a Eurocentric bias, see, for example, Amy Allen, *The End of Progress: Decolonizing the Normative Foundations of Critical Theory* (New York: Columbia University Press, 2017), 116.
11. Nancy Fraser, "Social Justice in the Age of Identity Politics: Redistribution, Recognition and Participation," in *Redistribution or Recognition? A Political-Philosophical Exchange*, ed. N. Fraser and A. Honneth (London: Verso, 2003), 7–109.
12. Lois McNay, *Against Recognition* (Cambridge: Polity, 2008).
13. Louis Althusser, "Ideology and Ideological State Apparatuses," in *Lenin and Philosophy and Other Essays* (New York: Monthly Review, 2001), 127–86.
14. See Judith Butler, *The Psychic Life of Power: Theories in Subjection* (Stanford: Stanford University Press, 1997), 106–31. See further the exchange between Honneth and Butler in this volume, in which Butler, among other things, reflects on the relation of her thought to Althusser.
15. Judith Butler, *Subjects of Desire: Hegelian Reflections in Twentieth-Century France* (New York: Columbia University Press, 1987).
16. Judith Butler, "Taking Another's View: Ambivalent Implications," in *Reification: A New Look at an Old Idea*, ed. M. Jay (Oxford: Oxford University Press, 2008), 97–119; Judith Butler; "Longing for Recognition," in *Undoing Gender* (New York: Routledge, 2004), 131–51.
17. See Bert van den Brink and David Owen, *Recognition and Power* (Cambridge: Cambridge University Press, 2007).

REFERENCES

Allen, Amy. *The End of Progress: Decolonizing the Normative Foundations of Critical Theory*. New York: Columbia University Press, 2017.

Althusser, Louis. "Ideology and Ideological State Apparatuses." In *Lenin and Philosophy and Other Essays*, 127–86. New York: Monthly Review, 2001.

Brandom, Robert. *Reason in Philosophy: Animating Ideas*. Cambridge, MA: Belknap, 2009.

van den Brink, Bert, and David Owen. *Recognition and Power.* Cambridge: Cambridge University Press, 2007.

Butler, Judith. "Longing for Recognition." In *Undoing Gender.* New York: Routledge, 2004.

Butler, Judith. *The Psychic Life of Power: Theories in Subjection.* Stanford: Stanford University Press, 1997.

Butler, Judith. Subjects of Desire: Hegelian Reflections in Twentieth-Century France. New York: Columbia University Press, 1987.

Butler, Judith. "Taking Another's View: Ambivalent Implications." In Reification: A New Look at an Old Idea, edited by M. Jay. Oxford: Oxford University Press, 2008.

Fraser, Nancy. "Social Justice in the Age of Identity Politics: Redistribution, Recognition and Participation." In *Redistribution or Recognition? A Political-Philosophical Exchange*, edited by N. Fraser and A. Honneth. London: Verso, 2003.

Hegel, Georg Wilhelm Friedrich. *Phenomenology of Spirit.* Translated by A. V. Miller. Oxford: Oxford University Press, 1977. First published in 1807.

Hegel, Georg Wilhelm Friedrich. *System of Ethical Life* (1802/3) *and First Philosophy of Spirit* (Part III of the System of Speculative Philosophy 1803/4). Edited and translated by H. S. Harris and T. M. Knox. Albany: State University of New York Press, 1979.

Honneth, Axel. *Recognition: A Chapter in the History of European Ideas.* Cambridge: Cambridge University Press, 2021.

Honneth, Axel. *The Struggle for Recognition: The Moral Grammar of Social Conflicts.* Cambridge: Polity, 1995. First published in 1992.

Kojève, Alexandre. *Introduction to the Reading of Hegel.* Edited by Allan Bloom. Translated by James H. Nichols Jr. Ithaca, NY: Cornell University Press, 1980.

Markell, Patchen. *Bound by Recognition.* Princeton, NJ: Princeton University Press, 2003.

McBride, Cillian. *Recognition.* Cambridge: Polity, 2013.

McNay, Lois. *Against Recognition.* Cambridge: Polity, 2008.

Neuhouser, Frederick. *Rousseau's Theodicy of Self-Love: Evil, Rationality, and the Drive for Recognition.* Oxford: Oxford University Press, 2010.

Oliver, Kelly. *Witnessing: Beyond Recognition.* Minneapolis: University of Minnesota Press, 2001.

Pippin, Robert B. *Hegel's Practical Philosophy: Rational Agency as Ethical Life.* Cambridge: Cambridge University Press, 2008.

Povinelli, Elizabeth A. *The Cunning of Recognition: Indigenous Alterities and the Making of Australian Multiculturalism.* Durham, NC: Duke University Press, 2002.

Sartre, Jean Paul. *Being and Nothingness: A Phenomenological Essay on Ontology.* New York: Washington Square, 1984.

Siep, Ludwig. *Anerkennung als Prinzip der Praktischen Philosophie.* Freiburg: Alber, 1979.

Taylor, Charles. "The Politics of Recognition." In *Multiculturalism: Examining the Politics of Recognition*, edited by Amy Gutmann. Princeton, NJ: Princeton University Press, 1992.

1

RECOGNITION BETWEEN POWER AND NORMATIVITY

A Hegelian Critique of Judith Butler

AXEL HONNETH

Dear Judith,

It took me a long time to realize how important the very idea of "recognition" is to your efforts to bring about a renewal of critical theory. This may have been due solely to my ignorance, but I suspect that many readers of your work have tended to overlook the central role of recognition in your own thinking. For you first started to make use of the term in *The Psychic Life of Power*—and there only vaguely—whereas it was terminologically absent from the earlier *Gender Trouble*; in the meantime, however, the importance of the notion for your theory has become too obvious to be overlooked, as is testified to by the growing literature on this topic within your work. I myself by now feel sufficiently familiar with your thought to start a small debate with you on the convergences and differences between our two approaches. Let me open my remarks with the unsurprising observation that, in the course of the development of your thought, the idea of recognition has undergone quite a drastic change, from a term helping to explain power relations to a notion designating a moral attitude; my suspicion is that these two different notions of recognition, the early one and the recent one, not only exclude each other but are both unsatisfactory in themselves. I know that this sounds like a very harsh objection, but I will try my best to explain my reservations.

I will start with what I take to be your initial view on recognition. Already, in *Gender Trouble*, you followed, to a certain degree—albeit without using the term explicitly—Althusser's appropriation of Hegel's idea of recognition, by claiming a close connection between "recognizing" a singular person or a group of persons and the ideological reproduction of a given social order; as a result of the attribution of specific, namely functionally required, role characteristics to certain individuals or groups, they start to become convinced that they actually possess these properties, and so become "happy slaves"—willingly performing the tasks or obligations required of them by the prevailing regime of power. Whereas Althusser's prime example was famously the police practice of hailing somebody ("Hey, you there"),[1] identifying him or her by this interpellation as a presumptive criminal, your central theme was the cultural reproduction of the existing gender order via the "normalizing" fixation of only two gender identities, by which people were unconsciously forced to adopt either the one or the other—and if they did not so adapt, as you laid out very illuminatingly, it came at the price of becoming "unintelligible" to the social public, therefore having no legitimate status within society and being liable to all kinds of punishment.[2] I'm not aiming to criticize this approach as such; on the contrary, I believe it was one of the most important contributions to the advancement of critical theory over the last few decades, elaborating a theme that, while present in this tradition, was never sufficiently articulated.[3] However, I have some reservations about the treatment of the idea of recognition in that earlier work which, even though it was not explicitly present, conceptually preconfigures its usage in your later works of the same period. First of all, you seem to conceive of such an attribution of fixed gender identities as a medium or cultural instrument that members of society have to adopt for reasons of social "survival"—not accepting the dominant schemes of gender identity would be disadvantageous, if not fatal, within the "compulsory system" of societal reproduction;[4] secondly, you presuppose that such attributions must necessarily have a "substantializing" effect, making those concerned believe that it is their "nature" or "substantive being" that is articulated by the respective attribution.[5] Taking both premises together, the conclusion is that the hegemonic attribution of certain properties (in this case fixed gender identities) to people functions as an ideological tool by inviting or priming them to adopt the (ritually repeated) characteristics in such a way that the origin of such identification becomes unknown. In your later book, *The Psychic Life of Power*,[6] another highly innovative and trailblazing work, it seems to me that you kept these two presumptions about the ideological functioning of power regimes, but started to frame them by approaching the Hegelian notion of recognition: by recognizing individuals who are in need of a social existence and assuring them continuity over time, social visibility, and a place to be, "regulatory power" ascribes certain forms of behavior to these individuals. Due to their "desire," individuals are prepared to adopt these behaviors, which then in turn once again makes them "happy slaves" of the existing order. I think I'm not wrong in supposing that the theoretical core of this approach was the result of an original attempt to synthesize elements of Lacan's version of psychoanalysis and Althusser's explanation of ideological reproduction: by being recognized as such and such an individual, having such and such typical, socially stereotyped properties, one at the same time becomes subjected to a given power regime, is "thrown" into it, and becomes a socially accepted and therefore visible "subject." Recognition, then, is the process of "subjectivation" in the double sense that the French and (probably) English languages allow: of, on the one hand, becoming subordinated to a given, hegemonic order, and on the other hand of becoming a "subject" in the first place, capable of understanding itself as socially accepted and, to a certain degree, "autonomous." From a distance, this idea might look like what Hegel had in mind when using the notion of "recognition," which for him also included the dimension of becoming part of a socially established order and of gaining a certain degree of freedom; however, I doubt that this captures the full meaning of Hegel's account of recognition. Let me explain where I see the main differences between your appropriation of it and Hegel's own concept; this might also help to highlight some of the differences between us.

Whenever Hegel makes use of the notion of recognition that he borrowed from Fichte, he seems to have a relationship in mind that is dyadic in a very specific sense: the granting of a certain normative status to the other has normative effects on both sides, on the receiver of such recognition, and on its giver; they do not remain the same sort of individuals they were before the event of recognition. This is so because to accord someone the normative status involved in granting recognition at the same time requires the dispenser to limit his or her own freedom, or, to use the Kantian phrase, "self-love," as it bestows a new kind of freedom or authority on the beneficiary; the concomitance of the two alterations is a necessary one since the second—being from now on granted a liberty one didn't possess before—is dependent on the first; namely, that the giver forbids themselves from acting in as free and unconstrained a manner as before. However, this implies that the mere act of ascribing a certain property or characteristic to someone isn't sufficient to call it an occurrence of recognition in the Hegelian sense; the only forms of such an ascription that can be labeled (Hegelian) recognition are those that grant the other a status or authority that instantaneously forces the subject of such an ascription to change its normative attitude by renouncing the boundlessness of its own actions—or, in short, to value the other in terms of the property or characteristic attributed to her. To my mind, the confusion of mere "ascription" with "recognition" has its origins in Althusser's famous article in which he labels every act of ascribing a certain (functionally required) property to individuals or groups with the notion of recognition, thus making no distinction between granting a normative status and the interpellation by certain authorities backed by state power. You seem to be more reluctant to make this simple equation of social recognition and attributing certain characteristics to individuals or whole groups of people; at least one can read your idea that such ascriptions have to guarantee people a legitimate place within society as an indication that recognition, as a normative category, has to be something more than simply the bestowing of certain social categories upon individuals or groups. Yet, in your earlier writings, it remained relatively unclear what kind of entitlement is warranted by such recognition and what sort of self-limitation is therefore required by the recognizer.

I guess the reason for this vagueness has to do with a lack of clarity in your use of the notion of recognition. This term has a long history, and in recent decades its usage has led to considerable confusion. As you are aware, the notion of recognition has a wider range of meanings in French and English than it does in German; where the German word normally conveys the normative meaning of granting somebody a certain status, entitlement, or right, and only sometimes also includes the idea of accepting an unpleasant state of affairs, in French and English "recognition" refers primarily to epistemic acts of reidentification and only secondarily to those normative attitudes or acts. My assumption now is that you tend to alternate between these two sets of meanings by sometimes stressing the cognitive component and sometimes emphasizing the normative component. Thus, you occasionally seem to say that, by such acts of recognition, people become "understandable," "intelligible," or "identifiable," as if referring to a cognitive accomplishment, while at other times you conceive of those acts as bringing about certain entitlements or as bestowing "a safe place" on people. It may be that I'm overemphasizing the distinction between the two meanings or that I'm not yet able to grasp the intricate relationship between them; right now, however, I'm quite convinced that your conflation of the cognitive and the normative side of recognition makes it very hard for you to get a clear picture of what recognition implies when understood, in the Hegelian sense, as an act of granting a normative status.

I can't resist adding a further comment on this point that seems to me to be of the highest importance for clarifying the differences between us. It may well be, or so I suspect at least, that your conflation of the two meanings does not result primarily from a linguistic confusion, but is due instead to the area in which you have (with good reason) chosen to apply the concept of recognition. If we want to explain the culturally deep-seated distinction between two gender identities, it may be advisable to conceive of it as a result of institutionally mediated acts of recognition; we then take as our point of departure the observation that it was through the repetition of such attributions of stable gender identities to two classes of social members that the common belief in the nature of this gender division was established. But, in this case, we are using the notion of recognition, as my formulation already indicates, exclusively in its epistemic meaning, since there is not yet any normative consequence associated with the "identification" of being either a "man" or a "woman." To explain then how such a moral charging of the two already-constituted gender identities became possible, it is again advisable to make use of the notion of recognition, but now in its normative meaning, because what henceforth has to be the focus of our attention are acts of recognition by which an unequal normative status was granted to the two genders. I'm not sure whether this analytical distinction between the two steps of explanation helps us to gain a better understanding of the two meanings of recognition that, in my view, have to be clearly distinguished: in the first case, groups of people are cognitively identified as possessing such and such stable properties and exhibiting such and such sets of behavior; in the second case, each of these groups is then recognized as deserving a certain normative status—and only this second kind of action or attitude is what Hegel called "recognition." As I have mentioned, it demands from the giver a self-constraint with regard to how to act or behave in the future, where this is an expression of the value attributed to the other; if sufficient self-limitation of one's freedom does not follow, we can speak of recognition becoming a form of ideology.[7]

If this interpretation of your early work is not completely wrong or misleading, then one might venture the following hypothesis as to your reasons for shifting unexpectedly to a more robustly moral account of recognition in your later works: since your early approach, or so one could argue, didn't provide a sufficient basis for evaluating the moral quality of social actions or behavior, you had to introduce a standard or a criterion that permitted such normative distinctions; for this, you again made use of the notion of recognition, but now in a moral sense closer to Levinas than to Hegel. Before I go on to challenge this normative shift, most clearly expressed in your marvelous Adorno Lectures in Frankfurt,[8] I should probably pause for a moment in order to clarify the thrust of the argumentation I'm presenting here. My intention is certainly not to quarrel with you about the correct understanding of Hegel's account of recognition; as we are both aware, there are too many alternative ways to understand what he had in mind when using the notion to be concerned about the one, true meaning. Instead, what I would like to find out in our discussion is how to make use of Hegel's idea of recognition such that it best and most profoundly serves the critical intentions of a theoretical tradition we both share; and it is with this agenda in mind that I am pursuing the present inquiry about the development of your thoughts concerning the role of recognition within social life. So far, I have come to the conclusion that, in your first books, recognition mainly serves the task of explaining how certain forms of power operate: following an approach similar to Althusser's, you seemed to believe that, by (the institutional) attribution of certain properties to people, they are compelled to unconsciously take on specific attitudes that help reproduce the prevailing order. My worry with regard to this proposal has been that it doesn't sufficiently allow us to distinguish between two varieties of such an attribution of properties: one, by which the recognizer—be it an institution or an individual person—is implicitly required henceforth to abstain from certain kinds of action, and another, where such a moral consequence is not an internal part of such an attribution. In insisting that Hegel would have called only the first of these two phenomena recognition, I didn't intend to identify the reason why we should prefer the first over the second; what I meant to say was that by not making such a distinction, we risk overlooking an important feature of our social life, namely the possibility of attributing properties to people that bear a moral significance, forcing us to change our attitude—there is a difference between addressing somebody as a "citizen" or a "friend" and addressing that same person as, let's say, a "soccer fan" or a "piano player," where no moral meaning requiring a certain kind of behavior of us is implied. In calling only the first two forms of address recognition, we make sure that, in these cases, the attribution of properties has the moral implication of granting the other a normative status we have to obey.

For the moment I will leave our discussion at this. Perhaps we will also have the opportunity to discuss the problems I see with your appropriation of Levinas at a later stage, but for now it seems most useful to me to first see whether this contribution has helped to make certain disagreements between us more clearly visible.

Yours,
Axel Honneth

NOTES

1. Louis Althusser, "On Ideology," in *Ideology and Ideological State Apparatuses* (London: Verso, 2014), 190–91.
2. Judith Butler, *Gender Trouble* (New York: Routledge, 1990), chapter 1.
3. Amy Allen, *The Politics of Our Selves. Power, Autonomy, and Gender in Contemporary Critical Theory* (New York: Columbia University Press, 2008).
4. Butler, *Gender Trouble*, 190.
5. Butler, *Gender Trouble*, 22–34.
6. Judith Butler, *The Psychic Life of Power: Theories in Subjection* (Stanford: Stanford University Press, 1997).
7. Axel Honneth, "Recognition as Ideology: The Connection Between Morality and Power," in *The I in We: Studies in the Theory of Recognition* (Cambridge: Polity, 2012), 75–97.

8. Judith Butler, *Giving an Account of Oneself* (New York: Fordham University Press, 2005).

BIBLIOGRAPHY

Allen, Amy. *The Politics of Our Selves: Power, Autonomy, and Gender in Contemporary Critical Theory*. New York: Columbia University Press, 2008.

Althusser, Louis. "On Ideology." In *Ideology and Ideological State Apparatuses*, 171–207. London: Verso, 2014.

Butler, Judith. *Gender Trouble*. New York: Routledge, 1990.

Butler, Judith. *Giving an Account of Oneself*. New York: Fordham University Press, 2005.

Butler, Judith. *The Psychic Life of Power: Theories in Subjection*. Stanford: Stanford University Press, 1997.

Honneth, Axel. "Recognition as Ideology: The Connection Between Morality and Power." In *The I in We: Studies in the Theory of Recognition*, 75–97. Cambridge: Polity, 2012.

2

RECOGNITION AND THE SOCIAL BOND

A Response to Axel Honneth

JUDITH BUTLER

Dear Axel,

I am glad to be in discussion with you. I would like to clarify from the outset that I do not understand myself to be producing a renewal of critical theory, although I am always glad to honor the debt I owe to that tradition. I note that many people wish to ally with critical theory even though there is disagreement about how it should be defined, and whether the definition should err on the side of inclusivity or exclusivity.

On the question of recognition, it is true that this theme was from the start an important one for me. The theme of recognition is linked to the problem of desire in my dissertation, and then again in the revised version that became *Subjects of Desire*.[1] The relation between desire and recognition struck me as important not only for understanding the French reception of Hegel, but for clarifying the philosophical stakes in certain arguments made by LGBTQ studies. In Hegel one can find that desire is to some extent a desire for recognition, but also that the potentially reciprocal form of recognition effects desire and makes its aims more expansive. Of course, the case would have to be made that what Hegel describes as desire (*Begierde*) gives us the structure for sexual desire. I note here that *Begierde* in Hegel gives us a general structure of consciousness, but also, implicitly, of reciprocal social relations. Even as the *Phenomenology of Spirit* leaves desire behind, it persists, for negation is cultivated into new forms, moving, for instance, in the space of a few pages from a potentially infinite consumption of objects to potentially self-destructive murder, to a self-deluded form of domination, to crafting an object that yields a reflection of one's own freedom as dependent on both objects and social relations.

Although it may not be clear how someone who wrote a dissertation on the French reception of Hegel, focusing on the trajectory of desire, embarks at about the same time on LGBTQ politics, I understood there to be a link. When sexuality and sexual orientation emerged as a human right, one key argument in favor of that position was that discrimination against individuals or groups on the basis of their sexual orientation demands understanding sexuality as a variable aspect of humans that deserves recognition not only through antidiscrimination law, but in public discourse more broadly. A more fundamental claim is presupposed by that rights claim, since desire itself carries with it a demand for recognition. Without social recognition for forms of desire that have been regularly and wrongly pathologized, criminalized, or effaced, the struggle for sexual justice cannot proceed. Of course, sometimes intimate dimensions of sexual desire may want nothing more than protection from public recognition. But for that right to privacy to be secured, a more general right to sexual freedom has to be affirmed. Thus, whether seeking to gain recognition, or elude its capture, sexuality is bound up with a desire for recognition. This poses a specific problem when, for instance, there is no available language in law or public life for the kind of recognition that is sought. Indeed, the LGBTQ movement does not always assume that recognition can be sought in existing terms. When such terms are not available, the demand for recognition can only be met by developing new terms, conventions, and new norms, that facilitate recognition through terms that reflect equality and freedom. The demand for recognition of the rights of sexual minorities was articulated within the 1980s and 1990s along with experimentation in new vernaculars. And this led some intellectuals in the emerging field of queer theory to consider the relationship between language and recognition. As activists were demanding full recognition, some academics pointed out that, for Lacan, misrecognition is a constitutive feature of human relations, and that the expectation of a full recognition of sexuality is a fantasy and an impossible ideal. Significantly, the notion of desire, even the coupling of desire with recognition, was central to Lacan's work. His departure from Hegel centered on the claim that full recognition was impossible, and the well-known "mirror stage" served as a demonstration of the view that whatever "reflection" one receives back from the mirror, or the other, is itself disfigured by an insuperable narcissism and eventual disappointment.

To evaluate the merits of this debate, we would first have to ascertain whether we find a notion of "full recognition" in Hegel. In my view, Hegel figures recognition as an ongoing dynamic in social relations, one that does not come to a teleological fulfillment at any certain time. Revising both Freud and Hegel through a structuralist vocabulary, Lacan sought to establish the imaginary dimension of the struggle for recognition, showing that an expectation of a full recognition is always disappointed in the end.

Although I have always been interested in this Lacanian challenge, I do not myself take a Lacanian approach. One problem with the Lacanian appropriation is that it underscored the structural necessity of "misrecognition," which implies that all forms of recognition are mistaken. In my view, recognition is always partial: there is, for instance, no recognition of all that a person is or may be, and in that sense, there is no capture of the person by existing terms available for the conferring of recognition. But the fact that recognition is partial does not make it false. It only makes it noncomprehensive. Hegel himself gives an account of misrecognition that the Lacanian position does not fully acknowledge (a failure of recognition, we might say). The Lacanian position was taken up by Althusser, of course, in his redefinition of ideology as a set of imaginary relations to the real conditions of existence. My own pathway was, however, different. I became more interested in the problem implicitly laid out by the demand for recognition originating in the LGBTQ movement: what are the existing norms that establish recognizability, that is, the field in which recognition proves to be possible? How do we measure their sufficiency or insufficiency? And how do new norms develop so that the political demand for LGBTQ rights and freedoms becomes legible, since a demand cannot be met without first being understood? I argue for a distinction between recognition and recognizability in the opening pages of *Frames of War*.[2] In this way, my own position is distinct from the Althusserians who identify a structural failure in all efforts to demand recognition. But my position is also not the same as the Deleuzians who argue that the Nietzschean critique of recognition is a subtle form of domination. Although I have argued that relying on *existing* gender categories for recognition may guarantee subjection, I do not think that all categories required for recognition necessarily guarantee subjection.

You suggest that in the course of my work "the idea of recognition underwent quite a drastic change, from a term helping to explain power relations to a notion designating a moral attitude." My response is that this formulation is only partially right, since I do not start with the idea of recognition as a term that explains power relations. In the earliest work on Hegel, recognition establishes the social relation between the I and the other, and so moves closer to a social ontology. In *Subjects of Desire*, the focus on power is not there, except toward the end of the manuscript. The idea that desire is a desire for recognition, and that recognition itself shapes the form of desire, is there from the start. Further, as subjects whose desire seeks recognition (as subjects who desire recognition), we are dependent on others to derive a sense of who we are. This leads to the general claim that the identity of the subject comes from elsewhere, and is not generated from within, nor accomplished through introspection. I take seriously the *ek-static* character of the subject, as illustrated by the opening scene of *Herrschaft und Knechtschaft*: we find ourselves first outside of ourselves—"außer sich gekommen"[3]—and that "outside" proves to be a necessary feature of our self-understanding. There is another who is structurally similar to me, and yet it does not fully extinguish my singularity or the difference between us. As a result, my singularity is bound to the other's singularity precisely through the differentiation process. This is one of the most important roles of determinate negation in social relations. As a result, whatever "social identity" may mean, it is not a seamless identification of persons with one another by virtue of an overarching category; rather, a primary dislocation of myself in or as the other provides a passionate—and ambivalent—basis for whatever social relation emerges between us. Only dislocated from myself can I then find myself as a social creature, which means that the self that I find in the course of dislocation and differentiation is and is not mine alone: I have become social in the course of my search for myself (or, rather, I discover that I have been social all along).

You formulate what you call a "harsh objection" to the two forms of recognition you identify in my work. So let me respond briefly to your characterization of those positions. You maintain that I follow Althusser in *Gender Trouble* by claiming that recognition for me involved the ideological reproduction of a social order. That claim would imply that recognition only serves that function. But my view is that the category by which one is named can be "resignified," and therefore depart from the mechanical or ideological reproduction of the norm. I do not use the term ideology in that book, and I don't believe that I engage with Althusser until later in my writing. Indeed, I did not read Althusser at all at the time that I wrote *Gender Trouble*, so you must assume that it entered into my way of thinking quite in spite of my actual formation and trajectory. It might matter as well that *Gender Trouble* (1989) follows *Subjects of Desire* (1990), so one question is how *Subjects of Desire* leads to *Gender Trouble*. It is true that *Gender Trouble* inaugurated a broader public understanding of my work and is often taken to be my earliest work, but for me it was a late development after an intensive engagement with German Idealism, phenomenology, and critical theory both in Germany as a Fulbright Scholar in Heidelberg and at Yale University, where I received all of my degrees. In *Gender Trouble*, I was concerned to show, among other things, that the available terms for establishing self-recognition as a woman were constraining for many who lived outside the heteronormative matrix (called "compulsory heterosexuality" at the time), and I called for more complex and inclusive terms so that those people who could not easily identify with the category of women still had a social place in language. The feminist movement in large part wanted to claim that feminism required a unified category of women, and yet many "women" could not easily identify with the terms on offer. My conclusion was not that all efforts to achieve recognition were ideologically suspect, but rather that new vocabularies and new social understandings of gender would promise or provide a form of recognition that would be less constraining. What I wanted was to help bring into public consideration ways of understanding gender that would more fully honor the lived complexity of gendered experience and prove to be less restrictive and constraining for those seeking to live their lives free of discrimination and violence. My argument was that it should be possible for all sorts of people to enter into the feminist movement without identifying with a restrictive category of gender, but I never thought all categories of gender are restrictive. And I certainly never thought that all forms of recognition were simply ways of interpellating individuals into existing ideological orders—that would amount to an indictment of the category of recognition itself. Rather, I sought to expand the vocabularies, the ways of understanding gender and its complexity, so that feminism did not require a premature and costly conformity to restrictive identity categories to make its claims.

My point, however, was to establish the play of freedom within forms of social construction. So though one comes into the world recognized as a specific gender, the meaning of that gender can be recrafted through time, especially in the context of social movements. Gender can also change, which we see in the trans movement. So no one is determined (in any causal sense) by the gender they are assigned. Thus, when you suggest that in response to being assigned certain genders or social identities, individuals or groups "start to be convinced of actually possessing these properties, and so become 'happy slaves,'" I think you have missed the aspect of the performative theory of gender that insists that freedom can be found within the scene of social constraints.

I am sure you will agree that "happy slaves" is not my term, but perhaps you are less convinced that it would never be my term or that it would never rightly characterize my views. Indeed, the characterization you offer assumes that I understand human conduct through a behaviorist model, which is not the case. The only argument I have made that comes close to the characterization you offer is that sometimes we do come to regard as an "essence" of our identity the effect of a reiterated embodied practice. Gender is performed a certain way over time; its effect is sedimented, and in that way can become naturalized as an essence, but not for all people or under all circumstances, and not consistently in any case. My argument against gender as an interior metaphysical essence gives us a way of understanding the enactment of gender norms as something other than an outward expression of such an internal essence. That we sometimes mistake an effect for a cause (an example of the rhetorical figure of metalepsis) does not mean that we always make that mistake, nor that we are the kind of creatures who are regularly mistaken about who they are. In fact, many people have anxiety about whether or not they are occupying gender in the "right" way, which means that internal to their own sense of self is a distance between lived experience and the requirements of the norm. Psychoanalysis enters here precisely because it documents the various ways in which we are unknowing about masculinity and femininity. What does a woman want? What does it mean to be a man? That we are creatures who ask questions such as these suggests that there is no naturalized understanding that is not beset by significant disturbances: anxiety, conflict, cross-identification, fantasy. People are not "unconsciously forced" to adopt gender roles; indeed, the unconscious very often contests the demands exercised by dominant norms on the psyche.

There is, however, a further point: the dominant ways in which we have been taught to understand gender as an expression of an interior essence relies on evidence that could just as well support the idea of gender as a reiterated cultural practice whose effects have become naturalized over time. The argument relies, by the way, on an appropriation of the concept of reification, which has been the focus of your recent work,[4] and an important legacy of critical theory.

That said, Althusser makes his first appearance only in *The Psychic Life of Power*, if I am correct. As I mentioned, he was not an influence on *Gender Trouble*. In fact, the performative theory of gender sought to show how it is possible to oppose such forms of power in the midst of undergoing those constraints. This is the central paradoxical structure of subjugation and agency—although we might say resistance. So we are not determined by the social order, and we do not only act out of the need for survival within its terms. Indeed, sometimes the very terms we are asked to occupy threaten our very ability to persist. I wanted to underscore at that time that we are able to occupy the categories by which we are constrained and give them new meaning. This is why I am sometimes accused of voluntarism. My actual view, however, is that agency is often possible within the scene of constraint, which means that forms of power, or ideological orders, do not act on us in a deterministic way. Although it is possible to lose one's life by virtue of being gay, lesbian, trans, bi-, queer, it is also possible to rise up within the scene of constraint. Many people insist on refusing that very bad deal which requires them to deny their mode of existence in order to survive in a given society. The paradox is that it is in the name of their own survival or persistence that they fight for another order.

Foucault, rather than Althusser, is more central to that early theory of gender. I do not think you will find citational evidence in *Gender Trouble* to support the claim that I see some form of power as "attributing" substantial identity to people, nor will you find any support for the claim that this form of power "makes people believe" false things about themselves. There is no source of power with such capacities. Neither will you find reference to a "hegemonic attribution of qualities" in *Gender Trouble.* The point was rather that, for Foucault, subjects are produced in discourse, but my point was that subjects also produce themselves, and that Foucault did not, at least in his early work, make enough room for this reflexive dimension. Performativity as a form of self-making adds an agentic dimension to the Foucaultian theory that it otherwise seemed to lack. Or so was my understanding. I also sought to bring a consideration of social exclusion and constraint into the picture by asking, what happens when the terms by which the subject is produced are those to which the subject objects or which constrain that subject in unlivable ways? What options are then open? Although we may well be formed within the terms of power, we also help to produce and reproduce those terms, and therein we can find agency, even forms of agency that subvert the terms by which we are conventionally restrained. Whereas for a structuralist position such as Althusser's the "reproduction" of ideology implies its unthinking replication and augmentation, I sought recourse to a poststructuralist understanding of "iterability" (derived from Derrida, but inflected by Husserl) to insist that reproduction can be a sense of agency, subversion, and change. This is why resignification takes the place of "reproduction" in the poststructuralist account that I gave. Resignification opens up the possibility of defeating the very order of power through its reiteration. Gender norms are "resignified" by bodies that are not supposed to embody them, and that can change the way we think about embodiment, norms, and social transformation.

It is, of course, true that Althusser becomes important in *The Psychic Life of Power*, but only because I am interested there in how guilt is mobilized as a psychic disposition that can keep the regulation of the subject in place. Whereas Althusser seeks to reinterpret Lacan for his own purposes, I move in another direction, returning to Freud. The return to Freud is a better route for those who wish to understand the mechanism of subjectivation. The problem is not that there are "typical" or even "stereotypical" ways of attributing gender. It is about subject formations within a field of power. It is true that some feminists have been concerned with criticizing typically masculine or feminine attributes in order to expand the possible ways of life for both genders. That is surely laudable. But mine is a different project concerned with subjectivation.

What do I mean by this term? Human beings come into the world through a gender matrix, such that that being called a girl or boy is a mandatory gateway for becoming human. In this way, gender is there as a matrix of subject formation—and so not merely a set of characteristics attributed to an already existing subject.

You write that

> "recognition, then, is the process of 'subjectivation' in the double sense that the French and (probably) English languages allow: of, on the one hand, becoming subordinated to a given, hegemonic order, and on the other hand of becoming a 'subject' in the first place, capable of understanding itself as socially accepted and, to a certain degree, 'autonomous.' From a distance, this idea might look like what Hegel had in mind when using the notion of 'recognition,' which for him also included the dimension of

> becoming part of a socially established order and of gaining a certain degree of freedom. . . . Whenever Hegel makes use of the notion of recognition that he borrowed from Fichte, he seems to have a relationship in mind that is dyadic in a very specific sense: the granting of a certain normative status to the other has normative effects on both sides, on the receiver of such recognition, and its giver; they do not remain the same sort of individuals they were before the event of recognition."[5]

So let us consider the relationship, then, between recognition and subjectivation, since I think the real difference between us surfaces there. I agree with your claim that when Hegel, borrowing from Fichte, describes recognition, he has in mind a dyadic relation, and neither of the individuals involved in reciprocal recognition remain the same after passing through that process or practice. So we agree that recognition transforms those who participate in it. What I am less sure about is whether each individual "grants" recognition to the other, and whether what is granted to the other is a moral value or normative standing.

I wonder whether perhaps your true argument is with Althusser rather than with me. This is not to say that you don't have true arguments with me, but to the degree that the Althusserian position that you critique is attributed to me, it is not quite the same as the position I actually hold. The misfire is interesting, but it is still a misfire. So perhaps it will be necessary to distinguish between your interesting critique of Althusser and my own position (which may well be deserving of another kind of critique). After all, I have sought to lay out an ethical position that could not be found in the Althusserian framework. In the grammar that you use to describe my position, there is some order of power (or capital) that occupies the grammatical position of the subject, and this subject acts to "attribute" qualities to people. This is the position, however, that Foucault already (rightly) criticized, arguing that Althusser did not appreciate deeply enough the problem of subject formation. In *Giving Account of Oneself*, I then argue that Foucault does not fully enough appreciate the relationship between subject formation (which is not the same as receiving or adopting attributions from some supervenient and countervailing "order of power") and ethical relationality.

Your Kantian effort to give a normative significance to recognition is surely admirable, and the world would be better if people were to adopt such an ethic. But that position is different from the relational ethics that I have sought to develop, one that oddly enough has some affinities with the Winnicottian strain in your argumentation. By virtue of the differences and the convergences, I see some possibilities where our dialogue might profitably begin.

In the Kantian reformulation of Hegelian recognition that you provide, the recognizer attributes a normative status—a value—to the one who is recognized, and, once that relation becomes reciprocal, both are transformed in the course of this process. I concur that the dyadic encounter is essential, but differently than in the way that you develop your position. I would start with the question: How do these two subjects emerge as subjects to begin with? Are they already formed and then encounter one another, or are they born into relations that they never chose and then become capable, in time, of giving and receiving esteem? Are they not also, and from the start, born into discourses—including social categories—that establish their intelligibility as human subjects? Gender, or rather the gender matrix, would be one such field of intelligibility that governs subject formation. If so, to what extent do they emerge as thinking and speaking beings by virtue of a formation at once social and psychological, bound up with an early formation in dependency and fraught with ambivalence? What role does that formation play in and for the subjects who can then, eventually, hopefully, deliberately and consciously confer or receive recognition? In a sense, they are already formed within a discourse that they come to use in a deliberate way (which does not mean that they blindly reproduce that discourse). Indeed, they may come up against the limits of that discourse as they seek to confer or receive recognition. Why use one name or category rather than another? What do I miss when I am recognized through certain discourses, and what do I gain?

Like you, I take very seriously the Hegelian claim that we are the sorts of creatures who desire recognition, and who come to understand ourselves in the social relations by which recognition is conferred and received. As a result, we come to understand ourselves as social creatures who are already related to those with whom we negotiate the terms of recognition. We belong to each other prior to the act of recognition that constitutes our value for each other. We do not make up those terms through which we are recognized since we are born into a language that precedes us and acts on us. But neither are we fully determined by such discourses; they can be resisted, resignified, dissolved, and new language can be wrought from and against the old.

We both base our understandings of recognition on psychoanalysis, but I emphasize a different part of the psychoanalytic tradition, one from which Winnicott clearly emerged (and only part of which he retained). The struggle for recognition is bound up with the problem of dependency, including unmanageable dependency, and so also with the ambivalence that Freud, following Hegel, understands as a constitutive feature of all love relations. In Hegel, the life and death struggle ends with the recognition that my life is bound up with the life of the other, that a social organization for our lives must be found that reflects and honors this insuperable interdependency. And though we can and do destroy one another, we are also at such moments destroying ourselves, not only making ourselves eligible for destruction as well, exposing ourselves to a reciprocal act of destruction, but because as social creatures, we are to some extent defined by our social bonds: any attack on that bond is an attack on the self. This is the "social" moment of psychoanalysis that both Klein and Winnicott surely both understood.

But this point cannot be reduced to the Hobbesian wager that if I seek to destroy the other, the other may decide it is better to destroy me first. The reason that Hegel gives us is that my life is bound up with the life of the other, that we are both bound to the earth and to the material objects that we consume and that support our common needs, and whose continuation depends upon our ethical stewardship. From this premise it follows that there is an ethical demand not to destroy the other and to build a social world in common that honors the social bonds that are the presupposition of our common life together, a common life necessarily marked by difference and conflict. So I seek to derive an ethical position from the interdiction against violence and destruction, or, rather, I base a politics of nonviolence on the postulate that the social bond is a necessary feature of who the subject is. I further argue that Hegel demonstrates this through his discussion of the "life and death struggle" in the *Phenomenology*.

You raise the question of whether there is an important difference between the cognitive and normative accounts of recognition. I would like to suggest that it might prove clarifying to consider this distinction differently. When I ask after the conditions under which some lives are established as "intelligible" and others "unintelligible," I am asking about the historical and discursive conditions of subject formation. This is not a cognitive attribution (a way that I think about the other centering on an attribute I see or confer on another), but, rather, a condition of subject formation. Cognitive attribution presupposes an existing subject who attributes intelligibility (or value) to another. This strikes me as an uncritical position to the degree that the subject is taken for granted and its formation, its condition of possibility, is not interrogated.

If, however, we ask the prior question, "Who emerges as an intelligible life?," or, "Who emerges as a recognizable subject?," we are asking about the matrices of subject formation, the fields of intelligibility and recognizability into which and by which any of us emerge. They make some of us very recognizable and cast some of us as nearly unrecognizable, depending on the terms of recognition themselves. They are fields into which we intervene, and they change with time. This is a different field of subjectivation than the one with which you begin. And though it has both cognitive and normative dimensions (What can I know? What do I value, and why?), both of those are dependent on fields of intelligibility that differentially produce the subjects who are more or less eligible for recognition. There is a problem of equality that enters into the situation that precedes the scene of recognition, one in which many people, on the basis of their class status, gender, or the forms of racial stratification to which they have been subjected, struggle for recognition precisely by seeking to change the terms by which recognition is conferred. The subject who confers recognition depends upon the availability of terms, and those terms belong to a life of discourse and power that does not exactly parallel the life of the subject. The intersection of the two, however, is obviously crucial to the scene of recognition itself.

Although I appreciate the way you describe the act of granting recognition, I think that recognition is not a punctual act, and it is not exactly performed by a subject for or on another subject. The structure of reciprocal recognition presupposes a "we" that is, in fact, formed through a set of ongoing relations. I think you agree with this conclusion, so I am not sure why we are asked to imagine individuals who grant recognition to one another. We can certainly start with the first person to understand how reciprocal recognition works, but in the end we are asserting something about the relation of equality that holds between us. When, for instance, I recognize another as someone whose life is as equally valuable as my own, I am not only "attributing" equality, but confirming a prior relationship that holds between us, even if I sometimes seek to deny it. In other words, if I maintain that my life or the lives of others who are like me are, in fact, more valuable than the life or lives of others, I am actively denying an equality that already exists between us as living human creatures. Sometimes this can take the form of treating others as unequal subjects. At other times it takes the form of treating others as if they are not living subjects at all; that is, as if they are the "socially dead," or the "uncivilized," or "undeveloped." In these latter instances, they have not yet been recognized as subjects worthy of an equal regard, but that is not because some subject has failed to attribute that quality to them. The very fact that recognition is reciprocal, or can be, presupposes a structural equality between subjects. When inequality structures social relations, it does so in part by allocating the status of the subject differentially. This form of power operates as a subjectivating matrix with strong normative implications. It is where I would begin the analysis. How people emerge as subjects with rights when they have not been accorded that recognition before is crucial here: we can see examples of that in the forms of resistance taken up by the stateless and the homeless. Their resistance must establish their status as subjects and militates against the negating effect of the ways in which they have been treated. They are struggling for recognition, but also struggling for an alteration of the terms such that recognition becomes possible for them.

I wonder whether we might agree that we have different conceptions of the normative operating in our work and that we have different ways of naming them. For instance, I note that there are two senses of the normative that are at stake. There is a normative aim in naming the "girl" or the "boy" to the extent that a set of expectations is also conveyed about how the girl or the boy should act, what they should become, and how they should conform to a norm of gender. So the act of ascription carries with it the force of prescription. This can also happen through racial appellation, depending on its rhetorical deployment. It does not just name a person, but implies something about character, life trajectory, potential, and worth.

If, however, we ask how ascription implies prescription, we enter into another sort of normative debate. Is it right that embodied lives should be constrained by such categories, or should they be free to develop vocabularies, wherever possible, that support a freer form of expression? I am, for instance, less convinced that the problem is the distinction between a cognitive and normative account of recognition than it is between two senses of the normative character of recognition. The Nietzscheans who claim that all recognition is a form of enslavement are wrong in part because they fail to understand the importance of reciprocal recognition as the basis for our social interdependency, and the ethicopolitical mandate to live together without mutual destruction.

I appreciate that you see the "more robust moral account of recognition in my later work." I do agree that I moved to a more explicitly normative position with *Precarious Life* and then in *The Psychic Life of Power*. You are surely right that in *Gender Trouble*, for instance, I could only develop a critique of gender norms through a theory that offered ways of acting against those norms and in favor of new gender possibilities. What I could not do, however, was explain how I thought social relations should take place, nor could I offer a vision or a measure for the social world that I wanted to come into being.

After the 1990s I moved from a negative understanding of normativity to a more positive one, or rather I developed a double vision that sought to account for both the positive and the negative senses of that term. You use the term "moral" to describe the kind of evaluation that you see as lacking in the earlier work. I also affirm the importance of moral philosophy and, in particular, a theory of moral sentiments that draws on psychoanalysis—on this we concur. The direction I take is different, however, because I think that a broader ethical philosophy can be derived from considering the interrelationship between (a) the interdiction on violence, and (b) the commitment to radical equality. My current work seeks to elaborate that inter-relationship.

Levinas remains important to the degree that he has elaborated an interdiction on doing violence to the other as a primary relationship, ethical in nature, which subtends social relations. Where I depart from Levinas, however, is precisely on the matter of recognition. He holds that the ethical relation is asymmetrical, but I continue to think that reciprocity is an ethical precept at the heart of social equality, and further that we cannot understand the ethical import of reciprocity without understanding its formulation as interdependency. The latter allows us to appreciate the human as one who is born in dependency (like many animals), and whose dependency is never fully overcome through versions of adult autonomy. Moreover, interdependency helps to explain the status of aggression as what Freud called an "unconquerable" feature of human psychic life, one with which we must struggle to arrive at an ethical position of nonviolence. In this way, I continue to think that negativity and destructiveness are important dimensions of the struggle for recognition, linking Hegel with a Freudian reflection on how best to curb human destructiveness (one might consult Freud's famous conversation with Einstein for this). So, for me, one of the salient differences between your position and mine has to do with the different ways that we think about negativity. In my view, the ethical relation among people depends on acknowledging and struggling against the threat of destruction, and that aggression is part of psychic and social life. But for you, negativity is conceptually separated from recognition, and you hold that negativity does not properly belong to the Hegelian elaboration of social relations. As I understand it, you refer to moral attitudes that are to be found in childhood, counterposing Winnicott to Klein (and the late Freud). But even Winnicott underscored the "mutilating" powers of the child, making room for aggression, although not as a drive, but as a feature of dependency and the struggle for individuation.

You rightly point out that there are various forms of recognition and that some of them have moral implications, but some of them do not. I think that is right. But to the extent that we address other beings on the presumption that they are like us in some way, the scene of address already establishes the expectation of communication. If someone uses an insulting term against another person, they generally assume that the other person can register the insult. I take it that the insult would not do its job if it were not registered by the addressee as insulting. Of course, if the other is assumed to be someone who is susceptible to hurtful language of that kind, that truth implies that the one who hurls the insult bears that same susceptibility. Perhaps we have to think about this linguistic vulnerability or susceptibility to the other as a precondition of recognition, one that has moral implications of its own. It helps to elaborate the exposure of one subject to another as an aspect of social ontology, if not ethical relationality. So what the scene of address implies about mutual exposure already bears moral implications, quite regardless of whether the content of the speech act bears on soccer or citizenship.

At the most basic level, recognition reveals something about who we are as social beings. The one who grants recognition is in need of being granted recognition, so that "one" is never exclusively active; it seeks to grant moral value at the same time that its own moral value has to be granted. "Granting" is neither a punctual nor a unilateral act. Perhaps I take my cue from a different Hegel. As already mentioned in the beginning, in the *Phenomenology of Spirit*, he tells us that we are each "outside ourselves" (*außer sich*), lost to the other, or lost "in" the other, which means that our first idea of individual autonomy turns out to be limited and false. If and when we recover a better idea of autonomy, it is one that accepts the fact that who we are is constituted in the course of our social exchanges, and that without becoming lost in the other, we stand no chance of knowing ourselves or achieving autonomy. This *ek-static* dimension of the subject means that we are given over from the start to another on whom we depend for our lives, and who has the capacity to destroy us, to let us live, to support us, to help us flourish. When we find a way to live among one another with a full understanding of our interdependency, and with a commitment to refrain from acts of destruction, we then are able to formulate and affirm a version of equality that acknowledges that profound and precarious form of interdependency. This last is a normative vision, one that departs from Levinas by insisting on reciprocity but also departs from Kant by insisting on interdependency, that is, the ways in which our lives are in each other's hands.

All best,
Judith Butler

NOTES

1. Judith Butler, *Subjects of Desire: Hegelian Reflections in Twentieth-Century France* (New York: Columbia University Press, 1987).
2. Judith Butler, *Frames of War: When Is Life Grievable?* (London: Verso, 2009).
3. G. W. F. Hegel, *Phänomenologie Des Geistes*, ed. Eva Moldenhauer and Karl Markus Michel, vol. 3, *Werke* (Frankfurt: Suhrkamp, 1986), 146; G. W. F. Hegel, *Phenomenology of Spirit*, trans. A. V. Miller (Oxford: Oxford University Press, 1977), 111.
4. Axel Honneth, *Reification: A New Look at an Old Idea* (Oxford: Oxford University Press, 2008).
5. See chapter 1, p. 24 in this volume.

BIBLIOGRAPHY

Butler, Judith. *Frames of War: When Is Life Grievable?* London: Verso, 2009.

Butler, Judith. *Subjects of Desire: Hegelian Reflections in Twentieth-Century France*. New York: Columbia University Press, 1987.

Hegel, Georg Wilhelm Friedrich. *Phänomenologie des Geistes*. Edited by Eva Moldenhauer and Karl Markus Michel. Vol. 3, *Werke*. Frankfurt am Main: Suhrkamp, 1986.

Hegel, Georg Wilhelm Friedrich. *Phenomenology of Spirit*. Translated by A. V. Miller. Oxford: Oxford University Press, 1977.

3

INTELLIGIBILITY AND AUTHORITY IN RECOGNITION

A Reply

AXEL HONNETH

Dear Judith,

Thank you very much for your elaborate reply. It has helped me better understand the aims you are pursuing with your notion of recognition. However, although I see more clearly now that I might have been a bit too hasty in ascribing to your writings a split between two phases—of which the first in my interpretation has an Althusserian flavor, whereas the second leans more toward Levinas's account—I'm still not completely convinced with regard to the way in which you are now attempting to defend the unity of your own account. Let me try to develop the doubts I still have in two steps: in (1) I will try to show that your own account seems to connect two very different understandings of the "function" of recognition which, however, do not easily fit together; it may be, as I will indicate, that these two rival notions stem from the different phases of your own philosophical development that I had earlier tried to differentiate. In (2) I will attempt to show that, in following the Hegelian account of recognition as the mutual granting of some kind of normative status, one is *required* to distinguish different modes of recognition from the outset; it is precisely the advantage of Hegel over

Kant, as I hope to be able to demonstrate, that the former believes that such recognition never appears "empirically" or "historically" in only one standard form; rather, it always already appears in socially embedded forms because there is nothing like a "pure" normative status. But before outlining these two reservations, let me emphasize that I found in your reply many formulations on the relevance and normative role of recognition within social life with which I see myself as being in full accord; this is especially true for your statement that there is not something like the idea of a "full" or final recognition in Hegel because he takes all institutionalized forms of recognition to be only provisional in view of the inexhaustible nature of our subjectivity—I couldn't agree more.

(1) Let me start from a relatively inconspicuous formulation you use at one point in your text in order to accentuate a certain difference between your account and my own. There you say that prior to being able to mutually recognize each other, subjects are always already thrown into social discourses by which they are constituted as "intelligible";[1] it is, to put it differently, the social categories comprised in such discourses that establish the "intelligibility" of subjects as human subjects. I have no reason to doubt the social fact you are referring to in this statement: when we grow up, we are involuntarily but inescapably categorized by different classificatory schemas that squeeze us into socially standardized types (male, white, brown-haired, tall, shy). "Intelligibility" thus means being transformed into a kind of social being that possesses characteristics that are understandable within a given social community. A subject would lack such "intelligibility" if it existed within its social community without obtaining such standardized characteristics. In this sense we are already socially "formed," constituted as having such and such properties, before even entering the

normative horizon of mutual recognition; and it is undoubtedly the case that these classificatory acts possess a "normative" power over us that is almost completely beyond our control and not subject to our will. But what I doubt is that this has anything to do with the kind of recognition Hegel has in mind; it is not the kind of "recognition" we refer to when speaking of the reciprocal granting of a normative status. The first type of "recognition"—to use a word here that I think is inadequate—the "recognition" by which we are classified by an existing vocabulary as such and such does not grant us any normative authority but instead deprives us in many cases (gender, color) of all legitimate chances to codetermine the norms in play. The first type of "recognition"—which for me is nothing other than the classificatory act of an attribution of certain standardized characteristics—limits the freedom of the subject, whereas the second type of recognition—the one for which I reserve this notion—allows (in certain gradations) for the exercise of such freedom.

It will not come as a surprise to you that I believe that this conflation of two different forms of treating subjects by using the same word for both of them can be seen as a remnant of an earlier lack of clarity on your part with regard to how exactly to understand the role of "recognition" within society: there was, on the one hand, the "Althusserian" tendency to identify such recognition with institutional acts of ascribing social categories to individuals and fixing the social identity of subjects by these categorizations; and on the other hand there was the tendency to perceive such recognition as the liberating act of granting subjects a certain space of normative authority that allows them to have a say on how to interpret and apply the norms governing the interaction. But independently of the question of whether I'm right in suspecting that the confusion between these two acts can be understood as resulting from a residue of Althusserianism in your work, I propose that we clearly differentiate between the two forms of treating people and call only the second one "recognition": there is the institutional ascription of social identities by the public use of identifying categories within social discourses, and there is the recognitive granting of a normative authority that requires of the "recognizer" that they limit their own space of freedom—and these acts of "recognition" can be performed by agents of different degrees of aggregation, be they individual subjects, social groups, or institutionalized organizations.

(2) When we follow this second account of "recognition," which describes the respective act as including a normative stance toward, or treatment of, the other, it soon becomes clear that it would be somewhat misleading to take only one form of such recognition into account. In taking the other as someone in possession of normative authority, in recognizing this other, there are different possibilities for granting him or her a legitimate claim to codetermine the norms we follow. These alternatives depend on the types of reasons I allow the other to bring forward in order to either interrogate or criticize the norms prevailing among us: it makes a huge difference whether this other is allowed to make use of his or her emotional sensitivities, to rely on socially agreed conventions, or to mobilize rights claims when questioning an existing interpretation or application of the norms governing our interactions. Hegel must have had something like these alternatives in mind when he set about distinguishing between various forms of recognition; as you know, he spoke of recognition never only in the singular but, from the beginning, solely in the plural, differentiating between love, rights, and something like public esteem. For me such distinctions are crucial; we can't analyze how recognition functions within society

without taking into consideration its variations in shape and form.

It is my vague impression that you restrict yourself mostly to a singular form of recognition, namely one that Hegel tends to refer to as legal respect; this would be a kind of recognition by which I grant the other the normative authority to codetermine how we, within our social community, should best conceive of the meaning and application of the legal rights we are supposed to understand as the product of our democratic "will formation." However, one might sometimes also get the impression that you favor another type of recognition, namely one that I would describe, with Hegel, as "love" or "care"—in such a case, I grant the other the normative authority to bring to bear his or her emotional sensitivities in order to put the norms regulating our personal interactions into question. The difference between the two attitudes of recognition seems obvious to me: in the first case I take the other as a person possessing the status of an equal bearer of rights, allowing him or her, by this attitude, to have an equal say on how we should best understand and apply the subjective rights established within our social community; in the second case, however, I take the other as someone deserving of my love and care, so that by holding this attitude I grant him or her the authority to criticize the rules prevailing among us by articulating his or her feelings and emotional reactions. I do not intend to immerse myself too deeply here in the question of precisely how to draw the lines between these different forms of recognition, but I would like to maintain that such distinctions are indispensable for any social analysis; if we refrain from attempting to distinguish the different shapes that social recognition can take, we will not be able to provide a satisfying picture of how it regulates and structures the conflicts and negotiations within a society. This all comes down to the question of whether you see the necessity and possibility of distinguishing between different forms of recognition within your own account of it; if you think such a step is superfluous and unnecessary, I would be very interested in your reasons for this claim.

Yours,
Axel Honneth

NOTE

1. See chapter 2, p. 46.

4

RECOGNITION AND MEDIATION

A Second Reply to Axel Honneth

JUDITH BUTLER

Dear Axel,

Thank you for your thoughtful reply. I am reminded of how difficult it is to move outside our theoretical frameworks to grasp the points that others are making within the terms that are most familiar and acceptable to them. It may be that we require a practice of translation or even a way to mark the impasse of translation as we proceed in conversations such as these. Let me reply first to your queries and objections and then summarize the difference, as I see it, between my view and yours.

First, I have never been committed to a unified account of this or that philosophical notion, since in the course of decades I have been most usefully challenged by critics and new paradigms and have found it necessary and important to revise my views. I believe that this willingness to change one's views testifies to the provocative and educative powers of intellectual dialogue, but also to the living character of thought itself. Forms of thinking that refuse to be revised by new challenges risk becoming ossified. They may then be "unified," but they are unfortunately also dead.

One way to handle your challenges would be to show that what I have to say fits within your framework, but I am not able to comply in such a way since I think the frameworks, though overlapping in part, are distinct. We agree that recognition appears in socially embedded forms and that it is inexhaustible. When, however, you describe one modality of recognition as a "mutual granting of normative status," it turns out that the differences between us attest to different understandings of what "socially embedded" means. A subject, for instance, can be embedded in history without being constituted or formed by history. In other words, there can be a relatively or absolutely asocial and ahistorical structure of the subject who is embedded in history. That would mean that social embeddedness is an extrinsic feature of the subject. I believe you hold to this view; for me, social embeddedness is intrinsic to subject formation.

We could, for instance, understand social inequality as unequal treatment, and we would, with such a formulation, surely capture one important sense of social inequality, but not all senses. If some fail to grant normative status to others, then they regard those others as not deserving of equal treatment. That is surely to be opposed. But if those "others" do not appear within the field of intelligibility, if they are not considered persons or humans at all, that can be the consequence of an inequality that follows from hierarchies implied by historically specific ideas of the human. Women and slaves were excluded from the category of the human, and now whole populations are considered lives to be managed by biopolitical means, often targeted in war or abandoned to disease. The problem is not just that some humans are treated with normative status, esteem, and dignity, while others are not. The problem, rather, is that there is a differential production of the human. When we ask who counts as human or even who counts as the subject, the very question points to the forms of inequality at work in the production of the human or the recognizable subject. This is different from unequal treatment which presumes that humans have already been constituted intelligibly within a social field, and we can then point to some humans who are treated with dignity where others are not. Of course, being part of a population targeted in war or abandoned to disease is to be treated without dignity. But that does not touch on the differential powers of racism, for instance, or the biopolitical forms of management that take place on the border, or under conditions of occupation. For that, we need to recognize the forms of power that establish certain subjects as recognizable as human and others less so, or not at all.

You suggest that I subscribe to two incompatible forms of recognition, but actually I distinguish between recognition and recognizability. My argument is that for the kind of recognition you describe to be possible, recognizability must first be established. To understand the epistemological conditions under which the differential production of the human takes place, or the differential production of the subject, we have to first understand that nexus of power and knowledge that constitutes various fields of recognizability. This move in the argument is Foucaultian, not Althusserian. And the idea of subject formation within grids of intelligibility is not Heidegger—who claims that *Dasein* is "thrown"—but rather an account of how the subject is produced within historical schemas. This would relate back to the idea of history and social relations as constituting the subject, rather than functioning only as an external form of its embeddedness.

Another consequence of this idea of social formation of the subject is the following. You note that we grow up unwillingly constituted by and within social categories. The paradox, I would add, is that the will is also formed through that very constitution.

So I may at first find that my freedom is restricted by the social categories into which I am born (religion, gender, race) only to find that I am able, through the inadvertent resources those categories provide, to remake them—or even to break with them. My freedom still depends on its social constitution—it does not exist in any asocial time and space. But restrictive categories can expose their historical malleability and revisability in the course of repetitive use, and subjects formed as intelligible within a given category can also break with it. That break is possible because such epistemes can be displaced, though very often not without great risk. I am sure that the theory of types, derived from sociology, cannot account for the categories and schemes by which the intelligibility of the subject is constituted. Nor do I think that the powers of normalization and biopolitical management and abandonment can be adequately accounted for by the pressure of "standardization" imposed by societies. The violence implied and enacted by being constituted (or deconstituted) in a zone of "nonbeing" that Fanon describes in *Black Skin, White Masks* is much more than the painful effects of types and standards.[1]

You maintain rightly that social classification alone does not endow any of us with normative status, and may even limit, or deprive us of, freedom. In this sense, in your view, the freedom of the subject transcends all social categorization. And when we confer recognition on one another, we acknowledge a dignity and freedom that transcends, or escapes from, all social categorization. Such a view is compatible with those forms of humanism that are blind to gender, race, or colonial formations. And yet, how then do we take account of those demands for recognition that seek freedom from colonial rule, the end to systemic racism, or the structural conditions of gender inequality? These demands cannot be countered simply by treating others with dignity, since they draw from policies and institutions which, though continued by individual subjects, exercise a form of power that is not reducible to individual acts. The recourse to an ethic that obligates us to treat one another with dignity, though surely laudable, does not address the systemic differentials of power by which some are produced as recognizable beings worthy of such treatment and others not. If the task is to separate those who make such demands from the historical conditions they seek to bring to light with such demands, then such a gesture surely fails to offer them the recognition they demand and may well contribute to forms of denial that are part of the original problem.

Even if we were to stay within the intersubjective framework implied by Hegel's analysis, we would still have to ask, through what language and medium does this "conferral of recognition" take place? Is the conferral of recognition possible if it is separated from language, media, discourse, or from the historically formative character not only of social categories but of social and economic conditions? Would it even be communicable without such mediations?

Although I do think that legal rights are important for minority and marginalized populations and for the very possibility of democracy, I am opposed to legal recognition serving as a model for all social recognition. I understand myself as describing a process that belongs to civil society and culture as well as law. Many social movements want to have recognition of a history that is not told, and many wish to achieve extrajuridical forms of recognition and justice. The LGBTQ movement surely seeks to achieve legal rights, but a more radical transformation of our idea of life forms, modes of intimacy and association, and ways of loving and living as an embodied person in the world are equally important, if not more so. The task is not just to bring each other "emotional sensitivities"—"I feel hurt when you call me that name or treat me with that presumption"—but in understanding the more pervasive structures of domination and exclusion, including the exclusions and hierarchies implied by historically contingent versions of personhood or, indeed, the human. Who counts as human is different from the question of what an already legible somebody who "counts" brings to others as an emotionally sensitive issue. Indeed, the micromanaging of modes of address, however important, is surely not the same as a systemic or structural understanding of oppression. The larger task is to understand how the one implies the other, and to develop a form of analysis and politics that responds to both.

On the one hand, you rightly insist on the reciprocal character of recognition, the fact that whatever one does the other potentially can do, and this structural equality serves as a guide both for assessing modes of inequality, and for understanding the normative potential of Hegel's theory of social relations. On the other hand, if we take recognition to be a "*Haltung*," a stand, or an attitude, it shifts our attention back to the individual subject who regards another in a certain way, and whose attitude is expressed or embodied in actions. At this point, recognition seems to be a moral stance of a subject toward others, but less of a social relation. You have, of course, written an entire book addressing this topic,[2] so I cannot do justice to your argument in these pages. There, your argument against Althusser (which is not really applicable to my views) is that recognition can be positive, a form of affirmation that facilitates the achievement of autonomy on the part of the other. I agree with this view. We are often empowered by recognition to gain greater autonomy, even though we sometimes need to change the terms by which we are recognized to achieve that autonomy. The problem I see is that it is the specific qualities of the other that are recognized, and I am not sure how this can work at a social and political level.

It describes a mode of intimacy that seems to escape the terms of social power, one in which we either recognize existing qualities, or, through our attribution, actualize them in the context of the exchange. As lovely as this intimate exchange may be, I am not sure that it responds to the demands for recognition that emerge from conditions of exclusion, for instance. In those cases, what is wanted is a fuller response to a condition that has been reproduced or neglected by those in power, and that would demand the recognition of a social history, an economic condition, and a mode of denial within the media and public policy that is complicit with the reproduction of this exclusion. I worry as well that only those who manifest "valuable human qualities" are worthy of recognition. But what about those who merely exist, or who manage to persist in stateless or precarious positions, and who want their lives to be recognized not because they have this or that feature, but because they are living creatures who deserve recognition for their struggle? We may or may not know the singular features of any number of people who demand recognition. They deserve it not because we know their features well, but because they are still alive enough to ask for recognition. That suffices, in my view.

Similarly, the ethics and politics of care is not simply a question of how one individual treats another. And, in my mind, it is not a question of who *deserves* love and care and who does not. If we sought to understand inequality, for instance, on the basis of who is regarded as deserving care and who is not, then we are left with the question of how to understand the formation of such a "regard." Is it always one subject who regards another in one way or another, or are there ways of regarding and treating that depend upon the formation of subjects who can enter into the sphere of appearance and so become "regarded" there? The epistemological encounter between two subjects comes up against its own limits as a model for social and political analysis, even for a contemporary account of recognition. Recognition can be part of a theory of justice or a political account of democracy, but it cannot give us the full terminology we need to analyze and oppose injustice and inequality. It does remind us of the social character of equality, and the potential of transformation when we struggle to secure both the life and freedom of each other. But we never transcend the social character of our freedom even as we seek to contest the terms that have restricted autonomy and secured inequality. We turn against one set of social norms only because we are facilitated by terms offered up by an alternative sociality or history. In this sense, we rely on the social schemes that are made available to us by converging historical currents to find our way and to facilitate our mutual transformation in the direction of greater freedom and equality.

My best,
Judith Butler

NOTES

1. Frantz Fanon, *Black Skin, White Masks* (London: Pluto, 1986).
2. Axel Honneth, *The I in We: Studies in the Theory of Recognition* (Cambridge: Polity, 2012).

BIBLIOGRAPHY

Fanon, Frantz. *Black Skin, White Masks*. London: Pluto, 1986.

Honneth, Axel. *The I in We: Studies in the Theory of Recognition*. Cambridge: Polity, 2012.

5

HISTORICIZING RECOGNITION

From Ontology to Teleology

LOIS MCNAY

1.

Feminists have long drawn attention to the inadequate way in which issues of gender inequality are treated in mainstream political theory. Although it is a central structuring feature of social life, political theorists have, in general, paid relatively little attention to the analysis of gender inequality or to the methodological and normative implications that it may have for their central concepts, categories, and mode of reasoning. Indeed, despite numerous feminist criticisms of the masculine bias of the seemingly objective abstractions of conventional political theory, as well as the increasing urgency of issues of growing inequality in a neoliberal era, the indifference to gender concerns persists in many areas of normative reasoning. Some may regard this indifference as a symptom of the abstract turn that political reasoning of all stripes has taken in the last thirty years or so, which has led to a "dismal disconnection" between theoretical enquiry and matters of pressing sociological concern.[1] In this regard, Axel Honneth's social theory of recognition is a notable exception to mainstream normative theorizing in that it has always accorded a central place to issues of gender inequality as part of a more general understanding of social justice. Honneth's Hegelian account of the family as a primary site of social freedom contrasts with the way it is typically treated in mainstream liberal theories as a quasi-natural, background institution. As a consequence, his thought productively crosses over with arguments of feminist ethicists and others that the largely undervalued care work carried out mostly by women, in and beyond the family, is of fundamental moral significance for any understanding of justice. The affinities with feminist theory are not limited to a shared intellectual focus on care, however, for Honneth's deliberate enshrining of an interpretative element at the heart of his recognition paradigm, in the form of a phenomenology of social experiences of injustice, concurs with an analogous orientation in feminist theory to recover, reexplore, and revalorize the neglected experiences of women. Finally, Honneth's methodological commitment to normative reasoning as socially reconstructive critique, rather than as what he calls "the groundless circularity" of moral constructivism, converges with the feminist suspicion of idealizing modes of political thinking. Both share the insight that, if it is to be politically effective, normative thought is better guided negatively by the analysis and critique of existing forms of injustice and inequality rather than by idealized, counterfactual scenarios of justice and equality. There are, in short, several potential ways in which recognition theory may be fruitfully drawn on by feminists to further develop an understanding of women's subordination in the context of a systematic social critique.

Yet, despite these interesting points of convergence, any feminist seeking to use Honneth's recognition theory as a tool in the analysis of gender inequality has to face a central theoretical difficulty which relates to the way in which he grounds his critical social theory in a transhistorical anthropology of recognition, or what I have called elsewhere an *ontology* of recognition.[2] The problem is, in a nutshell, that the dehistoricizing entailments of a reliance on ontology seem to markedly curtail the sensitivity to social variation and change that should characterize a disclosing social critique. How plausible is it, for instance, to explain the complex and multifarious dynamics of past and present struggles for freedom as ultimately driven by a psychologically invariant need for recognition, without thereby effacing their genuinely agonistic, polemical character and, ultimately, depoliticizing them? This tension between ontology and critical theory stems from Honneth's commitment—typical of Frankfurt School thinkers more generally—to the idea of emancipatory political thought as immanent social critique. This is to say that the values and principles that guide emancipatory critique are not derived from external moral standards, but rather have some kind of internal connection to the norms already embodied in the practices and struggles of a given age. The problem that arises for Honneth from the rejection of conventional notions of moral transcendence in favor of a method of immanent social reconstruction is that, without independent critical standards in which to ground itself, critique is potentially confined to a parochial hermeneutics, and its emancipatory force is drastically limited. If the normative claims of critique are to have relevance beyond their immediate context, they need to be based in principles that, although socially immanent, also have a generalizable or "quasi-transcendent" validity. Consequently, Honneth has always regarded the unearthing of such a "rational universal" as one of the fundamental tasks of critical theory and, in his early work, finds this organizing principle in the primary role that recognition plays in the formation and self-realization of the individual.[3] The psychological need for recognition is, in his view, not a contingent or culturally relative construct, but an ahistorical constant, and a fundamental prerequisite of healthy human self-development. On the basis of this ontogenetic claim, he develops his Hegelian social theory, which regards the developmental dynamic of modern societies as driven by the progressive, although not unfaltering, instantiation of ever more inclusive and differentiated forms of recognition.

The difficulty is, however, that ontology in this relatively strong sense does not sit easily with a social theoretical attentiveness to the specificity of social practice, and this has led to numerous criticisms of Honneth's work as psychologically reductive and naïve in its understanding of power and conflict, especially with regard to an appreciation of recognition as a normalizing mode of social control.[4] From a feminist perspective, Honneth's interpretation of the family in terms of recognition dynamics has been particularly problematic because it mystifies the historically variable, hierarchical, and often exploitative organization of its internal gender relations as an ethical mutuality of care. As Nancy Fraser, one of Honneth's most trenchant critics, puts it: "what Honneth calls affective care is actually women's labour, ideologically mystified and rendered invisible."[5] Honneth has always been mindful of this tension between social theory and ontology, but his efforts to overcome it have not, on the whole, been convincing. He has tended to resort to a circular mode of reasoning, amounting to a questionable form–content distinction where, although the desire for recognition is supposedly a universal "need anchored in human nature," it only ever manifests itself in variable, socially distinctive practices.[6] It is hard to see, however, how this circular logic is anything but self-canceling; the claim to historical specificity is surely undermined by the positing of a self-same desire for recognition that remains untouched through the course of history and that resurfaces, time and again, as the unvarying catalyst for social conflict and change.

In his more recent work, however, Honneth has revisited this troubling tension between historical openness and ontological closure, acknowledging that previously he had not perhaps thought through in sufficient detail whether the three principal domains of recognition (love, esteem, rights) should be conceptualized as "constants of human nature" or as the result of "historical processes."[7] His renewed attempts to address this dilemma involve a general reorientation of the recognition paradigm around an intensified emphasis on its contingent and historically variable elements.[8] On this historicized view, the recognition regimes of the lifeworld are explained not so much in terms of the externalization of a presocial need, but instead as "bundles of customs" whose significance is tied to the distinctive contribution they make to socialization processes in any given historical era, and which change over time. The fact that love, for example, until recently was linked to issues of utility suggests that it is more productive to conceptualize this particular recognition order less as a socio-ontological given and more in terms of changing historical circumstance. The stress that Honneth now places on the historical variability of intimate relations represents an especially significant shift in his thinking, for he had previously claimed that the sphere of love did not have the potential for normative development, and that only the spheres of law and achievement were amenable to the possibility of progressive change.[9] Similarly, the stress that was placed previously on generic psychological dynamics is replaced by a focus on the "social and experiential reality" of being recognized in certain ways and not in others as part of a process of social interaction played out in the "historically emergent *space of moral reasons*."[10]

Misrecognition is no longer thematized as a free-floating psychological injury; instead, it is seen as rooted in a historically specific "moral" experience tied to the biased or misplaced evaluations that individuals make of each other. As Honneth puts it, the "historically fuelled feeling that others unjustly fail to recognise certain aspects of who one is."[11]

Although historicizing recognition in this manner goes some way to mitigating the naturalizing effects of ontology upon critique, it brings back for Honneth the potential problem of cultural relativism. If recognition relations are to be understood primarily as socially variable configurations, then the transhistorical standards on which it is possible to judge whether they represent a contribution to human emancipation or not seem to recede. The advantage of the psychosocial anthropology of recognition is that it allowed for the evaluation of social arrangements on the grounds of the extent to which they promoted or blocked healthy self-realization. However, the displacement of ontological grounds potentially exposes immanent critique to the value relativism of the radical contextualist where, given their essential contingency, any recognition regime is as valid as any other, or, as Honneth puts it: "the validity of the recognitional attitude . . . would depend exclusively on the normative givens of the form of life in question."[12] Consequently, Honneth has to find alternative grounds to ensure the evaluative bite of his newly historicized paradigm, and he does so by resorting to the idea of progress: "I do not think we can do without a conception of progress if we are to avoid the relativism that would ordinarily accompany claims to the alterability of evaluative human qualities."[13] The idea of progress has always been present in Honneth's writing—it is inseparable from the influence of Hegel and to a lesser extent the functionalist sociology of Durkheim and Parsons on his thought—but it is only with his historicizing turn that it acquires an augmented normative status. It brings with it the potential problems of teleology and historical finalism and, needless to say, Honneth attempts to strip his version of progress of questionable spiritual metaphysics in order to acknowledge more effectively the "ineradicable element of historical revisability and openness" in processes of social development. Even in this weaker, more open form, however, Honneth still endorses a notion of the inevitability of progress. From a historical perspective, the discernible expansion and democratization of core relations of recognition in modern societies attests to the general fact of modernity's normative progress; it shows us that, as Honneth puts it, "prevailing values are normatively superior to historically antecedent social ideals or 'ultimate values.'"[14] Belief in the inexorability of progress is, according to Honneth, "an inevitable element of modernity's self-understanding," the result of a "centuries long learning process" and, given the immanent connection between critique and existing social values, "historical-teleological thinking" must necessarily also be an integral element of his own method.[15] But, of course, the fact of modernity's progress is no reason to complacently endorse the current order, which is always an imperfect instantiation of general values and ideals. The "moral surplus" that arises from the imperfect embodiment of ideals and values in the institutions and practices of the lifeworld supplies the normative perspective from which to measure the shortcomings of the existing social order, and to press for future corrective measures.

These are, in brief, the basic steps that Honneth takes to recalibrate his social theory such that its receptivity to sociohistorical variation is augmented and, correspondingly, its reliance on an ahistorical psychology of recognition is downplayed, if not entirely displaced. The question that arises is, then, how successful is such a move from ontology to teleology? To what extent does it allow Honneth to engage in social critique that is more alert to changing configurations of power, even though he still refers, albeit less frequently, to the "invariant dependence" of human beings on the experience of recognition? Does attaching a social theory of recognition to a thin idea of progress give it greater analytical and normative reach than when it is attached to a substantive, but arguably culturally specific ethical good of self-realization? Most significantly, does an intensified stress on the historicity of recognition relations, especially in the sphere of love, open up grounds for a renewed engagement between feminist and critical theory? In fact, as I will argue, the harnessing of recognition critique to the idea of modernity's inevitable moral progress commits Honneth to a developmental narrative that considerably underplays the significance of the negative tendencies and contradictions of social life by depicting them as historical residues that will wither away. Nowhere is this normative skewing more apparent than in the story Honneth tells of the development of gender relations within contemporary family life as a democratizing process based on the gradual unfurling of an ethical dynamic of reciprocal empowerment and authorization. Honneth's investment in such a notion of ethical mutuality leads him to mystify the asymmetrical character of gender relations in the family and consequently to underestimate the considerable barriers that these enduring asymmetries pose to the possibility of women's autonomous self-realization. Moreover, Honneth's normative interpretation of the family as turning essentially around an inner logic of care screens out the extent to which it is penetrated by other social and economic logics and, as a result, disregards the pivotal role it plays in the systemic production of gendered vulnerabilities and inequalities. Ultimately, this neglect throws into question the adequacy of a monistic theoretical frame based on recognition for addressing issues of gender inequality.

2.

It is the idea of autonomy that, according to Honneth, is the main criterion by which it is possible to judge how much moral progress a society has made. To evaluate, in his terms, the emancipatory potential of any particular regime of recognition, "every new evaluative quality whose confirmation through recognition increases a human subject's capacity for autonomy must be viewed as a progressive step in the historical process of cultural transformation."[16]More than any other ideal, it is that of individual autonomy that furnishes the "directional index" of progress in modern democracies, and the history of modernity can be reconstructed accordingly as its progressive, although not unhindered realization in different social and institutional forms. Naturally, for a Hegelian like Honneth, autonomy is not to be understood in monologic or negative terms as sovereign agency, but rather as a fundamentally relational and intersubjective achievement. As that which signifies the capacity for self-realization, autonomy is constituted and sustained by the life-world processes of mutual recognition embedded in the three core spheres of social practice: personal relations, market interactions, and political life. Each sphere is characterized by a distinctive practice, set of norms, and personality type, and qualifies as ethical insofar as it is structured around a core dynamic of "reciprocal empowerment and authorisation."[17] In following a "socially practised morality," any individual in the group may appeal to the practice's governing norms as part of an inclusive process of deliberation, to ensure a fairer and more reciprocal distribution of tasks and duties. The fundamental function of such a deliberative ethical practice is to bring about an ever improved alignment of individual autonomy with a willingness to assume the obligations and duties that are required of subjects in their social roles, to eliminate, in Honneth's words "[the] gulf separating duty and inclination, reason and sensibility."[18] When individuals feel that their intentions and purposes are fully supported and appreciated in the social order, it becomes more likely that they will be able to develop their personalities and aims in harmony with those of other social actors, and that they will experience their social duties not as imposed and self-negating burdens, but as fulfilling their inclinations and sensibilities. Again, in keeping with his Hegelian roots, Honneth regards intimate and familial relations of care and duty as the fullest expression of this ethical dynamic of "reciprocal self-subjection," as the "epitome of democratic virtues" and, consequently, as the primary grounds of social freedom.[19]

Honneth's fear is that, under the atomizing effects of intensifying materialist individualism, the ethical bonds of social freedom are being neglected and progressively eroded. This threat notwithstanding, he offers a generally optimistic account of the evolution of familial and intimate relations in the postwar period as the "democratization of love," characterized as the faltering but ultimately steady uncovering of the ethical mutuality that lies at their core. In the last fifty years of so, intimate relations have become institutionally decoupled from marriage and have attained an independent legitimacy. Same sex relationships exemplify this democratic progress insofar as they are acquiring ever greater social acceptance culminating, in many countries, in the legal recognition of gay marriage. At the same time, the internal structure of the heterosexual family unit has undergone a corresponding liberalization, moving from a rigid nuclear model to embrace complicated and extended patterns of intimacy captured under the term "patchwork" families. Diversification of the family structure has been accompanied by a dismantling of its organization around traditional and fixed gender roles, giving way to more fluid notions of partnership and shared responsibility, and this, in turn, has brought about an attenuation or "levelling" of the gendered division of labour.[20] This gender equalization has been intensified by women's presence in the workforce, which has replaced conventional ideas of the stay-at-home mother with those of the "career mother."[21] The democratization of the family structure has not been without setbacks; for example, liberalization has been accompanied by rising divorce rates and familial bonds of mutuality are under threat from pathological social tendencies toward a growing purposeless or emotional anomie where individuals find it increasingly difficult to form lasting attachments and emotional ties. Despite this, Honneth concludes that, on balance, democratizing trends in the family and intimacy more generally are historically inevitable: "almost all empirical data indicates that this new ideal is inevitable, because the non-coercive power to assert a normative surplus exercises a permanent pressure that will sooner or later destroy any remains of traditional practices."[22] Progress is inexorable because, as the norms of familial intimacy are contested and revised over time, there is a "socialising feedback effect" which correspondingly alters the desires and expectations of participants, and leads to the dropping away of "ethically faded or withered norms."[23]

Honneth's depiction of the recent evolution of family life as a process of ethical purification is undoubtedly appealing, but how plausible is it? There are a number of respects in which his story could be complicated, the most significant of which pertain to its disregarding of those more negative features of family life that are ineluctably bound up with the reproduction of persistent gender inequalities. So, for instance, there is little sociological evidence to suggest that the gender division of labor is being extensively renegotiated, or that fathers are now playing a significantly increased role financially or with regard to child-care after divorce. The overwhelming majority of single parent families (around 90 percent) are still headed by women.[24] Women's greater presence in the work force is not really accurately captured either in the idea of the career mother, since the majority of jobs they undertake are low paid, part time, relatively unprotected, and clustered in low prestige, gendered areas of, for example, the care and service industries. It is also arguable that Honneth misdiagnoses the main threat to family life, which is not so much an atomizing emotional anomie but rather the stresses that arise from increasing levels of poverty and growing social inequality, threats that are being intensified by the erosion of welfare support and other public services in Western democracies, trends that disproportionately affect women.[25]

The problem is not just that Honneth fails to pay sufficient attention to these negative tendencies but that, because of the biasing effects of the idea of the inevitability of progress, he has to imply that they are obsolete residues of traditional dynamics or anomalous deviations that will fade away from the largely emancipatory developmental path of modern democracies. Given the persistent nature of many gender inequalities, however, it is possible to argue that these regressive features are as intrinsic a part of familial dynamics as the progressive ones that are one-sidedly foregrounded, and that overall the developmental trajectory of the sphere of intimacy is much more uneven, nonsynchronous, and contradictory than Honneth allows. Despite formal gender equality in most areas of social life, for instance, there is little evidence to suggest that rates of domestic violence are declining; indeed, a recent study in the UK has suggested that levels of domestic violence against women and children in the family were on the increase.[26] Many experts fear that the actual rate of domestic violence is in fact far higher than official figures because of the widely acknowledged problem of underreporting where women only go to the police and other authorities only after enduring repeated assaults.[27] These facts are not unknown but are worth repeating to contest Honneth's skewed narrative of progress where negative features in the family are viewed as dysfunctions that will inevitably drop away with the gradual purification of socially instantiated ethical practice. In the light of these negative tendencies, an alternative feminist account of the development of the modern family might replace the story of ethical progress and democratization with one of the succession of different eras of patriarchy: from the direct domination of paternal and then fraternal/husband forms to the indirect oppression of public patriarchy that typifies contemporary modernity.[28]

Honneth's tendency to drastically underestimate negative, gendered tendencies endemic in the family is symptomatic of a deeper problem with his method of normative reconstruction, namely that it idealizes social institutions and practices. By depicting the family as, in essence, an ethical mutuality, he mystifies the far more contradictory reality it has for women when viewed from a perspective concerned with gendered inequality. From this perspective, the "reciprocal self-subjection" and "deliberative autonomy" that is presented as the animating rationale of family life has always in fact been structured around hierarchical, nonreciprocal relations of gender. If he is to successfully avoid the charge of mystification, Honneth needs to pay more attention, inter alia, to the fundamental ways in which intimate sex-affective dynamics underpin general processes of gender socialization that maintain the "soft domination" of male privilege.[29] In an era when patriarchy is no longer functionally necessary for social reproduction, it is the internalization of a heteronormative "sex/affective system" that is a key factor in sustaining what Butler terms the "passionate attachments" of subjects to their own gendered subordination and the universal fact of male domination. The endemic nature of domestic violence, for instance, can only really be properly understood in the context of a ubiquitous societal valorization of masculinity. There is a connection, albeit not a direct causal one, between male violence on the one side, and patriarchal "scripts" of male entitlement, aggression, and independence, and female passivity, dependence, and duty to care, on the other: "the social constructions of romantic love, idealized masculinity, and women's social responsibility for men's emotional lives provide the discursive context for batterers' anger and frustration, remorse, appeals to sympathy, and shifting of blame."[30] Honneth acknowledges in principle that if social freedom is to be properly protected and enhanced, then it is vital to reflect on "the ways in which a society's recognitional infrastructure can leave the autonomy of individuals unacceptably vulnerable."[31] Yet his idealized and degendered account of recognition bonds in the family permits little, if any, reflection on the special vulnerabilities of gender that are directly and indirectly associated with conventionally structured intimacy.

Such a disregard is evident, for example, in his sanitized depiction of the sex-affective triangle of father-mother-child as an ethical bond of care where duty and obligation are aligned with autonomous self-realization. Arguably, there is no such alignment, actual or potential, for the woman in this triad because the bonds that Honneth hopefully describes as "reciprocal self-subjection" are in fact better understood as asymmetrical and nonreciprocal, creating a far more ambivalent and constraining emotional and practical reality. Compared to the father, a structural contradiction marks the mother's sex-affective interests in the family; the greater investment she is conventionally expected to make in emotional bonds with the child, while undoubtedly rewarding, also puts her in a self-sacrificing role with regard to other aspects of her self-realization. Moreover, the feminized nature of nurturing means that she is expected to attend to her husband's emotional needs in addition to those of the child. Consequently, the woman tends to carry the burden of responsibility for the emotional welfare of the family as a whole and thereby places herself in the self-abnegating position of "adjudicating actual and potential conflicts in the sex/affective family triangle."[32] Differently put, the alignment that Honneth posits between obligation and self-realization does not exist—and historically has never done so—for the woman in the family. Rather, she is confronted with a dilemma where the more she conforms to feminized norms of care, the more likely it is that she narrows down possibilities for autonomous self-fulfillment. Contra Honneth's progressive narrative of ethical purification, it is not clear whether these entrenched sexual and affective dynamics are simply outmoded symbolic dysfunctions that will gradually wither away, so much as deep-rooted expressions of the "compulsory" heteronormativity that enduringly shapes most areas of social life.

Honneth might well respond that, because his social critique has explicitly normative aims, the reconstruction of the family as an ethical institution must necessarily be selective, and therefore the omission of these regressive features is warranted. The problem is, however, that if the reconstruction is idealized to the degree that it is descriptively far removed from the actuality of contemporary family life, then it risks losing the "objective foothold in pre-theoretical practice" that he regards as the distinguishing feature of critical theory. What distinguishes Critical Theory from other conventional forms of political thinking is its "intramundane transcendence," which implies that, as he puts it, "its innermost core is dependent upon a quasi-sociological specification of an emancipatory interest in social reality itself."[33] If, however, the reconstructed ideal is normatively sanitized to the point that its connection to social reality is tenuous, Honneth comes close to a position that he explicitly wants to avoid, namely, the devising of ethical principles that have a tenuous relevance to actual social practice. This is not to deny that there are normative aspects to intimate interactions, but rather to claim that they are bound up far more closely with gendered asymmetries of power than Honneth's sanitized depiction of family life would suggest. It is somewhat ironic that Honneth criticizes Habermas's colonization of the lifeworld thesis for externalizing power with regard to the family and failing to recognize its internal contradictions and paradoxes, and yet, in the end, his narrative of the inevitability of progress finishes in a not-so-dissimilar romanticization.[34]

3.

My criticism so far casts doubt on the success of Honneth's attempt to historicize recognition by attaching it to an idea of progress, but it does not necessarily invalidate the basic parameters of the paradigm itself. Shortcomings in a recognition theoretic construal of gender asymmetries in the family and the barriers these present to women's autonomous self-realization might, in principle, be overcome if Honneth were able to develop a less strongly normative and more differentiated account of power. A more radical criticism of the recognition paradigm would maintain, however, that, even with revision, it is an inadequate vehicle for addressing gender inequalities because it fundamentally misrecognizes the distinctive way in which these are reproduced. What recognition monism configures in psychological terms as generalized patterns of misrecognition and lack of sensitivity to women's needs in the sphere of intimacy is better understood in sociostructural terms as systemically generated oppression. Feminists tend to agree that the persistence of gender inequalities in advanced democracies is, to a large extent, the work of interlocking, impersonal systemic tendencies—oppression—rather than direct domination. Moreover, the family plays a pivotal role in these impersonal cycles of subordination, or what Susan Okin famously described as "a cycle of socially caused and distinctly asymmetric vulnerability by marriage."[35] The gendered division of labor, revolving around women's traditional responsibility for childcare, helps shape labor markets that disadvantage women, resulting in unequal power in the marketplace, which, in turn, reinforces and exacerbates unequal power in the family. Not only does vulnerability in marriage increase over time as the gap between spouses' earnings widen, but it is also often dramatically worsened by divorce and separation, which invariably brings a drop in women's living standards. Recent feminist work attests to how the globalizing tendencies of neoliberal capitalism have only intensified and made more complex this systemic cycle of gender vulnerability.[36] As Iris Marion Young puts it: "all women, even unmarried women and even women who are not mothers, are made vulnerable to domination, exploitation, and deprivation by these structural processes, which pivot around the gendered division of labour in the family."[37]

By treating familial dynamics in isolation from other social and economic forces, and focusing on internal interpersonal ethical bonds at the expense of the external connections the family has with other structures, Honneth effectively renders the systemic nature of gender subordination invisible. For instance, his reconstruction of the deliberative core of family life, where individuals may appeal to latent norms of mutual respect and care to ensure a reciprocal distribution of tasks and duties, seems naïve and orthogonal to what often practically determines the division of labor in this realm, namely the general economic disadvantage of women. The structural constraints produced by employment opportunities and lack of state attention to domestic work and childcare mean that even less-traditional, egalitarian-minded couples often fall into a conventional gender division of labor against their best ethical intentions. They usually choose to develop the husband's skills rather than the wife's because doing so ensures greater economic security.[38] Families then are penetrated by, interact with, and reinforce sociostructural dynamics; they can be, in Fraser's words "sites of labor, exchange, calculation, distribution and exploitation."[39] Given this, Honneth's emphasis on enhancing ethical dynamics of mutuality and care seems, at best, an indirect way of promoting women's autonomy. Arguably the latter is more effectively promoted through an array of measures that focus more directly on breaking the entrenched systemic cycles that perpetuate gendered vulnerabilities. From this perspective, it is not so much more recognition that women need but greater economic independence and practical emancipation achieved through measures such as increasing women's wages, provision of affordable childcare, enhanced welfare support for single parent families and carers, extending educational and training opportunities, greater state intervention into private marital relations to provide security for battered women, and so on.[40] Such corrective measures might, of course, have the secondary effect of enhancing ethical mutuality in the family, but their main focus is breaking structurally generated inequalities of gender. So, for instance, on the issue of overcoming inequity in the provision of care, compare the way in which recognition critique frames the issue as a reciprocal relation of nurturance with feminist approaches that center, instead, on analyzing the political economy of existing regimes of care. On this latter approach, care is understood not only as an affective bond, but also as a cluster of diverse practices including nonrelational domestic labor (laundry, cooking, etc.), that is, as "care work," carried out largely by working class and migrant women, and that is undervalued, poorly paid, and maldistributed. This disaggregation of care and attentiveness to its multifarious social dynamics engenders, in turn, a series of normative proposals—breaking care work down into its constituent elements, provision of "doula rights," greater protection for migrant labor, not allowing market forces exclusively to adjust the pay of care workers, increased public spending on care facilities, and so on.[41] The detailed and pluralist nature of these proposals contrasts with Honneth's rather one-dimensional framing of care in terms of securing the interpersonal affective grounds for social freedom. Recognition monism may well be conceptually elegant, but ultimately it is too tangential and schematic an approach to yield an adequate critique of complex inequalities such as gender.

4.

Honneth's questionable idealization of familial relations reveals the shortcomings in his attempt to historicize recognition via the move from ontology to teleology. Although, on the face of it, the idea of progress seems to be more compatible than a foundational psychology with an enhanced emphasis on the historical variability of recognition regimes, it tends, in fact, toward an undertheorization of the contradictions, "negative" tendencies, and matters of deep difference and conflict that characterize the present moment. Does this mean then that Honneth's method of normative reconstruction is intrinsically flawed in so far as its necessarily selective nature—its focus on progressive ethical dynamics at the expense of others—will always inevitably lead to a questionable idealization of social life? Does attentiveness to the contradictions and negative aspects of social life mean that effective critique should relinquish any guiding sense of progress and confine itself to limited and relativist evaluations of local practices and circumstances? This is not necessarily the case insofar as the purifying tendencies in Honneth's work stem not so much from the idea of progress itself but rather from the way in which it is generalized as a unilinear narrative about the inevitability of certain developments in modernity. This grand narrative of progress is problematic not only because it has dehistoricizing effects, but also because, when it is tied so closely to the development of modernity, it seems inevitably to entail the troubling colonial implication that the non-West is comparatively immature and normatively underdeveloped.[42] This does not mean, however, that the idea of progress should be abandoned altogether; instead, it is to suggest that it should be conceptualized in a less grandiose fashion, as uneven, multilayered, and potentially reversible processes rather than as a single, unifying historical trajectory. It is possible for critique to work with a more limited and "deflationary" notion of progress that allows the acknowledgment of advances that have been made in certain areas, and according to certain standards currently regarded as important, but without having to connect this to an overarching teleology.[43] The position of women has undoubtedly improved in the postwar period in significant respects but, in others, there has been little improvement, and this is glaringly apparent in the persistence of certain forms of gender subordination (widening pay gap, levels of domestic and sexual violence, sexualized commodification). Moreover, the creation, by capitalism, in its globalizing, neoliberal phase, of new types of social vulnerability and precariousness—many of which disproportionately affect women—suggests that progress is not as straightforwardly cumulative and inevitable as Honneth implies, but rather a far more discontinuous, fragile, and staccato process. Gaps between formal and substantive freedoms may be mitigated in some areas, but, given the pace and unplanned nature of social change, they perpetually resurface in new, unforeseen guises in others.

Honneth might well respond that the cost of adhering to such a circumscribed notion of progress is too great because it involves the loss of the "rational universal," context-transcending perspective that he believes is necessary for a normative social theory to have critical purchase. There is good reason, however, to question this false and somewhat overplayed antithesis between universalism and historicism to which Honneth resorts. To accept that critique is always situated does not necessarily relegate it to "disorder and contingency," nor is it to deny that, as Foucault puts it "the work in question has its generality, its systematicity, its homogeneity, its stakes." Dispensing with a "rational universal" does not mean that immanent critique is condemned to an undiscriminating relativism for this negates the many important, often emancipatory, critical insights delivered by hermeneutically informed perspectives including comparative, historical, and genealogical approaches.[44] There are clearly better and worse interpretations of the world and their merits can be decided, inter alia, by debate on the relative explanatory force of one account over another. In short, immanent critique does not need a rational universal in order to aspire to generalized validity, clarity, internal rigor, systematic analysis, correspondence with facts, and so forth.

In any case, given its dehistoricizing effects and normative vagueness, it is not clear what a rational universal—in the form of a master narrative of progress that reinstates recognition monism—really adds to critique. In this regard, Honneth's own earlier work on social theoretical negativism may be instructive. Following Adorno, Honneth holds that a commitment to negativity should be the animating methodological impulse of critique for it is the sensitivity to suffering that enables us to question the world in the first place. By attending to negative experiences—a phenomenology of injustice—it becomes possible to acquire an understanding of the deeper systematic sources of inequality and subordination that render a given social order deficient.[45] Honneth discusses negativism mainly with regard to the descriptive orientation of disclosing critique but, on its own, he does not think that it can provide normative resources to help us to decide how to intervene in the world or justify our actions. It may tell us what is wrong with the world, but ultimately it is a "parasitical critical procedure" that needs supplementing with some kind of transhistorical normative principle of progress, recognition and so on.[46] But is it really the case that what Adorno calls an unalleviated consciousness of negativity is really so normatively insufficient? For negativism is never a simple negation, a form of naysaying. As Judith Butler points out, "it is important to remember that the no delineates and animates a new set of positions for the subject; it is inventive and, in that sense, operates as a determinate negation."[47] Critique's methodological focus on negative power relations goes hand in hand with an "epistemic negativism"; it might not be possible to know what the good is prior to its realization in certain circumstances, but we do know what the bad is because it is instantiated in the world and confronts us in an immediate and visceral fashion.[48] It is the avoidance or mitigation of the latter that helps to inform our judgments about how to practically orient ourselves with regard to others, that provides us, in other words, with an "orientational" normativity whose evaluative standards are derived from an attentiveness to the repressed particularity of existing forms of oppression and domination.[49] This negativist orientation is exemplified in the type of contextually grounded but systematic evaluative reasoning that characterizes the work on care, discussed earlier, as well as many other instances of feminist normative thought on tackling gender inequality. Critique, on this view, is what Iris Marion Young describes as "theorising with practical intent," a mode of thinking that aims not "to develop systematic theories that can account for everything in a particular field" but rather follows a line of solving "particular conceptual or normative problems that arise from a practical context."[50] Given the constraints that a theoretical commitment to the inevitability of progress imposes on Honneth's thought, it might be this negativist orientation that, in the end, proves to be a more productive route for developing normative social critique in a world permeated by hierarchically ordered differences, and worsening inequality.

NOTES

1. Marc Stears "The Vocation of Political Theory: Principles, Empirical Inquiry and the Politics of Opportunity," *European Journal of Political Theory* 4, no. 4 (2005): 326.

2. Lois McNay, *Against Recognition* (Cambridge: Polity, 2009).
3. Axel Honneth, "A Social Pathology of Reason: On the Intellectual Legacy of Critical Theory," in *The Cambridge Companion to Critical Theory*, ed. F. Rush (Cambridge: Cambridge University Press, 2004).
4. E.g., Bert van den Brink and David Owen, *Recognition and Power: Axel Honneth and the Tradition of Critical Social Theory* (Cambridge: Cambridge University Press, 2007); Nancy Fraser and Axel Honneth, *Redistribution or Recognition? A Political-Philosophical Exchange* (London: Verso, 2003).
5. Fraser and Honneth, *Redistribution or Recognition*, 220.
6. Fraser and Honneth, *Redistribution or Recognition*, 131–32.
7. Axel Honneth, "Grounding Recognition: A Rejoinder to Critical Questions," *Inquiry* 45, no. 4 (2002): 501.
8. The fullest expression to date of this historical shift in Honneth's thinking is Axel Honneth, *Freedom's Right: The Social Foundations of Democratic Life* (Cambridge: Polity, 2014).
9. Axel Honneth, *The Struggle for Recognition: The Moral Grammar of Social Conflicts* (Cambridge: Polity, 1995), 176.
10. Honneth, "Grounding Recognition," 503.
11. Honneth, "Grounding Recognition," 504.
12. Honneth, "Grounding Recognition," 508.
13. Honneth, "Grounding Recognition," 510.
14. Honneth, *Freedom's Right*, 4.
15. Honneth, *Freedom's Right*, 4, 18.
16. Honneth, "Grounding Recognition," 510–11.
17. Axel Honneth, "The Normativity of Ethical Life," *Philosophy and Social Criticism* 40, no. 8 (2014): 819.
18. Honneth, "Normativity of Ethical Life," 821.
19. Honneth, *Freedom's Right*, 175.
20. Honneth, *Freedom's Right*, 161.
21. Honneth, *Freedom's Right*, 159.
22. Honneth, *Freedom's Right*, 164.
23. Honneth, "Normativity of Ethical Life," 823.
24. "Single Parents: Facts and Figures," Media Center, Gingerbread, updated September 2019, https://www.gingerbread.org.uk/what-we-do/media-centre/single-parents-facts-figures/.

25. I have discussed these negative tendencies in more detail in Lois McNay, "Social Freedom and Progress in the Family: Reflections on Care, Gender and Inequality," *Critical Horizons* 16, no. 2 (2015): 170–86.
26. HM Inspectorate of Constabulary, "Everyone's Business: Improving the Police Response to Domestic Abuse," HMIC 2014. See also European Union Agency for Fundamental Rights, *Violence Against Women: An EU-wide Survey*, 2014.
27. "How Common Is Domestic Abuse?," Information and Support on Domestic Abuse, Women's Aid, updated March 2019, https://www.womensaid.org.uk/information-support/what-is-domestic-abuse/how-common-is-domestic-abuse/#1447951162114-dd9bc8fd-c7ad.
28. Ann Ferguson, "On Conceiving Motherhood and Sexuality: A Feminist Materialist Approach," in *Feminist Social Thought: A Reader*, ed. Diana Tietjens Meyers (London: Routledge, 1997), 50–57.
29. E.g., Marilyn Friedman, "Autonomy and Male Dominance," in *Autonomy and the Challenges to Liberalism: New Essays*, ed. J. Christman and J. Anderson (Cambridge: Cambridge University Press, 2005).
30. Nancy Hirschmann, *The Subject of Liberty: Toward a Feminist Theory of Freedom* (Princeton, NJ: Princeton University Press, 2003), 128.
31. Joel Anderson and Axel Honneth, "Autonomy, Vulnerability, Recognition, and Justice," in *Autonomy and the Challenges to Liberalism: New Essays*, ed. J. Christman and J. Anderson (Cambridge: Cambridge University Press, 2005), 142.
32. Ferguson, "On Conceiving Motherhood and Sexuality," 47.
33. Axel Honneth, *Disrespect: The Normative Foundations of Critical Theory* (Cambridge: Polity, 2007), 65.
34. E.g., Martin Hartmann and Axel Honneth, "Paradoxes of Capitalism," *Constellations* 13, no. 1 (2006): 41–58.
35. Susanne Moller Okin, *Justice, Gender, and the Family* (New York: Basic Books, 1989), 4. E.g., Iris Marion Young, "The Gendered Cycle of Vulnerability in the Less Developed World," in *Toward a Humanist Justice: The Political Philosophy of Susan Moller Okin*, ed. Debra Satz and Rob Reich (Oxford: Oxford University Press, 2009), 223–37; Ann Cudd, *Analyzing Oppression* (Oxford: Oxford University Press, 2006).

36. E.g., Alison Jaggar, *Gender and Global Justice* (Cambridge: Polity, 2014).
37. Jaggar, *Gender and Global Justice*, 225.
38. Young, "Gendered Cycle of Vulnerability," 228.
39. Nancy Fraser, *Unruly Practices: Power, Discourse and Gender in Contemporary Social Theory* (Cambridge: Polity, 1989), 120.
40. E.g., Beate Roessler, "Work, Recognition, Emancipation," in *Recognition and Power: Axel Honneth and the Tradition of Critical Social Theory*, ed. B. van den Brink and David Owen (Cambridge: Cambridge University Press, 2007), 135–63.
41. E.g., Eva Feder Kittay, "The Moral Harm of Migrant Carework: Realising a Global Right to Care," in *Gender and Global Justice*, ed. Alison Jaggar (Cambridge: Polity, 2014); Kathleen Lynch, John Baker, and Maureen Lyons, *Affective Equality: Love, Care and Injustice* (Basingstoke: Palgrave Macmillan, 2009); Joan Tronto, "Democratic Care Politics in an Age of Limits," in *Global Variations in the Political and Social Economy of Care: Worlds Apart*, ed. S. Razavi and S. Staab (London: Routledge, 2012).
42. Amy Allen, *The End of Progress: Decolonizing the Normative Foundations of Critical Theory* (New York: Columbia University Press, 2016).
43. Allen, *End of Progress*, 9.
44. Michel Foucault, "What Is Enlightenment?," in *The Foucault Reader*, ed. P. Rabinow (London: Penguin, 1984), 317.
45. Honneth, "A Social Pathology of Reason," 338ff.
46. Axel Honneth, *Pathologies of Reason: On the Legacy of Critical Theory* (New York: Columbia University Press, 2009), 48.
47. Judith Butler, "Critique, Dissent, Disciplinarity," *Critical Inquiry* 35, no. 4 (2009): 792.
48. Fabian Freyenhagen, *Adorno's Practical Philosophy: Living Less Wrongly* (Cambridge: Cambridge University Press, 2013), 3–4.
49. E.g., Albena Azmanova, *The Scandal of Reason: A Critical Theory of Political Judgment* (New York: Columbia University Press, 2012), 131.
50. Iris Marion Young, *Intersecting Voices: Dilemmas of Gender, Political Philosophy, and Policy* (Princeton, NJ: Princeton University Press, 1997), 5.

BIBLIOGRAPHY

Allen, Amy. *The End of Progress: Decolonizing the Normative Foundations of Critical Theory*. New York: Columbia University Press, 2016.

Anderson, Joel and Axel Honneth. "Autonomy, Vulnerability, Recognition, and Justice." In *Autonomy and the Challenges to Liberalism: New Essays*, edited by J. Christman and J. Anderson, 127–49. Cambridge: Cambridge University Press, 2005.

Azmanova, Albena. *The Scandal of Reason: A Critical Theory of Political Judgment*. New York: Columbia University Press, 2012.

van den Brink, Bert, and David Owen. *Recognition and Power: Axel Honneth and the Tradition of Critical Social Theory*. Cambridge: Cambridge University Press, 2007.

Butler, Judith. "Critique, Dissent, Disciplinarity." *Critical Inquiry* 35, no. 4 (2009): 773–97.

Cudd, Ann. *Analyzing Oppression*. Oxford: Oxford University Press, 2006.

European Union Agency for Fundamental Rights. *Violence Against Women: An EU-Wide Survey*. 2014.

Feder Kittay, Eva. "The Moral Harm of Migrant Carework: Realising a Global Right to Care." In *Gender and Global Justice*, edited by Alison Jaggar. Cambridge: Polity, 2014.

Ferguson, Ann. "On Conceiving Motherhood and Sexuality: A Feminist Materialist Approach." In *Feminist Social Thought: A Reader*, edited by Diana Tietjens Meyers, 39–63. London: Routledge, 1997.

Foucault, Michel. "What Is Enlightenment?" In *The Foucault Reader*, edited by P. Rabinow. London: Penguin, 1984.

Fraser, Nancy. *Unruly Practices: Power, Discourse and Gender in Contemporary Social Theory*. Cambridge: Polity, 1989.

Fraser, Nancy and Axel Honneth. *Redistribution or Recognition? A Political-Philosophical Exchange*. London: Verso, 2003.

Freyenhagen, Fabian. *Adorno's Practical Philosophy: Living Less Wrongly*. Cambridge: Cambridge University Press, 2013.

Friedman, Marilyn. "Autonomy and Male Dominance." In *Autonomy and the Challenges to Liberalism: New Essays*, edited by J. Christman and J. Anderson. Cambridge: Cambridge University Press, 2005.

Hartmann, Martin and Axel Honneth. "Paradoxes of Capitalism." *Constellations* 13, no. 1 (2006): 41–58.

Hirschmann, Nancy. *The Subject of Liberty: Toward a Feminist Theory of Freedom*. Princeton, NJ: Princeton University Press, 2003.

HM Inspectorate of Constabulary. "Everyone's Business: Improving the Police Response to Domestic Abuse." HMIC, 2014.

Honneth, Axel. *Disrespect: The Normative Foundations of Critical Theory*. Cambridge: Polity, 2007.

Honneth, Axel. *Freedom's Right: The Social Foundations of Democratic Life*. Cambridge: Polity, 2014.

Honneth, Axel. "Grounding Recognition: A Rejoinder to Critical Questions." *Inquiry* 45, no. 4 (2002): 499–519.

Honneth, Axel. "The Normativity of Ethical Life." *Philosophy and Social Criticism* 40, no. 8 (2014): 817–26.

Honneth, Axel. *Pathologies of Reason: On the Legacy of Critical Theory*. New York: Columbia University Press, 2009.

Honneth, Axel. "A Social Pathology of Reason: On the Intellectual Legacy of Critical Theory." In *The Cambridge Companion to Critical Theory*, edited by F. Rush. Cambridge: Cambridge University Press, 2004.

Honneth, Axel. *The Struggle for Recognition: The Moral Grammar of Social Conflicts*. Cambridge: Polity, 1995.

Jaggar, Alison. *Gender and Global Justice*. Cambridge: Polity, 2014.

Lynch, Kathleen, John Baker, and Maureen Lyons. *Affective Equality: Love, Care and Injustice*. Basingstoke: Palgrave Macmillan, 2009.

McNay, Lois. *Against Recognition*. Cambridge: Polity, 2009.

McNay, Lois. "Social Freedom and Progress in the Family: Reflections on Care, Gender and Inequality." *Critical Horizons* 16, no. 2 (2015): 170–86.

Okin, Susanne Moller. *Justice, Gender, and the Family*. New York: Basic Books, 1989.

Roessler, Beate. "Work, Recognition, Emancipation." In *Recognition and Power: Axel Honneth and the Tradition of Critical Social Theory*, edited by B. van den Brink and D. Owen, 135–63. Cambridge: Cambridge University Press, 2007.

Stears, Marc. "The Vocation of Political Theory: Principles, Empirical Inquiry and the Politics of Opportunity." *European Journal of Political Theory* 4, no. 4 (2005): 325–50.

Tronto, Joan. "Democratic Care Politics in an Age of Limits." In *Global Variations in the Political and Social Economy of Care: Worlds Apart*, edited by S. Razavi and S. Staab. London: Routledge, 2012.

Young, Iris Marion. "The Gendered Cycle of Vulnerability in the Less Developed World." In *Toward a Humanist Justice: The Political Philosophy of Susan Moller Okin*, edited by Debra Satz and Rob Reich, 223–37. Oxford: Oxford University Press, 2009.

Young, Iris Marion. *Intersecting Voices: Dilemmas of Gender, Political Philosophy, and Policy*. Princeton, NJ: Princeton University Press, 1997.

6

RECOGNIZING AMBIVALENCE

Honneth, Butler, and Philosophical Anthropology

AMY ALLEN

In her response to Axel Honneth's 2005 Tanner Lectures, *Reification: A New Look at an Old Idea*, Judith Butler criticized Honneth for having an overly optimistic philosophical anthropology.[1] In *Reification*, Honneth had argued for an antecedent form of recognition that is a necessary precondition not only for the three forms of recognition delineated in his previous work—love, rights, and solidarity—but also for the cognition of objects. This antecedent form of recognition consists in a primordial acknowledgment of another human as a human, rather than as an object. In his defense of this account of antecedent recognition, Honneth drew on the work of developmental psychologists and attachment theorists to support his underlying claim about ontogenesis: the developing child becomes able to perceive the world of objects as a meaningful world only on the basis of stable attachments to a primary caregiver.[2] Butler aimed her critique of Honneth, in part, at this use of attachment theory, which she characterized as a selective reading of psychology and psychoanalysis.[3] As Butler saw it, Honneth's claim about primary attachment amounted to the positing of an "Arcadian myth" of a "genuine bond" between parent and infant that precedes and serves as the foundation of the social.[4] According to Butler, this myth downplays significantly the fundamentally ambivalent nature of our primary attachments, and, as a result, of the structure of the psyche. As she puts it, "we are beings who, from the start, both love and resist our dependency, and whose psychic reality is, by definition, ambivalent."[5] Moreover, Butler was concerned that Honneth's reliance on this myth leads him to adopt a problematic form of moral idealism: "If we prioritize care and attachment, is that a way of making sure we are, from the start, 'necessarily' good and become contingently bad under only certain social conditions?"[6]

In his response, Honneth attempted to sidestep Butler's criticism by emphasizing that the topic of his Tanner Lectures—the antecedent form of recognition that is denied in instances of genuine reification—has no normative content whatsoever. Rather, it functions as a precondition for the normative structures of recognition and intersubjectivity that make up the rest of his theory. As he put the point, "in the context of my theory of recognition, the form of recognition dealt with in these lectures is only intended as a necessary prerequisite of all human communication, one which consists in experiencing the other in a way that is not connected with normative implications or even positive attitudes."[7] In my view, Honneth's reply is convincing as far as it goes; Butler's critique does seem to be based on the incorrect assumption that his account of antecedent recognition has normative content. However, as Christopher Zurn has recently pointed out, even if Honneth's response to the charge of anthropological optimism is convincing as far as his account of antecedent recognition is concerned, the charge may still stand with respect to his tripartite account of individual and social recognition, inasmuch as the latter account centers on the concepts of love, rights, and esteem, each of which has an undeniably normative character.[8] As Zurn explains, each of these three forms of moral recognition "essentially involves a particular kind of other-regarding attitude that seeks at the least to positively evaluate, and at most to protect and promote, those characteristics of the other which are recognized: their needs and emotions, their moral autonomy, and their distinctive contributions to collective endeavors."[9] As we will see, this tripartite account is also based on Honneth's reading of attachment theory and of psychoanalysis.

In what follows, I would like to pick up on Zurn's point and argue for what I take to be the correct and insightful kernel of Butler's criticism of Honneth. As I see it, her criticism is properly directed not at his account of antecedent recognition, but rather at Honneth's account of love, which, in his theory, is the primordial—first and most basic—form of normatively inflected *mutual* recognition. I shall argue that Honneth's account of love does entail an overly optimistic philosophical anthropology, according to which the parent–infant bond is understood as a blissful and unambivalent fusion that serves as the paradigm case for Honneth's normative conception of recognition. After arguing that Butler's criticism is more aptly directed at Honneth's account of love, I will discuss the implications of this criticism for his theory of recognition. Given the centrality of love, and the related philosophical anthropology that he develops out of this account to Honneth's normative account of recognition, restricting the scope of the Butlerian critique to this aspect of his theory does not diminish the force of the criticism. On the contrary, this critique has potential implications for the normative, social-theoretical, and metanormative dimensions of his project. Finally, I will conclude by considering how the lack of ambivalence in Honneth's conceptions of love and recognition might be connected to the similarly insufficiently ambivalent discussion of gay marriage in his most recent work.

LOVE

In Honneth's theory of recognition, familial love is the first and most basic form of recognition. Love enables the individual to develop the basic sense of self-confidence that is a precondition for the other, more complex and mediated, forms of recognition: legal rights and social esteem. The paradigm case of love, for Honneth, and thus the paradigm case of the most basic form of recognition, is the bond between "mother"[10] and infant. In his early work, Honneth drew on the object relations psychoanalysis of D. W. Winnicott to characterize this relationship as one of symbiotic fusion and mutual dependency. Thus, in *The Struggle for Recognition*, Honneth described the "mother"–infant relationship as one in which "both partners to interaction are entirely dependent on each other for the satisfaction of their needs and are incapable of individually demarcating themselves from each other."[11] As Honneth told the story at this point, this early stage of "mother"–infant fusion lasts for several months and gradually gives way to one in which the "mother" and child come to see each other as distinct entities who are nonetheless dependent on one another's love and recognition for their basic self-confidence.

This hypothesis of symbiosis or primary fusion, however, came under serious pressure in the mid-1980s with the infant research of Daniel Stern.[12] Stern's work claims to show that even very young infants—just a few weeks old—have a primary sense of self-awareness or a core self, that is, an awareness of themselves as distinct from their caregivers, and that the relationship between infant and caregiver is best understood not as one of symbiosis or fusion but rather as one of reciprocal interaction. As Stern put it in his 1985 classic, *The Interpersonal World of the Infant*:

> There is no symbiosis-like phase. In fact, the subjective experiences of union with another can occur only after a sense of a core self and a core other exists. Union experiences are thus viewed as the successful result of actively organizing the experience of self-being-with-another, rather than as the product of a passive failure of the ability to differentiate self from other.[13]

With this argument, Stern challenged decades of psychoanalytic orthodoxy, starting with Freud's theory of primary narcissism and running through post-Freudian currents of psychoanalysis as diverse as the ego psychology, object relations, and Lacanian schools.[14] He also posed a serious challenge to Honneth's recognition framework, insofar as that framework started with the assumption of symbiotic fusion.[15]

In more recent work, Honneth has acknowledged that, by substantiating the existence of an "elementary sense of self" on the part of very young infants, Stern's research calls into question the assumption that young infants are incapable of distinguishing themselves from their environment, thus, casting doubt on "the entire idea of an initial phase of imagined omnipotence."[16] In light of these considerations, Honneth has more recently rethought his conception of primary fusion and its role in his recognition theory. In response to Stern's research, Honneth gives up the idea that infants exist in a *state* of fusion with their caregivers; nevertheless, he retains as a hypothesis a belief in the existence of "momentous *episodes* of fusion with primary objects."[17]

Such a hypothesis is not, as Honneth sees it, incompatible with the findings of infant research since it presupposes the truth of Stern's view that infants are able to experience themselves as distinct from their environment. Experiences of merger and fusion are irregular and episodic—they are experienced, for example, in moments when the infant is nursing or being held—but we can nevertheless posit them as occurring. In such episodes, infants experience themselves as fused with their caregivers, such that the caregiver's actions seem to be direct extensions of the infant's own needs and desires. Moreover, Honneth argues that these episodes are characterized by "the elation of pleasurable expansion/fusion" on the part of the infant, such that the gradual realization that the caregiver exists as an independent entity is experienced as a painful loss, that is, as "a negative phase of separation/non-fusion."[18]

However, contra psychoanalysts such as Joel Whitebook, Honneth thinks that it is misleading to characterize these states of fusion using the term "omnipotence."[19] For Honneth, infants must separate themselves not from a state of fantasied omnipotence but, more neutrally, from "beloved objects occasionally experienced as fused with their own experience."[20] If fusion is no longer a state of omnipotence, but rather an episodic occurrence of merger, its breakup will no longer be the traumatic blow to primary narcissism that it was once assumed to be by psychoanalysts.[21] Nevertheless, Honneth characterizes the fusion experience as an intense feeling of physical and mental security on the part of the infant; hence, he maintains, the rupture of fusion through the intervention of the independent reality of the caregiver causes in the infant "a tense unity of fear and pain, anger and sorrow."[22] In Honneth's framework, the fear, pain, anger, and sorrow that result from the rupture of fusion are the source of negative affects such as aggression. In other words, Honneth understands aggression as a byproduct of the negative affects generated by the breakup of fusion episodes, rather than "as an elementary component of our being equipped with drives."[23] This is his way of accounting for what he calls "the psychoanalytical 'sting' of negativity."[24] In Honneth's view, we can understand this negativity as "an unavoidable result of the unfolding of our socialization process as internalization,"[25] that is, as the result of the inevitable inadequacy of the primal interaction between infant and caregiver. The "life-long influence of early expectations of security" thus represents for Honneth "an infinite source of antisociality, because each act of resistance to the independence and uncontrollability of the other, who thereby embodies sociality, is new."[26]

Despite all of these modifications to his theory and the role of primary fusion in it, however, Honneth remains committed to its core idea, namely that we can understand "infants' sporadic experiences of fusion as the 'zero-point' of all experiences of recognition."[27] This means, I take it, that fusion gives us a primordial experience of a completely unmediated being together with another person. In such a state of being together, a relation of recognition is neither, strictly speaking, possible—for recognition presupposes two differentiated subjects who recognize each other as such—nor necessary—for it is precisely the blissfulness of this unmediated being together with another person that relations of recognition strive, necessarily unsuccessfully, to recapture. And yet, as the zero point of all experiences of recognition, not only does fusion with the primary caregiver provide the paradigm case of all relations of recognition, but also the inevitable and necessary loss of fusion furthermore generates in individuals a motivation to seek recognition. As such, the breakup of fusion provides the impetus or motor that drives both individual and social struggles for recognition. "As deep-seated feelings of security lost forever," Honneth writes, "they compel us to strive for those fractured forms of intersubjectivity that take on the form of mutual recognition between mature subjects."[28]

Having clarified Honneth's recently revised conception of parental love and its relation to his theory of recognition, we are now in a position to rearticulate the Butlerian critique of Honneth. First, Butler is quite right to suggest that Honneth's account of the parent–infant bond downplays ambivalence, making it a secondary, derivative phenomenon. In Honneth's view, the parent–infant relationship is initially characterized by episodes of pleasurable fusion that are subsequently, but inevitably, broken up *from the outside*, that is, by the demands of the external world that must be met by the parent. This causes fear, pain, anger, sorrow, and disappointment in the child, and it is these negative affects, in turn, that give rise to aggression and antisociality. In her critique of Honneth, Butler suggests a more ambivalent conception of the parent–infant bond, in which aggression arises *from within* the structure of that relationship, as a result of the intrinsic difficulties of forming a bond or attachment under conditions of radical asymmetry and dependency. For Butler, the very fact of the infant's primary dependency on the caregiver "produces the permanent necessity of aggression, of breaking and separating,"[29] precisely because children must resist their radical dependence on their caregivers in order to become their own people. The interesting point of contrast here is that Butler's more ambivalent account provides a reason for why the child would seek to break up the primary attachment in the first place, and the reason is that that attachment is formed under conditions of radical dependency.[30] For Butler, then, aggression is already *internal* to the primary attachment relation, and it is the result of the radically asymmetrical nature of that relationship. Whereas Honneth posits aggression as the result of the loss of love, triggered by the negative affects generated by the painful breakup of episodic fusion, a breakup that comes to that relationship *from the outside*, from the demands of the external world, for Butler, the radical asymmetry of the parent–infant bond generates aggression as it were *from the inside* of that relationship. In her view, aggression thus remains installed in love as a permanent possibility.[31] And if love is the most primordial form of recognition, and the relationship that provides the paradigm for all recognition relations, then aggression will remain installed in the higher, more complex, and institutionally mediated stages of recognition as a permanent possibility as well.

Second, Butler is also on to something important with her worry that Honneth's account of the parent–infant bond has normative implications, although, as I discussed above, the problem arises not, as she claims, at the level of Honneth's account of antecedent recognition, but rather in his account of love. Moreover, the specific way that she formulates this charge is not quite fair to Honneth. Recall that Butler suggested that Honneth's use of attachment theory commits him to positing an essential goodness to human beings that is only corrupted or made bad by contingent social conditions. However, even if we were to equate aggression with badness and love with goodness—which is a problematic equation but nonetheless seems to be what Butler tacitly presupposes here—then although Butler is correct to say that Honneth views love/goodness as primary and aggression/badness as derivative, he clearly doesn't view the latter as derived from *contingent* social conditions. Rather, he sees it as the *inevitable* or *unavoidable* result of the structure of our socialization process; on his account, episodes of fusion *must* give way to a more differentiated experience that conforms to the dictates of the reality principle. Whether Honneth's account of love in terms of fusion posits a primordial goodness to individuals is also far from clear. What is clear, however, is that his account of love as fusion serves as the paradigm case for his normative conception of recognition and its inevitable loss, which in turn provides the impetus that drives individual and social struggles for recognition. Fusion is, as he says, the "'zero point' of *all* experiences of recognition."[32] Thus, fusion is deeply entangled with the core of Honneth's social theory, even if sometimes only tacitly and implicitly, in ways that I will explore further in the next section.

RECOGNITION

In his recent critical appraisal of Honneth's *oeuvre*, Zurn suggests that there is not much at stake for Honneth in this debate about primary narcissism, infantile omnipotence, and the degree of negativity, aggression, or ambivalence inherent in primary love relationships. Hence, he counsels Honneth to resist the urge to develop a full-blown philosophical anthropology, and to rest content with a more limited moral anthropology that acknowledges affective negativity without attempting to offer an explanatory account of the conditions of its emergence. According to Zurn, this would allow Honneth to sidestep the ongoing thorny, technical disputes between competing schools of thought in psychology, psychoanalysis, and infant research into which he has repeatedly been drawn.[33] The core idea of a more minimal moral anthropology, according to Zurn, would be the claim that, in addition to affective negativity, "pro-social emotions central to our positive recognition of others are also real and effective elements of our psychological makeup, crucial to the psychological anchoring of morally valid treatment of others."[34] Such a minimal anthropology would thus hold simply that love and mutual recognition exist alongside affective negativity. Zurn maintains that this minimal claim about the existence of prosocial emotions is all that Honneth needs to make his philosophical point that the intersubjective bonds made possible by such prosocial emotions are necessary in order for infants to develop into social and moral subjects. In relation to this point, it is notable that much of Honneth's recent work focuses on the social and institutional dimensions of the development of relations of recognition over time and leaves aside the psychological and anthropological story.[35] This might lead one to think that he has taken Zurn's advice and jettisoned his stronger anthropological assumptions. However, Honneth continues to defend his psychoanalytically grounded philosophical anthropology.[36] This at least suggests that he thinks that this anthropology—and particularly its claim about fusion as the "zero point" of recognition— is doing important work for him. Which raises the question: what sort of work is it doing?

My suggestion is that this story does a lot of (sometimes implicit) work in three different aspects of Honneth's theory: the normative, the social-theoretical, and the metanormative. Its normative role is, I think, clear from the claim that the love between the "mother" or primary caregiver and infant is the zero point of all relations of recognition. This means that Honneth's account of fusion functions as the paradigm or ideal against which all other normative recognition relations will be measured. In addition, at the social-theoretical level, fusion provides the impetus for the ongoing individual and social struggles for recognition that fuel social and moral progress on Honneth's account. As I discussed earlier, Honneth claims that the breakup of even episodic occurrences of primary fusion with the "mother" is such a painful loss and it produces so much anxiety on the part of the infant that it creates in individuals a strong and persistent drive to recover that lost state. In other words, as a result of the loss and pain incurred by the breakup of our episodic experiences of primary fusion, individuals have an inbuilt psychological motivation to strive to recover the kind of blissful, unmediated being together with another person that we experienced in those episodes. Of course, once we become differentiated individual subjects, we can never fully regain such a state of fusion; the best we can hope for are the mediated forms of being together with others that Honneth, following Hegel, thinks are characteristic of mutual recognition.[37] In this sense, Honneth's story is very much a story of paradise lost, as Jonathan Lear has argued.[38] But the crucial point is that Honneth needs his strong philosophical anthropology to explain not only what recognition—his core normative notion—is, but also what gives rise to and sustains the ongoing individual and social struggles for recognition that are so central to his social theory.[39] As such, fusion seems to be doing important work for Honneth at both the normative and social-theoretical levels of his theory.

Although this point is somewhat more ambiguous, Honneth's strong philosophical anthropology is also arguably closely related to his metanormative strategy for grounding his core normative principles. Even in his early work, Honneth's attempt to articulate a formal conception of ethical life rests at least in part on his philosophical anthropology, which, via its reconstruction of universal features of individual identity development, maintains that prosocial intersubjective relations of love, respect, and esteem are necessary conditions for the development of individual autonomy.[40] To be sure, Honneth's overall metanormative strategy for grounding normativity remains a bit unclear.[41] What is clear is that Honneth is firmly committed to grounding his critical norms immanently, within the existing social world. This stance rules out both moral realist and Kantian constructivist strategies for grounding normativity, since the former denies the relevance of, and the latter abstracts away from, the rootedness of norms within the social world. However, the commitment to ground norms immanently, within the existing social world, leads to worries about conventionalism: how do we know that the critical norms that we find within our social world are themselves good, that they are not just what we happen to do around here? On one reading of Honneth, it seems as if his reconstructed philosophy of history—in which history is read as a conflict-ridden, and often interrupted, but nonetheless unstoppable and progressive learning process—is what steps in to solve this problem. On that reading, the claim that our norms are the result of a progressive historical learning process reassures us that they are not just what we happen to do around here.

However, this strategy raises the further question of how we are to know what counts as genuine historical progress, especially if the normative standards by which we make judgments of progress and regress are themselves immanently grounded and, thus, outcomes of the very historical processes that we seek to judge. At key moments, in response to this worry, Honneth appeals to his philosophical anthropology to address this question, arguing that the criteria of inclusion and individualization can undergird such judgments: historical developments that increase inclusion and individualization are progressive, those that don't are not.[42] Inclusion refers to expanding the scope of individuals who are granted various forms of recognition, and individualization refers to the idea that recognition is granted based more on individual characteristics or personality traits (rather than, say, on the basis of one's position within a status order).[43] These criteria are derived from Honneth's philosophical-anthropological account of recognition, which has emphasized from the beginning these two poles of recognition: through the various spheres of recognition, individuals are both *included within* communities of love, rights, and solidarity, and *recognized as* unique individuals; ideally, societies should be structured such that all subjects are recognized as "both autonomous and individuated, equal and particular persons."[44] This basic dialectic of inclusion and individualization follows directly from Honneth's account of the breakup of primary fusion. In the wake of that breakup, individuals strive to balance their drive to recover symbiosis with their need for independence; that is, they strive to be included in relations of recognition in which they will be recognized for their uniqueness as individuals.[45]

In sum, Honneth seems to need his strong philosophical-anthropological story about episodic primary fusion in parent–child relationships in at least three ways. At the *normative* level, fusion serves as the paradigm of all experiences of recognition, which is his core normative concept. At the *social-theoretical* level, the breakup of fusion provides an explanation of the telos and impetus of both individual and social struggles for recognition. Finally, at the *metanormative* level, it generates the criteria of inclusion and individuation to which Honneth frequently appeals in his attempts to ground normativity immanently without lapsing into conventionalism.

So what happens if Honneth has this account wrong? What if the primary "mother"–infant relationship is best characterized not as a relationship of blissful fusion that must inevitably be broken up, but rather as one of thoroughgoing ambivalence from the start? What if Butler is right that "the struggle between love and aggression, attachment and differentiation, is coextensive with being human?"[46] Let me take the three points articulated above in reverse order. First, if Honneth's strong—and overly optimistic—philosophical anthropology is playing an important metanormative role in grounding his basic norms of inclusion and individuation, and if that philosophical anthropology is open to doubt, then he might need a different strategy for grounding normativity.[47] Second, without his strong philosophical anthropology, he would have a difficult time maintaining the teleological nature of his theory of recognition. That is to say, without his story of episodic-yet-blissful fusion he doesn't obviously have a way of positing a telos toward which struggles for recognition aim, nor does he have a way of accounting for the impetus or motor that drives such struggles. I'm not convinced that this would be a bad thing since this aspect of his theory seems a bit too metaphysically loaded for my taste; still, jettisoning it would require a significant revision of his theory. Taking these first two points together might point Honneth in the direction of a much more contingent, consistently contextualist conception of normativity that also understands normativity itself as a more ambivalent phenomenon, necessarily entangled with relations of power, aggression, and violence.[48]

Third, and finally, if Honneth's account of the paradigm case of recognition were to change, then his account of recognition itself, his core normative concept, would have to change as well. As it stands now, Honneth is unwilling to acknowledge that there is any aggression or will to domination internal to structures of recognition themselves, just as he is unwilling to acknowledge any primary, internal ambivalence in his paradigm case of love. Ambivalence and aggression are, for him, secondary; they are the inevitable result of the pain and anxiety generated by the loss and breakup of primary fusion experiences. Similarly, in Honneth's work, recognition is, by definition, an unambivalently positive phenomenon. Although Honneth has acknowledged various critics of recognition, including Judith Butler, who have presented a more ambivalent conception of recognition as both a norm to which we aspire, and simultaneously a vehicle for domination, he has responded to such critics by attempting to distinguish between true and false, or ideological forms of recognition.[49] I don't think that this attempt succeeds,[50] but even if it did, note that it entails holding fast to the claim that true or genuine or nonideological recognition is untainted by aggression or the will to domination.[51] In other words, it entails holding fast to the claim that recognition is not *in itself* an ambivalent phenomenon; it is a positive phenomenon that may sometimes be made to serve the ends of domination or ideology. However, if love is the structural core of recognition for Honneth,[52] and if, as Butler suggests, aggression is installed within love as a permanent possibility, then his attempt to relegate aggression to a position external to recognition relationships—to a force that impinges upon such relationships from the outside, turning them to the ends of domination—seems problematic. On the other hand, if Honneth's overly optimistic account of primary parental love were to be replaced with a more ambivalent account, then the door would be open for a more ambivalent—and ultimately richer and more convincing—conception of recognition.

MARRIAGE

As I have already indicated, the Butlerian critique of Honneth's conception of love that I have been elaborating here has broad implications for his overall normative theory. If Butler's alternative conception of love, in which aggression remains installed within love as a permanent possibility, were to be taken instead as the structural core and paradigm case of relations of recognition, then this raises the possibility that even higher, more complex, more institutionally mediated forms of social and political recognition will remain fundamentally ambivalent as well. To see why such a richer and more ambivalent account of more institutionally mediated forms of recognition would be desirable, and how the lack of such an ambivalent account is rooted in Honneth's philosophical anthropology, let's consider the example of his recent discussion of gay marriage.

In his 2014 magnum opus, *Freedom's Right*, Honneth offers a normative reconstruction of the realization of social freedom in European modernity in the spheres of the family, the state, and the market. With respect to the family, Honneth cites the cultural and legal recognition of gay relationships and the push for the expansion of marriage rights as the culmination of a progressive "democratization" of romantic love that has taken place over the last two centuries.[53] In Honneth's reading, the historical trends are such that the "source of the reasons used to justify excluding homosexual couples from the legal privileges of officially sanctioned marriage will dry up,"[54] and the only options that will remain will be either abolishing marriage altogether or extending marriage rights to all intimate life partnerships.[55]

This discussion of gay marriage is part of Honneth's larger attempt to offer a normative reconstruction of the core social practices and institutions of modernity that vindicates them by showing them to be realizations of social freedom. There is much to discuss with respect to this ambitious project, but the details of this larger story need not concern us here. In his discussion of gay marriage, Honneth emphasizes the normative obligations, shared past, and future-oriented character of intimate relationships, and in so doing, he clearly takes committed, monogamous, long-term relationships as the paradigm cases for intimate relationships. Moreover, he maintains that such relationships play a crucial social role inasmuch as they protect the natural neediness of individuals, and thus provide "a specific experience of mutual recognition from which they derive elementary self-confidence";[56] in this way, they serve as the foundation of our modern form of ethical life and its expression of social freedom. As a result of these claims, Honneth leaves himself vulnerable to the queer-left criticism that his defense of gay marriage as a further step in the democratization of romantic love is both heteronormative—in that it implicitly privileges a bourgeois-romantic conception of heterosexual marriage—and homonormative—in that it implicitly privileges those queer relationships that most closely approximate this heterosexual norm.[57] Honneth's account thus seems guilty of obscuring the ambivalent effects of state recognition of marriage in general, and for sexual minorities in particular. By contrast, Judith Butler expresses these ambivalent effects well in her discussion of gay marriage:

> To be legitimated by the state is to enter into the terms of legitimation offered there, and to find that one's public and recognizable sense of personhood is fundamentally dependent on the lexicon of that legitimation. It follows that the delimitation of legitimation will take place only through an exclusion of a certain sort. . . . The sphere of legitimate intimate alliance is established through the producing and intensifying [of] regions of illegitimacy.[58]

The point that I want to make is that Honneth's insufficiently ambivalent reading of gay marriage as an unproblematic marker of historical progress is systematically related to his insufficiently ambivalent conception of recognition and, ultimately, to the account of fusion that serves as its paradigm case. To be sure, with the discussion of gay marriage, we have shifted levels of analysis from the horizontal relations of recognition that obtain between individual subjects to the vertical relations of legal recognition conferred upon individuals by the state. However, the same basic logic that structures Honneth's account of horizontal, intersubjective recognition can be seen to structure his account of vertical, legal, or state recognition as well. Recall that in Honneth's account, fusion is blissful, however fleeting, and its loss is inevitably and deeply painful. The pain and anxiety generated by that loss compel us to attempt to recover as much as we can of that primordial experience. Although intersubjective recognition, social integration, and legal inclusion are necessarily second best and incomplete—precisely because they are *mediated* forms of being together with another, whereas the fusion experience that we are striving to recover is a pure, *unmediated* being together with another—and although they must be balanced with individualization, that is with the recognition of subjects as unique and distinct individuals, they are still the goods that orient our individual and social strivings. Thus, the general logic that structures Honneth's account of recognition across both the horizontal and vertical dimensions is a logic of fusion according to which integration and inclusion into social structures and institutions of recognition are understood as unequivocally good, while their lack is seen as unequivocally bad. This logic and these assumptions have the effect of obscuring from Honneth's view the exclusionary aspect of forms of recognition, including (but not limited to) vertical, legal recognition by the state. In other words, Honneth fails to appreciate the ways in which inclusion and social integration can be highly problematic *in and of themselves*, as the case of gay marriage shows.

In Butler's work, by contrast, inclusion and social integration are much more ambivalent phenomena. They may be necessary for our social survival, and yet they are only possible through mechanisms of constraint (of ourselves) and exclusion (of others)[59]—that is, through what the members of the early Frankfurt School would have called the domination of inner and outer nature. On Butler's view, we cannot help but want to be included, to be recognized, and indeed this desire is so strong that we are likely to accept recognition on whatever terms are offered to us, even if they require identifying with an injurious name; and yet we cannot also help but feel the force of such integration as both a violation of our uniqueness and particularity and a redrawing of the circle of inclusion such that some others are now on the outside. As she puts it: "Recognition is at once the norm toward which we inevitably strive . . . [and] also the name given to the process that constantly risks destruction and which, I would submit, could not be recognition without a defining or constitutive risk of destruction."[60]

Moreover, although Butler is very aware of the dangers attendant upon being rendered socially unrecognizable, she is also aware that social unrecognizability or unintelligibility carries with it a certain productive political potential. She writes:

> On the one hand, it is important to mark how the field of intelligible and speakable sexuality is circumscribed, so that we can see how options outside of marriage are becoming foreclosed as the unthinkable, and how the terms of thinkability are enforced by the narrow debates over who and what will be included in the

> norm. On the other hand, there is always the possibility of savoring the status of unthinkability, if it is a status, as the most critical, the most radical, the most valuable.[61]

Hence Butler has, whereas Honneth does not, a way of explaining why the politics of unrecognizability figured as the site of pure resistance—instantiated, for example, in the refusal of legal recognition on the terms offered by the state—retains a certain persistent appeal and efficacy.

As Butler rightly argues, recognizing this ambivalence at the heart of the question of legal recognition of gay marriage does not automatically entail a particular political stance "for" or "against." We may be for or against gay marriage in a variety of different senses or contexts, and for a variety of different reasons, and perhaps even both at the same time—for example, one could be for it on the grounds that such a stance is politically necessary as a counterweight to the widespread homophobia that motivates much opposition to gay marriage, and simultaneously against it in the sense that one is against marriage altogether as an oppressive or patriarchal or simply outmoded institution.[62] What it does mean is that we should be much more cautious than Honneth is about reading the inclusion of gays and lesbians within the legal sphere of marriage rights as a clear and unambiguous instance of historical progress. A more ambivalent conception of recognition, grounded in a more complex and ambivalent understanding of love as its primordial, paradigmatic form and structural core, would, I think, lead to a more cautious and ambivalent assessment of gay marriage as well.

I have argued that, although Butler's critique of Honneth's overly optimistic philosophical anthropology was misplaced against its original target, the account of antecedent recognition offered in his Tanner Lectures, her critique is correct and insightful when applied to his conception of parental love as the paradigm case of mutual recognition. I have also shown that this critique, even if restricted in focus to Honneth's account of love, has important implications for his theory as a whole, by showing what work his strong philosophical-anthropological account of parental love is doing at the normative, social-theoretical, and metanormative levels. The upshot of this discussion is that if Honneth gives up on his account of the primary object relation as being constituted by episodic yet blissful fusion, he may have to rethink his normative conception of recognition, his social-theoretical account of how struggles for recognition are motivated and sustained and of the telos toward which they aim, and his metanormative conception of normativity. So, the stakes of the debate are high. Finally, I have considered how Honneth's lack of a sufficiently ambivalent conception of recognition plays out in the discussion of a particular social-political issue, namely, gay marriage. Although this part of the paper shifts to the level of vertical, legal recognition by the state, I have tried to show that the same logic of fusion that one finds in Honneth's account of love is operative there as well, and that this logic has the effect of obscuring the exclusionary and problematic aspects of legal recognition and inclusion, both of which are central to the debate within queer theory over gay marriage.

In the end, I am arguing for a richer, more ambivalent conception of recognition. It may well be true that recognizing ambivalence in this way will unsettle our normative and critical categories and even lead to a kind of normative undecidability. Like Butler, and unlike Honneth, I see this undecidability as enabling and productive for critique. As Butler puts it: "I may feel that without some recognizability I cannot live. But I may also feel that the terms by which I am recognized make life unlivable. This is the juncture from which critique emerges."[63]

NOTES

Thanks to the coeditors of this volume and to Robin Celikates for helpful comments and suggestions on earlier drafts of this essay, and to Nicole Yokum for research assistance.

1. As Honneth himself notes, this criticism was echoed in the responses of the other two commentators on the Tanner Lectures, Raymond Geuss and Jonathan Lear. See Axel Honneth, "Rejoinder," in *Reification: A New Look at an Old Idea*, ed. Martin Jay (Oxford: Oxford University Press, 2008), 147ff. For a more recent version of this argument, see Danielle Petherbridge, *The Critical Theory of Axel Honneth* (Plymouth, UK: Lexington, 2013).
2. See Honneth, *Reification*, 41–46.
3. Judith Butler, "Taking Another's View: Ambivalent Implications," in *Reification*, 106.
4. Butler, "Taking Another's View," 108.
5. Butler, "Taking Another's View," 106.
6. Butler, "Taking Another's View," 108.
7. Honneth, "Rejoinder," 148.
8. Christopher Zurn, *Axel Honneth: A Critical Theory of the Social* (Cambridge: Polity, 2015), 47.
9. Zurn, *Axel Honneth*, 47.
10. In his early work, Honneth refers to the primary caregiver as the "mother," even as he acknowledges that the person who fulfills this function for the infant need not be the biological mother, and need not be female. Hence, he places "mother" in scare quotes. See Axel Honneth, *The Struggle for Recognition: The Moral Grammar of Social Conflicts*, trans. Joel Anderson (Cambridge, MA: MIT Press, 1995), 192n12. For ease of understanding, I will follow Honneth's locution. Butler rightly takes Honneth to task for his assumption that the parent–infant relationship is always a dyadic one, and suggests that this sort of parenting practice is socially and culturally contingent. See Butler, "Taking Another's View," 107–8.
11. Honneth, *The Struggle for Recognition*, 99.
12. At stake here are complex methodological debates about the status of clinical versus empirical research methods in psychoanalysis. By citing Stern, I don't mean to be taking his side in those debates. Rather,

I am simply trying to reconstruct the evolution of Honneth's views of fusion. The best overview of the debate between classical psychoanalysis and empirical infant research is André Green and Daniel Stern, *Clinical and Observational Psychoanalytic Research: The Roots of a Controversy*, ed. Joseph Sandler, Anne-Marie Sandler, and Rosemary Davies (New York: Routledge, 2000).

13. Daniel Stern, *The Interpersonal World of the Infant: A View from Psychoanalysis and Developmental Psychology* (New York: Basic Books, 1985), 10.
14. Melanie Klein is a notable exception to this psychoanalytic orthodoxy—indeed, her rejection of primary narcissism was one of the major sticking points in her famous debate with Anna Freud. For a discussion of Klein's position on primary narcissism, see Amy Allen and Mari Ruti, *Critical Theory between Klein and Lacan: A Dialogue* (New York: Bloomsbury, 2019), chapter 2; and Amy Allen, *Critique on the Couch: Why Critical Theory Needs Psychoanalysis* (New York: Columbia University Press, 2021), chapter 1. Not coincidentally, I think, Klein is also increasingly central to Butler's reading of psychoanalysis. On this point, see Judith Butler, "To Preserve the Life of the Other," in Butler, *The Force of Non-violence: An Ethico-Political Bind* (London: Verso, 2020).
15. Although Honneth didn't seem to see it that way at the time, since he cited Stern favorably—if a bit anachronistically—as having paved the way for object relations theory in his initial discussion of Winnicott. See Honneth, *The Struggle for Recognition*, 97.
16. Honneth, "Facets of the Presocial Self: Rejoinder to Joel Whitebook," in Honneth, *The I in We: Studies in the Theory of Recognition*, trans. Joseph Ganahl (Cambridge: Polity, 2012), 222.
17. Honneth, "Facets of the Presocial Self," 226.
18. Honneth, "Facets of the Presocial Self," 226.
19. See their published dialogue: "Omnipotence or Fusion? A Conversation Between Axel Honneth and Joel Whitebook," *Constellations* 23, no. 2 (June 2016): 170–79.
20. Honneth, "Facets of the Presocial Self," 227.
21. See Honneth, "Facets of the Presocial Self," 227–28.
22. Honneth, "Facets of the Presocial Self," 227–28.
23. Honneth, "The Work of Negativity: A Psychoanalytical Revision of the Theory of Recognition," in *Recognition, Work and Politics: New*

Directions in French Critical Theory, ed. J-P. Deranty, D. Petherbridge, J. Rundell, and R. Sinnerbrink (Leiden: Brill, 2007), 134.

24. Honneth, "The Work of Negativity," 134.
25. Honneth, "The Work of Negativity," 135.
26. Honneth, "Facets of the Presocial Self," 229.
27. Honneth, "Facets of the Presocial Self," 229.
28. Honneth, "Facets of the Presocial Self," 229.
29. Butler, "Taking Another's View," 108.
30. Although Butler at one time seemed to conflate the child's radical dependency with subordination—suggesting that subjection is per se subordinating—in her more recent work, she has clarified that a child's radical dependency merely renders her vulnerable to exploitation and subordination. See Butler, "Introduction," in *Senses of the Subject* (New York: Fordham University Press, 2015). For her earlier conflation of dependency with subordination, see Butler, *The Psychic Life of Power: Theories in Subjection* (Stanford: Stanford University Press, 1997). For a critique of this conflation, see Allen, *The Politics of Our Selves: Power, Autonomy, and Gender in Contemporary Critical Theory* (New York: Columbia University Press, 2008), chapter 4.
31. As Butler puts it elsewhere, reading Hegel in a Kleinian fashion, "love has within it a hostile element." Butler, "To Sense What Is Living in the Other: Hegel's Early Love," in *Senses of the Subject*, 104.
32. Honneth, "Facets of the Presocial Self," 229. Emphasis added.
33. Zurn, *Axel Honneth*, 48–49.
34. Zurn, *Axel Honneth*, 49.
35. The anthropological story is missing entirely from Honneth's magnum opus, *Freedom's Right: The Social Foundations of Democratic Life*, trans. Joseph Ganahl (New York: Columbia University Press, 2014), and also from his more recent *The Idea of Socialism: Towards a Renewal* (Cambridge: Polity, 2017).
36. Most notably in his debate with Whitebook, "Omnipotence or Fusion?," published in 2016.
37. Presumably we could at least recover that state of fusion in episodic form by becoming "mothers," since Honneth still seems to presuppose that the episodes of fusion experienced by infants in moments of being held or nursed are *mutual*, that is, that both parties experience them as such. I think this is a romanticized and idealized vision of

"mother"ing, but I'm going to set this issue aside. For a compelling discussion of the complexities of maternal ambivalences, see Sarah LaChance Adams, *Mad Mothers, Bad Mothers, and What a "Good" Mother Would Do: The Ethics of Ambivalence* (New York: Columbia University Press, 2014).

38. Jonathan Lear, "The Slippery Middle," in Honneth, *Reification*.
39. Indeed, Honneth reiterates this connection in his debate with Whitebook: "the social patterns of recognition, those forms of institutionalized recognition in which we grow up, are always something which we, in certain moments of life, can't experience as fully satisfying. They all equally fall short of that quality of fusion. All patterns of recognition are patterns of relationships between independent subjects, and therefore there is probably a certain drive from rebellion against the existing forms of recognition, which also can explain why we are never fully content with even the highly-developed forms of differentiated patterns of recognition" (Honneth in Honneth and Whitebook, "Omnipotence or Fusion?," 176.) Thanks for Robin Celikates for drawing my attention to this passage.
40. See Honneth, *The Struggle for Recognition*, chapter 9.
41. On this point, see Zurn, "Anthropology and Normativity: A Critique of Axel Honneth's 'Formal Conception of Ethical Life,'" *Philosophy and Social Criticism* 26, no. 1 (2000): 115–24.
42. See, for example, Axel Honneth, "The Normativity of Ethical Life," *Philosophy and Social Criticism* 40, no. 8 (2014): 817–26.
43. See Fraser and Honneth, *Redistribution or Recognition?*, 184–86.
44. Honneth, *Struggle for Recognition*, 175.
45. See Honneth, *Struggle for Recognition*, chapter 5. It isn't clear to me that Honneth can employ these criteria of inclusion and individualization while remaining faithful to his conception of immanent critique and without running afoul of his own critique of Kantian constructivism, but I set these issues aside. I discuss the issue of Honneth's strategy for grounding normativity at length in Allen, *The End of Progress: Decolonizing the Normative Foundations of Critical Theory* (New York: Columbia University Press, 2016), chapter 3.
46. Butler, "Taking Another's View," 109.

47. For an extended critique of Honneth's philosophical anthropology in relation to his normative ambitions, see Petherbridge, *The Critical Theory of Axel Honneth*.
48. Obviously much more would need to be said than I have space for here about what such an account might look like. I have tried to sketch the contours of such a conception of normativity in Allen, *The End of Progress*, chapters 5 and 6.
49. See Honneth, "Recognition as Ideology," in *Recognition and Power: Axel Honneth and the Tradition of Critical Social Theory*, ed. Bert van den Brink and David Owen (Cambridge: Cambridge University Press, 2007).
50. For my critique of this attempt, see Amy Allen, "Recognizing Domination: Recognition and Power in Honneth's Critical Theory," *Journal of Power* 3, no. 1 (2010): 21–32.
51. Obviously, aggression and domination are not the same thing, but I am assuming here that the will to dominate others is one manifestation of aggression, though certainly not the only possible manifestation.
52. See Petherbridge, *The Critical Theory of Axel Honneth*, 84.
53. Honneth, *Freedom's Right*, 144.
54. Honneth, *Freedom's Right*, 150.
55. For criticisms of Honneth's rather optimistic reading of the historical trajectory of marriage and the family, see Lois McNay, "Social Freedom and Progress in the Family: Reflections on Care, Gender, and Inequality," *Critical Horizons* 16, no. 2 (May 2015): 170–86, and Zurn, *Axel Honneth*, 31–32.
56. Honneth, *Freedom's Right*, 154; see also Honneth, *The Struggle for Recognition*, 95–107.
57. See Lisa Duggan, "The New Homonormativity: The Sexual Politics of Neoliberalism," in *Materializing Democracy: Toward a Revitalized Cultural Politics*, ed. Russ Castronovo and Dana Nelson (Durham, NC: Duke University Press, 2002).
58. Judith Butler, *Undoing Gender* (New York: Routledge, 2004), 105.
59. The best articulation of this position is found in Butler, *The Psychic Life of Power*.
60. Butler, *Undoing Gender*, 133.
61. Butler, *Undoing Gender*, 106–7.

62. Butler, *Undoing Gender*, 109.
63. Butler, *Undoing Gender*, 4.

BIBLIOGRAPHY

Allen, Amy. *Critique on the Couch: Why Critical Theory Needs Psychoanalysis*. New York: Columbia University Press, 2021.

Allen, Amy. *The End of Progress: Decolonizing the Normative Foundations of Critical Theory*. New York: Columbia University Press, 2016.

Allen, Amy. *The Politics of Our Selves: Power, Autonomy, and Gender in Contemporary Critical Theory*. New York: Columbia University Press, 2008.

Allen, Amy. "Recognizing Domination: Recognition and Power in Honneth's Critical Theory." *Journal of Power* 3, no. 1 (2010): 21–32.

Allen, Amy, and Mari Ruti. *Critical Theory Between Klein and Lacan: A Dialogue*. New York: Bloomsbury, 2019.

Butler, Judith. "Introduction," in *Senses of the Subject*. New York: Fordham University Press, 2015.

Butler, Judith. *The Psychic Life of Power: Theories in Subjection*. Stanford: Stanford University Press, 1997.

Butler, Judith. "Taking Another's View: Ambivalent Implications." In *Reification: A New Look at an Old Idea*, edited by Martin Jay. Oxford: Oxford University Press, 2008.

Butler, Judith. "To Preserve the Life of the Other." In *The Force of Nonviolence: An Ethico-Political Bind*. London: Verso, 2020.

Butler, Judith. *Undoing Gender*. New York: Routledge, 2004.

Duggan, Lisa. "The New Homonormativity: The Sexual Politics of Neoliberalism." In *Materializing Democracy: Toward a Revitalized Cultural Politics*, edited by Russ Castronovo and Dana Nelson. Durham, NC: Duke University Press, 2002.

Green, André, and Daniel Stern. *Clinical and Observational Psychoanalytic Research: Roots of a Controversy*, edited by Joseph Sandler, Anne-Marie Sandler, and Rosemary Davies. New York: Routledge, 2000.

Honneth, Axel. "Facets of the Presocial Self: Rejoinder to Joel Whitebook." In *The I in We: Studies in the Theory of Recognition*, translated by Joseph Ganahl. Cambridge: Polity, 2012.

Honneth, Axel. *Freedom's Right: The Social Foundations of Democratic Life.* Translated by Joseph Ganahl. New York: Columbia University Press, 2014.

Honneth, Axel. *The Idea of Socialism: Towards a Renewal.* Cambridge: Polity, 2017.

Honneth, Axel. "The Normativity of Ethical Life." *Philosophy and Social Criticism* 40, no. 8 (2014): 817–26.

Honneth, Axel. "Recognition as Ideology." In *Recognition and Power: Axel Honneth and the Tradition of Critical Social Theory*, edited by Bert van den Brink and David Owen. Cambridge: Cambridge University Press, 2007.

Honneth, Axel. "Rejoinder." In *Reification: A New Look at an Old Idea*, edited by Martin Jay. Oxford: Oxford University Press, 2008.

Honneth, Axel. *The Struggle for Recognition: The Moral Grammar of Social Conflicts.* Translated by Joel Anderson. Cambridge, MA: MIT Press, 1995.

Honneth, Axel. "The Work of Negativity: A Psychoanalytical Revision of the Theory of Recognition." In *Recognition, Work and Politics: New Directions in French Critical Theory*, edited by J-P. Deranty, D. Petherbridge, J. Rundell, and R. Sinnerbrink. Leiden: Brill, 2007.

Honneth, Axel, and Joel Whitebook. "Omnipotence or Fusion? A Conversation Between Axel Honneth and Joel Whitebook." *Constellations* 23, no. 2 (June 2016): 170–79.

LaChance Adams, Sarah. *Mad Mothers, Bad Mothers, and What a "Good" Mother Would Do: The Ethics of Ambivalence.* New York: Columbia University Press, 2014.

McNay, Lois. "Social Freedom and Progress in the Family: Reflections on Care, Gender, and Inequality." *Critical Horizons* 16, no. 2 (May 2015): 170–86.

Petherbridge, Danielle. *The Critical Theory of Axel Honneth.* Plymouth, UK: Lexington, 2013.

Stern, Daniel. *The Interpersonal World of the Infant: A View from Psychoanalysis and Developmental Psychology.* New York: Basic Books, 1985.

Zurn, Christopher. "Anthropology and Normativity: A Critique of Axel Honneth's 'Formal Conception of Ethical Life.'" *Philosophy and Social Criticism* 26, no. 1 (2000): S. 115–24.

Zurn, Christopher. *Axel Honneth: A Critical Theory of the Social.* Cambridge: Polity, 2015.

7

HOW SHOULD WE UNDERSTAND THE AMBIVALENCE OF RECOGNITION?

Revisiting the Link Between Recognition and Subjection in the Works of Althusser and Butler

KRISTINA LEPOLD

The claim that recognition is ambivalent has featured prominently in debates on recognition in recent years.[1] As key sources for this claim, defenders and critics alike often cite the works of Louis Althusser and Judith Butler. In particular, Althusser and Butler are interpreted as making a connection between recognition and subjection. The claim is that, on Althusser's and Butler's accounts, recognition somehow goes hand in hand with subjection, and this connection is supposed to explain Althusser's and Butler's ambivalent view of recognition.

In the literature, the link between recognition and subjection in Althusser and Butler has mainly been construed in two ways, each of which involves a slightly different understanding of subjection. One interpretation holds that, according to Althusser and Butler, recognition by others is ontologically constitutive of subjects and is therefore a form of subjection that harms individuals in their capacity to choose themselves.[2]

The other interpretation holds that, according to Althusser and Butler, recognition can be functional for the subjection of individuals to others because it can make them adopt subordinating self-understandings.[3]

Such interpretations raise two kinds of questions. On the one hand, we may ask whether these interpretations are adequate as interpretations of what Althusser and Butler have to say about recognition, and more specifically about how it is linked to subjection. On the other hand, we may wonder whether the views that emerge from these interpretations are convincing, in particular whether the picture of recognition they reveal is one we can endorse on independent grounds. In this chapter, I will be primarily concerned with the question of the adequacy of the two interpretations of the connection between recognition and subjection in Althusser and Butler. Nevertheless, what I will have to say bears on the second question as well.

In my view, both interpretations fall short as interpretations of what Althusser and Butler say, and this has a lot to do with the respective understandings of the notion of subjection that underlie them. Whereas the first interpretation must be rejected in its entirety because it builds on a false background assumption that informs an inadequate understanding of subjection as the violation of a person's autonomy, the second interpretation is more promising because it captures an important aspect of Althusser's and Butler's views; however, it is also based on a flawed understanding of the notion of subjection, which it portrays as subjection or subordination to others. Through a critical discussion of both interpretations, I will develop an alternative interpretation of the link between recognition and subjection in Althusser and Butler which builds on a more adequate understanding of subjection as subjection to social norms. On the proposed interpretation, recognition occurs against the backdrop of individuals' subjection to prevailing social norms which may be part of problematic social arrangements. Although I will not be able to argue for this separately here, this interpretation is not only more adequate, but it also offers a more compelling overall account of the ambivalence of recognition.

THE ONTOLOGICAL INTERPRETATION: RECOGNITION AS SUBJECTION

The first interpretation of the link between recognition and subjection in Althusser and Butler can be called "ontological" and has been advanced by a range of authors.[4] It asserts that recognition by others is ontologically constitutive of subjects, and therefore that Althusser and Butler regard it as a form of subjection that harms individuals in their capacity to choose themselves. In order to make it easier to follow the discussion, I would like to begin by reformulating the first interpretation as an argument.

According to the first interpretation:

P_I1. Both Althusser and Butler conceive of recognition as the identification of an individual as X by others.

P_I2. In both of their accounts, the recognition or identification of an individual as X by others constitutes this individual ontologically as X.

P_I3. According to both Althusser and Butler, to be constituted as X by others is to be subjected.

C_I. Therefore, according to Althusser and Butler, the recognition by others represents a form of subjection that harms individuals in their autonomy.

Let me address each of these premises in turn:

P_I1. At first sight, premise P_I1 appears to be correct: both Althusser and Butler conceive of recognition as identification, a conception of recognition that differs from more evaluative ones according to which person A recognizes person B not only by identifying B as X, but by affirming or approving of B as X.[5] On closer inspection, however, P_I1 proves to be problematic, because it rests on an unwarranted background assumption. Showing this will be important for the assessment of the argument as a whole.

As support for the truth of P_I1, authors often draw on an everyday scene which Althusser describes in what is arguably the best-known passage from his work. In the scene, a police officer hails a passerby by shouting, "Hey, you there!"[6] For our purposes, it is sufficient to note that this hailing by the police officer is interpreted as an act of recognition in the sense of identification. That is, various authors suppose that the passerby is recognized or identified by the police officer as X, that is, as someone specific who is answerable to the law.[7]

Authors who defend this interpretation generally acknowledge that Althusser does not offer the hailing by the police officer as an illustration of recognition, but as an illustration of *interpellation*. As Althusser writes, the "very precise operation which I have called *interpellation* or hailing . . . can be imagined along the lines of the most commonplace everyday police (or other) hailing."[8] That Althusser speaks of interpellation rather than of recognition has not been a cause for concern, since it is assumed that for Althusser interpellation and recognition are essentially the same. In my view, however, this assumption is unwarranted.

Let us examine what Althusser says more closely. Is there some indication that interpellation is not exactly the same as recognition? To quote the surrounding passage from Althusser's "Ideology and Ideological State Apparatuses": the "very precise operation which I have called *interpellation* or hailing . . . can be imagined along the lines of the most commonplace everyday police (or other) hailing: 'Hey, you there!' Assuming the theoretical scene I have imagined takes place in the street, the hailed individual will turn round. . . . Because he has recognized that the hail was 'really' addressed to him, and that 'it was *really him* who was hailed.'"[9] On a careful reading, although Althusser speaks of recognition here, he treats it as something distinct from interpellation. The police officer hails a passerby who, as a result, recognizes that he has been hailed or, to be more precise, *recognizes himself* as X in the hail and turns around. In other words, recognition is not performed by the representative of the law—he or she performs an interpellation—but by the hailed or interpellated individual, and it appears to refer to an act of *self-identification*.[10] To sum up, then, contrary to the assumption that informs P_I1, interpellation and recognition appear to be two different things. Nevertheless, it is true that Althusser conceives of recognition as identification. The identification in question, however, is not an identification by others, but primarily a self-identification.

Let us turn to Butler where we find a very similar situation. Commentators usually assume that "the central figure in Butler's account of recognition is that of 'interpellation'"[11] and suggest that through "recognition-interpellation"[12] persons are identified as X. Regarding interpellation—which she sometimes also calls "address"—Butler writes in her oft-cited introduction to *Excitable Speech* that "the Althusserian reversal of Hegel seems appropriate: the address constitutes a being within the possible circuit of recognition," and she adds a few lines later that "to be addressed is not merely to be recognized for what one already is, but to have the very term conferred by which the recognition of existence becomes possible."[13] Admittedly, these are just two remarks quoted with little surrounding context. Nevertheless, I think that they provide a first indication that for Butler interpellation and recognition are two different things. More specifically, it appears that for Butler, just as for Althusser, interpellation is something that precedes recognition.

Regarding Butler's understanding of recognition, I want to suggest that, like Althusser, she understands recognition as identification, although unlike Althusser she is primarily interested in processes of *interpersonal* recognition. According to Butler, person A successfully recognizes person B if A is able to identify or cognize B as X. In her work, recognition is related to the notion of intelligibility. As she writes, "intelligibility is . . . that which is produced as a consequence of recognition according to prevailing social norms."[14] Thus, a person is intelligible if she can be recognized or identified as X. For instance, a person is intelligible if she or he can be recognized or identified as unambiguously female or male in the light of dominant gender norms—a case of particular importance for Butler's work.[15] Therefore, while it is true that Butler conceives of recognition as the identification of an individual as X by others, she does not do so because she equates recognition with interpellation, which is the background assumption underlying P_I1.

P_I2. Turning to premise P_I2, it states that, in both Althusser's and Butler's accounts, the recognition or identification of an individual as X by others constitutes this individual ontologically as X. Let us unpack the content of P_I2. To hold that recognition constitutes an individual ontologically as X is to say that recognition makes an individual into X. This does not seem an instance of *ex nihilo* creation, but one of ontological change: a preexisting individual is said to acquire a determinate identity or to become a subject through the recognition of others. Primarily with reference to Butler's account, but also to Althusser's, Bertram and Celikates write, for instance, that "the 'recognition of X as Y' makes it so that X is determined or regarded as Y,"[16] and a few lines later they add that, "[o]n this view, we are made into fathers, citizens, entrepreneurs."[17] Jaeggi also notes that the hail of the police officer "makes the passerby into 'someone.'"[18] And Deines concludes that individuals "only become subjects by being recognized."[19]

It is here that the unwarranted equation of recognition and interpellation begins to become a serious problem. As we saw in the previous section, Althusser is primarily concerned with recognition as self-identification, which appears to be an epistemic relation: insofar as one recognizes oneself in Althusser's sense, one knows "'it's me,'"[20] "'I am here, a worker, a boss or a soldier!'"[21] While there is a sense in which this epistemic relation is at the heart of what it is to be a subject, the important point is that for Althusser one is not made into a subject through the recognition of others. Premise P_I2 therefore appears to miss the mark. Similarly, on Butler's account, recognition appears to denote an epistemic relation, which in her case is a relation between persons. If person A is able to recognize B as X, that is, as this or that subject, this is a matter of ascertaining what B is. This means that recognition seeks to determine epistemically "the content" of the other's "personhood,"[22] a content which crucially precedes the act of recognition. Therefore, I believe that, as regards the accounts of both Althusser and Butler, P_I2 must be rejected: neither Althusser nor Butler hold the view that the recognition by others *makes* persons ontologically into X, that is, into particular subjects who understand themselves in certain ways.

However, given the confusion surrounding interpellation and recognition, it is easy to see how one might come to embrace P_I2. In the passage already quoted at length, Althusser continues: "Assuming the theoretical scene I have imagined takes place in the street, the hailed individual will turn round. By this mere 180-degree physical conversion, he becomes a *subject*. Why? Because he has recognized that the hail was 'really' addressed to him, and that 'it was *really him* who was hailed.'"[23] If one mistakenly construes the hail or interpellation as an act of recognition, one might interpret this quotation as stating that the passerby—who is said to "become . . . a *subject*"—is made into a subject or has an identity imposed on him by being recognized. Some passages from Butler's work lend themselves to such a misinterpretation.[24]

Let us now ask whether it would at least be correct to say that the hail or interpellation, in contrast to recognition, makes individuals into particular subjects, or Xs. In my view, even claiming that interpellation makes individuals into subjects or imposes identities on them is not entirely correct. Yes, it is true that the passerby in Althusser's scene becomes a subject after having been hailed or interpellated, insofar as he recognizes himself in the hail. But, strictly speaking, this happens because the passerby is susceptible to the hail and turns around. That is, the passerby actively responds. His becoming a subject does not happen automatically simply because he has been interpellated. As Butler writes, interpellation is only the "*demand* to align oneself with the law,"[25] so that "the turn towards the law is not necessitated by the hailing."[26]

I would like to take this opportunity to say something more about the somewhat arcane notion of interpellation. According to Althusser and Butler, the demand involved in interpellation sometimes takes the form of a literal speech act uttered—as in Althusser's scene, for instance—by a police officer who calls on a passerby to stop and thereby show himself to be a good citizen. However, this should not lead us to ignore the important point that interpellation is, in Butler's words, a "continuous and uninterrupted process"[27] that does not require such speech acts to be effective. In their everyday social lives, individuals are always already involved in a number of practices and institutions. Expressed in general terms, practices are patterned activities that assign positions or places to individuals. Using a slightly different terminology we already drew upon earlier,[28] one might also say that they confer or offer terms to individuals through which they can understand who or what they are, and, connected with this, what they ought to do. Taking the example of Christian practices, Althusser observes that, in order to make them "speak," these practices "say" something along the following lines to those who participate in them: "this is who you are . . . , you were created by God for all eternity . . . ! This is your place in the world! This is what you must do!"[29] In other words, the social world in the form of its manifold practices *interpellates* individuals all the time, although for the most part implicitly. The social world constantly "asks" individuals to be certain kinds of persons and to comply with the corresponding social expectations, that is, it exerts subtle—and sometimes not so subtle—pressure on individuals to act in accordance with it. This is why Butler describes interpellation as the "demand to align oneself with the law,"[30] where "law" here refers to the prevailing social norms. In responding to myriad such demands in everyday social life, often unaware, individuals become particular subjects who understand themselves in certain ways, that is, who recognize themselves in Althusser's sense as X—for example, as a father or citizen—and who are "recognizable"[31] as such for others.[32]

P_I3. The final premise on which the first interpretation rests is that, according to both Althusser and Butler, to be constituted as X is to be subjected. It is easy to see what premise P_I3 is supposed to add to the picture: if recognition is an operation of identification (P_I1), and if the identification of a person as X constitutes this person as X (P_I2), then arguing that to be constituted as X is to be subjected (P_I3) would support the conclusion that recognition is a form of subjection.

Again, let us first try to clarify what this third premise involves. Deines writes that, for Butler, "the introduction into the dominant normative structures" represents a "form of basal subjection."[33] On Deines's reading, Butler chooses to use the term "subjection" because the introduction into the dominant normative structures is something that happens *to* individuals, that is, without their willing it or having any control over it whatsoever. In line with this, Jaeggi explains, with regard to both Butler and Althusser, that individuals are subjected because they are "being decided upon."[34] Thus, Deines and Jaeggi ascribe to Butler and Althusser the view that the act through which individuals are made into someone represents, and is also experienced as, a form of subjection because it impairs individuals in their capacity as autonomous beings.[35]

However, we have already seen in our discussion of P_I1 and P_I2 that for Althusser and Butler individuals are not simply made into subjects by others—neither through recognition nor through interpellation, at least not in any straightforward manner. Therefore, there is no obvious candidate for an act of the kind assumed by P_I3 that would represent, and be experienced as, a form of subjection in the sense of a violation of one's autonomy. In short, P_I3 appears to lack any plausible basis.

But where does this leave us? After all, both Althusser and Butler speak of "subjection."[36] However, given that a notion of subjection as an act that harms persons in their capacity as autonomous beings does not seem to have any place in Althusser's or Butler's accounts, subjection must mean something else. As our discussion of interpellation showed, the subjects who recognize themselves in Althusser's sense, or who are recognizable for others in Butler's sense, come into being by responding to interpellation, that is, to a myriad normative demands in social life. What does this involve more specifically? As Butler puts it in one place, "the status of the subject [is acquired] in and through *compliance* with the interrogative law."[37] Thus, one becomes a subject by assuming the place one is assigned and by acting accordingly. To judge from Butler's writings, it is clear that she views this as an ongoing and emphatically prereflexive process whose more profound effects take some time to materialize. Butler writes, for example, that there is a "performing" which "works the subject into its status as a social being"[38] and that "[t]his is not simply to act according to a set of rules, but to embody rules in the course of action."[39] Now, as I want to suggest, subject formation according to both Althusser and Butler involves *subjection* precisely because it involves complying with what Butler calls "the interrogative law." That is, for Althusser and Butler, "compliance with the interrogative law" is nothing other than "subjection to the law by which the subject is produced."[40] One becomes a subject who recognizes oneself as X, or who is recognizable for others as X, by complying with or subjecting oneself to the prevailing social norms. In other words, the subjects who recognize themselves or are recognizable for others are subjects in both senses of the term. As Althusser explains: "In the ordinary use of the term, subject in fact means: 1) a free subjectivity, a center of initiatives, author of and responsible for its actions; 2) a subjected being, who submits to a higher authority."[41] On this reading, therefore, subjection is not something that individuals passively undergo. Quite the contrary, subjection in the sense of subjection to social norms is something that *individuals actively carry out*. They respond to the constant demands of the social world to be certain kinds of subjects, although they do so for the most part on a prereflexive level.

Before concluding the first part of this chapter, we must be careful not to overlook one further important point to which the quote from Althusser draws our attention—namely, that the subjection to larger social norms, against the backdrop of which recognition takes place, is usually concealed by this very same recognition. As we have just seen, according to Althusser, individuals are subjects in the twofold sense of the term, that is, they comply with prevailing social norms, but are at the same time subjects in the philosophical sense who assume as a matter of course that they are this or that particular person and act as they see fit. Indeed, insofar as we recognize ourselves in Althusser's sense, "for you and for me, the category of the subject is a primary 'obviousness' . . . it is clear that you and I are subjects (free, ethical, etc.)."[42] For subjects who recognize themselves as this or that particular kind of person, the prior subjection that makes this recognition or self-identification possible in the first place is thus concealed. Similarly, Butler thinks that in recognizing others as male or female, for instance, we are inclined toward a "substantializing view,"[43] and assume that being a woman or man is their essence. Hence here, too, recognition involves a reification or even a naturalization of what is recognized and thus a forgetting of the subjection that precedes it.

We can now summarize the discussion so far. The first interpretation, according to which Althusser and Butler hold that recognition is a form of subjection because it constitutes individuals ontologically as X, and thereby harms them in their capacity as autonomous beings, has considerable flaws, all of which are related to the unwarranted equation of recognition with interpellation. Therefore, the first interpretation of the link between recognition and subjection must be rejected as inadequate. For Althusser and Butler, it does not seem to be the case that recognition makes persons into particular subjects in an ontological sense, thereby robbing them of their freedom to choose who they want to be. Rather, on the alternative interpretation developed above, recognition, for Althusser and Butler, which they understand primarily in epistemic terms, takes place against the backdrop of subjection, and subjection must be understood in turn in terms of the individuals' active compliance with prevailing social norms. On this interpretation, individuals become subjects who recognize themselves, or can be recognized by others, by subjecting themselves to social norms; however, this subjection is simultaneously concealed by recognition.

I would now like to build on this alternative interpretation when turning to the second interpretation of the link between recognition and subjection in Althusser and Butler.

THE FUNCTIONAL INTERPRETATION: RECOGNITION AS FUNCTIONAL FOR SUBJECTION

The second interpretation of the link between recognition and subjection in Althusser's and Butler's work is somewhat less prominent than the one examined in the previous section. I call this second interpretation "the functional interpretation." This label seems apt because, according to this interpretation, recognition can prove *functional* for the subjection of individuals, that is, it can help or facilitate their subjection, where to be subjected is equated with holding a subordinate social position.[44] To begin with, I will again state the interpretation we are considering in the form of an argument. According to the second interpretation:

> **P_{II}1.** For Althusser and Butler, recognition by others can make persons adopt certain self-understandings or identities.
>
> **P_{II}2.** Both Althusser and Butler believe that self-understandings or identities can be subordinating or subjecting.
>
> **C_{II}.** Therefore, according to Althusser and Butler, recognition can be functional for the subordination or subjection of individuals to others.

I will now discuss each of these premises in turn:

P_{II}1. Premise P_{II}1 states that, according to Althusser and Butler, recognition can make persons adopt certain self-understandings or identities. Thus, Honneth interprets Althusser as saying that "forms of recognition . . . employ methods of ritual affirmation in order to create a [particular] self-image."[45] From this quotation, Honneth might appear to be defending an interpretation of the kind we discussed in the first part of this chapter, according to which recognition makes persons into X, and other passages in the text seem to confirm this. Nevertheless, in the same text, Honneth also explains that "through processes of reciprocal recognition, subjects *are encouraged* to adopt a particular self-conception."[46] This at least suggests an interpretation of Althusser according to which individuals are not simply made into X by means of recognition, but it is rather the *prospect* of receiving recognition as a certain kind of person that gives individuals a reason to develop and maintain particular self-understandings.[47] With respect to Butler's account of recognition, Allen offers a similar reading. Here, it is more specifically the fact that "social recognition" is said to be tantamount to "having a social existence at all"[48] that explains why individuals "attach"[49] themselves to particular social norms and identities that promise recognition. Allen draws on this account to elucidate specifically how children develop particular "psychic attachment[s]."[50]

I believe that premise $P_{II}1$ is in part correct and that it adds an important aspect to our understanding of the link between recognition and subjection in the works of Althusser and Butler. It is not clear to me whether Althusser really believes that it is the prospect of recognition which makes individuals develop particular self-understandings, given that, for Althusser, recognition is essentially self-recognition and synonymous with identifying oneself as X;[51] as far as Butler is concerned, however, there can be no doubt that the promise of recognition plays a crucial role in individuals' motivation to develop and maintain particular self-understandings. As Allen explains, according to Butler only lives that can be recognized are "intelligible and hence livable."[52] In her early work on gender, for example, which I discussed in the first part of this chapter, Butler points out that a person's gender can only be recognized if it "maintain[s] relations of coherence and continuity among sex, gender, sexual practice, and desire,"[53] that is, only if it is unambiguously male or female. Persons with genders that are not unambiguously male or female cannot be recognized and are thus unintelligible and as a consequence are "regularly punish[ed]"[54] and violently excluded from the social realm.[55] Therefore, the subjection to social norms often takes place under compulsion. Subjection, by which one becomes recognizable for others, may be a "strategy of survival"[56] of which persons are to varying degrees aware. As Paddy McQueen has stressed, especially those who find it difficult to comply with the prevalent gender norms and identify as male or female will feel the force exerted by the existing forms of recognition.[57]

$P_{II}2$. Let us now turn to premise $P_{II}2$, which states that both Althusser and Butler believe that self-understandings or identities can be subordinating or subjecting. Again, let us first unpack this premise a bit further. Honneth interprets Althusser's point as stating that there are self-conceptions that "conform . . . to social expectations" and are "seamlessly integrated into a system based on the prevailing division of labor."[58] By this Honneth means more specifically that individuals might "voluntarily take on tasks or duties that serve society,"[59] that is, work primarily for the good of others, because of their self-understandings. In a similar vein, according to Allen's reading of Butler, there can be "identit[ies] based on subordination"[60] or "subordinating mode[s] of identity."[61] Allen explains what she means by this with reference to feminine gender identities. Feminine gender identities are identities that involve "attachment to pernicious and subordinating norms of femininity"[62] which prescribe, among other things, docility, a caring attitude toward others, and a feminine appearance.[63] As I understand Allen, such gender identities are subordinating or subjecting because they lead one to act in ways that are primarily directed to what others think and to what is good for them, that is, because they are fundamentally other-directed.

According to Honneth's and Allen's readings of Althusser and Butler, therefore, self-understandings can be subordinating or subjecting when they lead one voluntarily to accept a subordinate position in an asymmetrical relationship with others. In other words, both Honneth and Allen assume that the subordination or subjection Althusser and Butler are talking about is ultimately a *subordination or subjection to others*. By contrast, on the reading developed in the first part of this chapter, subjection is another term for "compliance with the interrogative law."[64] One is "a subjected being" insofar as one "submits to a higher authority."[65] Thus, according to my interpretation, Althusser and Butler are primarily interested in the *subjection to social norms* when they speak of subjection or subordination, not in the subjection to others.

What this difference involves can be illustrated by returning to the feminine gender identities that, for Allen, are a prime case of subjection or subordination in Butler's sense, because they make their bearers willingly accept a subordinate position vis-à-vis others. These subordinating identities can be contrasted with "non-subordinating forms of identity,"[66] which appear, by contrast, to be forms of identity that allow their bearers to be confident, to be assertive regarding their own projects, and the like. Masculine gender identities can be plausibly regarded as nonsubordinating identities in that sense.[67] I have no doubt that identities can differ in respects such as these, but on the reading of subjection proposed in the first section, individuals are subjected regardless of their particular identities. As we saw there, being a subject who understands oneself in certain ways is based on, or presupposes, a prior subjection to prevailing social norms. On my interpretation of Althusser and Butler, therefore, feminine *as well as masculine subjects* in Allen's sense would count as being subjected because they comply with, or are subjected to, different social norms that makes them feminine and masculine in the first place.

To conclude the second part of this chapter, the second interpretation, according to which Althusser and Butler hold that recognition plays, or can play, a functional role in the subjection of individuals, draws our attention to an important point—namely that the prospect of recognition, at least according to Butler, can prove vital in motivating or prompting persons to develop specific self-understandings. This insight will have to be integrated into the alternative interpretation I began to develop in the first part of this chapter. In my view, however, the second interpretation goes astray where it takes Althusser's and Butler's talk of subordination or subjection to refer to the subordination or subjection of individuals to others, instead of primarily to the subjection to social norms. Although it may be the case that the subjection to social norms will result in a person being subordinate to others, the important prior point is the subjection to social norms, and how it can be facilitated by the prospect of recognition.

WHAT MAKES RECOGNITION AMBIVALENT?

From the discussion in the first and second sections of this chapter, an alternative interpretation of the link between recognition and subjection in the works of Althusser and Butler has emerged. Let me recapitulate what this alternative interpretation involves by also stating it in the form of an argument:

P_A1. Both Althusser and Butler conceive of recognition as identification in an epistemic sense.

P_A2. Subjects who recognize themselves in Althusser's sense, or are in Butler's sense recognizable for others, have become what they are by subjecting themselves to larger social norms, although this is usually concealed in the operation of recognition.

P_A3. The prospect of recognition can even actively encourage individuals to develop specific self-understandings, at least according to Butler.

C_A. Therefore, according to Althusser and Butler, recognition in the sense of identification takes place against the backdrop of a prior subjection to social norms that, at least according to Butler, recognition may actively encourage.

One important question still needs to be addressed regarding this alternative interpretation. Unlike with the other two interpretations I examined in this chapter, where it was easy to see why recognition would be ambivalent simply because of its link to subjection, it is not immediately clear why this would hold for our favored interpretation, even though it also connects recognition with subjection. The reason is that, unlike the other two interpretations, each of which understands subjection as a problematic thing-in-itself, on the proposed interpretation subjection seems to have lost much of its pejorative meaning. According to the first interpretation, recognition subjects individuals, and subjection basically means an external infringement on a person's capacity to choose him- or herself, whereas on the second interpretation, recognition is functional for the subjection of individuals and being subjected means occupying a subordinate position vis-à-vis others. According to our favored interpretation, by contrast, recognition takes place against the backdrop of a prior subjection to norms that recognition simultaneously conceals and may even actively encourage. But "subjection" is understood here as the subjection to or compliance with social norms, and in itself such subjection does not appear to be problematic. The question that still needs to be addressed is therefore: Why is the picture of recognition that emerges from the alternative interpretation of the link between recognition and subjection in the works of Althusser and Butler an ambivalent one?

Taking our cue from the discussion in the second section of this chapter, I want to venture the hypothesis that, according to Althusser and Butler, *whether or not recognition is ambivalent depends on the particular social norms to which individuals subject themselves.* In the second section I discussed, among other things, Allen's example of feminine gender identities. She argues that these are subordinating identities, but her analysis suggests that nonsubordinating identities can exist as well. If it is true that, as Althusser and Butler suggest on my reading, one becomes a particular kind of person through subjection to social norms, then the differences between identities to which Allen draws our attention can be explained at least in part by the particular norms in play. In other words, the subjection to some norms will mean that individuals develop identities that Allen would describe as subordinating, while the subjection to other norms will not lead them to develop subordinating identities. Viewed in this light, we can draw the more general conclusion that subjection to certain norms will prove problematic because of how it affects the individuals themselves. However, it is important to recognize that the subjection to particular social norms may also prove problematic because of the negative consequences it has for others. Men who follow certain norms of masculinity that lead them to treat women in demeaning ways would be a case in point. Thus, to formulate this hypothesis in more general terms, recognition will count as ambivalent insofar as it takes place against the backdrop of prior subjection to norms that are part of problematic social arrangements.

As a final step, let us turn to Althusser's and Butler's accounts to see whether they provide support for the proposed interpretation. In his essay "Ideology and Ideological State Apparatuses" from which I have already quoted extensively, Althusser is primarily concerned with the question of how capitalist production can continue to run smoothly. This requires, among other things, that everyone—that is, "the exploited (the proletarians),. . . the exploiters (the capitalists), . . . the exploiters' auxiliaries (the managers), or . . . the high priests of the ruling ideology (its 'functionaries'), etc."[68]—fulfill their tasks in the social division of labor. Sometimes, as Althusser observes, this is ensured by force. "But the vast majority of (good) subjects work all right 'all by themselves.'"[69] In other words, they voluntarily participate in a social order that, under conditions of capitalism, is an order of "class oppression and . . . exploitation."[70] According to Althusser, this is explained by the fact that individuals have subjected themselves not only to some norms in general, but specifically to the norms of the capitalist division of labor and the recognition that occurs on this basis. Prima facie, this appears to lend credence to the idea that, for Althusser, recognition in this case is ambivalent because of the norms that form the backdrop in which it takes place.

However, the point that Althusser is making here can be understood in two ways.[71] On the one hand, Althusser could be interpreted as saying that as soon as persons recognize themselves as this or that particular kind of person, for instance as a capitalist or a worker, they will conceive of themselves as "a free subjectivity, a centre of initiatives, author of and responsible for its actions,"[72] whereas in reality they are "subjected being[s]"[73] who are always already acting in line with the social demands they are confronted with. That is, they *think* they act "'all by themselves,'"[74] but this is an illusion implanted in them retroactively at the moment of their recognition or self-identification. On this reading, their recognition would not possess any real efficacy. On the other hand, Althusser could be interpreted as saying that once persons recognize themselves as this or that particular kind of person, they really become "centres of initiatives."[75] In other words, their self-identification changes something about how they are in the world and becomes the basis for acting " 'all by themselves' "[76] as objectively required of them. I think that the latter assumption would be far more plausible, but I am afraid that this is not what Althusser has in mind, since he stresses again and again the "imaginary" character of people's "relationship to their real conditions of existence."[77] With regard to Althusser, therefore, we may conclude that it is not altogether clear after all whether recognition as he understands it can ever count as ambivalent. For although recognition takes place against the backdrop of norms that we may describe as being part of problematic social arrangements, by itself it does not *add* anything to the reproduction of the arrangements.[78]

Let us turn to Butler, and to her analysis of the binary gender order in particular, where it is a different story. For Butler, the binary gender order is a social order in which there are only two genders that are defined in opposition to each other: men and women. The binary gender order is problematic, since genders that undermine this opposition by not exhibiting the unity of sex, gender, and desire have no place. In Butler's view, the binary gender order is upheld mainly in two ways. On the one hand, as we noted earlier, different or alternative genders are "regularly punish[ed]"[79] in social life: because they appear to be unnatural or as "developmental failures or logical impossibilities,"[80] they are not allowed to exist. On the other hand, the binary gender order is upheld because it continuously enlists a large number of individuals to participate in it. According to Butler, this cannot be explained without reference to subjection and recognition. As we have seen, it is by subjecting oneself to the dominant gender norms that one becomes a woman or a man, and thus recognizable for others, and recognition plays a double role here. The desire to be recognized, especially when the alternative is being unintelligible and therefore nonexistent, as in the case of gender, plays a key role in motivating or prompting individuals to subject themselves to the dominant gender norms in the first place. But recognition also conceals the subjection to the dominant gender norms insofar as, in recognizing others as women or men, people tend to take a "substantializing view of gender."[81] Thereby, recognition contributes to the belief in the naturalness of the binary gender order,[82] which shields it from critical questions. At least for Butler, therefore, recognition is (or at least can be) ambivalent because it actively participates in two different ways in the reproduction of a problematic social arrangement.

NOTES

I am grateful for the many discussions of this chapter's theme I have had in recent years with Axel Honneth, Martin Saar, and Tobias Wille. Sanford Diehl, Sally Haslanger, Mirjam Müller, Tommie Shelby, Titus Stahl, and Tobias Wille read an earlier draft of this chapter and provided helpful feedback, for which I would like to thank all of them. I am also grateful for a discussion of this paper at MIT's WOGAP in September 2019, and for the insightful suggestions and questions of the participants. I would also like to thank Ciaran Cronin for his help with copyediting this chapter.

1. See, among others, Kelly Oliver, *Witnessing: Beyond Recognition* (Minneapolis: University of Minnesota Press, 2001); Patchen Markell, *Bound*

by Recognition (Princeton, NJ: Princeton University Press, 2003); Stefan Deines, "Verletzende Anerkennung: Über das Verhältnis von Anerkennung, Subjektkonstitution und 'sozialer Gewalt,'" in *Verletzende Worte: Die Grammatik sprachlicher Missachtung*, ed. Steffen Herrmann, Sybille Krämer, and Hannes Kuch (Bielefeld: Transcript, 2007), 275–94; Axel Honneth, "Recognition as Ideology," in *Recognition and Power: Axel Honneth and the Tradition of Critical Social Theory*, ed. Bert van den Brink and David Owen (Cambridge: Cambridge University Press, 2007), 323–47; Amy Allen, "Recognizing Domination: Recognition and Power in Honneth's Critical Theory," *Journal of Power* 3, no. 1 (2010): 21–32; Amy Allen, "Dependency, Subordination, and Recognition: On Judith Butler's Theory of Subjection," *Continental Philosophy Review* 38 (2006): 199–222; Rahel Jaeggi, "Anerkennung und Unterwerfung: Zum Verhältnis von negativen und positiven Theorien der Intersubjektivität," unpublished manuscript (Goethe University Frankfurt, 2009); Estelle Ferrarese, "Judith Butler's 'Not Particularly Postmodern Insight' of Recognition," *Philosophy and Social Criticism* 37, no. 7 (2011): 759–73; Cillian McBride, *Recognition* (Cambridge: Polity, 2013); Danielle Petherbridge, *The Critical Theory of Axel Honneth* (Lanham, MD: Lexington, 2013); Steffen K. Herrmann, "Anerkennung und Abhängigkeit: Zur Bindungskraft gesellschaftlicher Ungleichheitsverhältnisse nach Hegel," *Deutsche Zeitschrift für Philosophie* 62, no. 2 (2014): 279–96; Titus Stahl, "Anerkennung, Subjektivität und Gesellschaftskritik," *Deutsche Zeitschrift für Philosophie* 62, no. 2 (2014): 239–59; Georg Bertram and Robin Celikates, "Towards a Conflict Theory of Recognition: On the Constitution of Relations of Recognition in Conflict," *European Journal of Philosophy* 23, no. 4 (2015): 838–61; Paddy McQueen, "Honneth, Butler and the Ambivalent Effects of Recognition," *Res Publica* 21 (2015): 43–60; Paddy McQueen, *Subjectivity, Gender and the Struggle for Recognition* (Basingstoke: Palgrave Macmillan, 2015); Kristina Lepold, "An Ideology Critique of Recognition: Judith Butler in the Context of the Contemporary Debate on Recognition," *Constellations* 25, no. 3 (2018): 474–84; Kristina Lepold, *Ambivalente Anerkennung* (Frankfurt: Campus, forthcoming in May 2021).

2. For this interpretation, see firstly Deines, "Verletzende Anerkennung"; Jaeggi, "Anerkennung und Unterwerfung"; Bertram and Celikates,

"Towards a Conflict Theory of Recognition"; but also Ferrarese, "Judith Butler's 'Not Particularly Postmodern Insight' of Recognition"; and Oliver, *Witnessing: Beyond Recognition.*

3. See Honneth, "Recognition as Ideology"; Allen, "Recognizing Domination" and "Dependency, Subordination, and Recognition."
4. See Deines, "Verletzende Anerkennung"; Jaeggi, "Anerkennung und Unterwerfung"; Bertram and Celikates, "Towards a Conflict Theory of Recognition"; but also Ferrarese, "Judith Butler's 'Not Particularly Postmodern Insight' of Recognition"; Oliver, *Witnessing: Beyond Recognition.*
5. See Axel Honneth "Grounding Recognition: A Rejoinder to Critical Questions," *Inquiry* 45 (2002): 505; Heikki Ikäheimo and Arto Laitinen, "Analyzing Recognition: Identification, Acknowledgement, and Recognitive Attitudes Towards Persons," in *Recognition and Power: Axel Honneth and the Tradition of Critical Social Theory*, ed. Bert van den Brink and David Owen (Cambridge: Cambridge University Press, 2007), 33–56.
6. Louis Althusser, "Ideology and Ideological State Apparatuses," in *On the Reproduction of Capitalism*, trans. G. M. Goshgarian (London: Verso, 2014), 264.
7. Jaeggi, "Anerkennung und Unterwerfung," 6; see also Bertram and Celikates, "Towards a Conflict Theory of Recognition," 844; and Ferrarese, "Judith Butler's 'Not Particularly Postmodern Insight' of Recognition," 761.
8. Althusser, "Ideology and Ideological State Apparatuses," 264.
9. Althusser, "Ideology and Ideological State Apparatuses," 264.
10. Althusser, "Ideology and Ideological State Apparatuses," 263.
11. Deines, "Verletzende Anerkennung," 282; my translation.
12. Jaeggi, "Anerkennung und Unterwerfung," 9; my translation.
13. Judith Butler, *Excitable Speech: A Politics of the Performative* (New York: Routledge, 1997), 5.
14. Judith Butler, "Introduction: Acting in Concert," in *Undoing Gender* (New York: Routledge, 2004), 3.
15. See Judith Butler, *Gender Trouble: Feminism and the Subversion of Identity* (New York: Routledge, 2006), 23; Lepold, "An Ideology Critique of Recognition," 475–76.

16. Bertram and Celikates, "Towards a Conflict Theory of Recognition," 843.
17. Bertram and Celikates, "Towards a Conflict Theory of Recognition," 844.
18. Jaeggi, "Anerkennung und Unterwerfung," 6; see also Ferrarese, "Judith Butler's 'Not Particularly Postmodern Insight' of Recognition," 762.
19. Deines, "Verletzende Anerkennung," 282.
20. Althusser, "Ideology and Ideological State Apparatuses," 263.
21. Althusser, "Ideology and Ideological State Apparatuses," 267.
22. Judith Butler, *Giving an Account of Oneself* (New York: Fordham University Press, 2005), 31.
23. Althusser, "Ideology and Ideological State Apparatuses," 264.
24. See, for instance, Butler, *Excitable Speech*, 2–5.
25. Judith Butler, *The Psychic Life of Power: Theories in Subjection* (Stanford: Stanford University Press, 1997), 107; emphasis mine.
26. Butler, *Psychic Life of Power*, 108; with regard to Butler, this is acknowledged by Ferrarese, "Judith Butler's 'Not Particularly Postmodern Insight' of Recognition," 764.
27. Butler, *Excitable Speech*, 27.
28. See Butler, *Excitable Speech*, 5.
29. Althusser, "Ideology and Ideological State Apparatuses," 266.
30. Butler, *Psychic Life of Power*, 107.
31. Butler, *Psychic Life of Power*, 130.
32. Sally Haslanger, "Taking a Stand: Second-Order Pathologies or First-Order Critique," in *Debating Critical Theory: Engagements with Axel Honneth*, ed. Julia Christ, Kristina Lepold, Daniel Loick, and Titus Stahl (Lanham, MD: Rowman and Littlefield, 2020), 43–45.
33. Deines, "Verletzende Anerkennung," 285; see also Ferrarese, "Judith Butler's 'Not Particularly Postmodern Insight' of Recognition," 764–65; and Oliver, *Witnessing: Beyond Recognition*, 61–69.
34. Jaeggi, "Anerkennung und Unterwerfung," 7.
35. This also explains why authors who have defended this interpretation find the resulting picture of recognition philosophically implausible. Both Deines and Jaeggi argue that Althusser and Butler are committed to an untenable notion of autonomy (Deines, "Verletzende Anerkennung," 287–89; Jaeggi, "Anerkennung und Unterwerfung," 15);

Bertram and Celikates think that such an account leaves too little room for practical criticism and struggles (Bertram and Celikates, "Towards a Conflict Theory of Recognition," 844–45).

36. See, e.g., Althusser, "Ideology and Ideological State Apparatuses," 236, 267–69; Butler, *Psychic Life of Power*, 10–13, 28.
37. Butler, *Psychic Life of Power*, 118; emphasis mine.
38. Butler, *Psychic Life of Power*, 119.
39. Butler, *Psychic Life of Power*, 119. It should be noted that, in these passages, Butler is in fact offering an interpretation of Althusser, albeit one which seems to be deeply indebted to her own account of how the (gendered) subject comes into being through manifold performances (see Butler, *Gender Trouble*, and Butler, *Bodies That Matter: On the Discursive Limits of "Sex"* (New York: Routledge, 2011)).
40. Butler, *Psychic Life of Power*, 118.
41. Althusser, "Ideology and Ideological State Apparatuses," 269.
42. Althusser, "Ideology and Ideological State Apparatuses," 262.
43. Butler, *Gender Trouble*, 33.
44. See Honneth, "Recognition as Ideology"; Allen, "Recognizing Domination," and "Dependency, Subordination, and Recognition." On some views, the first and second interpretation that I distinguish in this chapter might actually be connected in such a way that recognition is conceived as producing subordinate subjects (see, e.g., Bertram and Celikates, "Towards a Conflict Theory of Recognition," 843–44, who seem to suggest such a reading). I cannot explore this interpretive option here.
45. Honneth, "Recognition as Ideology," 325.
46. Honneth, "Recognition as Ideology," 323; italics mine.
47. In light of two very recent texts by Honneth—namely, his exchange with Butler in the present volume and his most recent book *Recognition* (Cambridge: Cambridge University Press, 2020)—I now think that Honneth is in fact defending the first interpretation of Althusser and not the interpretation according to which the prospect of recognition can motivate individuals to become certain kinds of persons. His earlier text, "Recognition as Ideology," from which I am quoting here, is less clear in this respect.
48. Allen, "Dependency, Subordination, and Recognition," 206.

49. Allen, "Dependency, Subordination, and Recognition," 206.
50. Allen, "Recognizing Domination," 26.
51. In fact, it seems that Honneth's interpretation of Althusser already presupposes far more of Honneth's own account of recognition than his text would at first sight suggest. This becomes apparent when Honneth writes, among other things, that recognition leads to "a feeling of self-worth" (Honneth, "Recognition as Ideology," 326) which may explain the motivational force of the prospect of receiving recognition.
52. Honneth, "Recognition as Ideology," 326.
53. Butler, *Gender Trouble*, 23.
54. Butler, *Gender Trouble*, 190.
55. See also Lepold, "An Ideology Critique of Recognition," 476.
56. Butler, *Gender Trouble*, 190.
57. McQueen, "Honneth, Butler and the Ambivalent Effects of Recognition," and *Subjectivity, Gender and the Struggle for Recognition*. In his reading of Butler, McQueen also appears to equate recognition with interpellation (see, e.g., McQueen, "Honneth, Butler and the Ambivalent Effects of Recognition," 48, 50). As I explained in the first part, I do not think that this is an adequate interpretation of Butler. However, I agree with McQueen's general conclusion that processes of recognition may exert disciplining pressure. Furthermore, although I concede that recognition may often occur together with interpellation, it is important to distinguish these two operations analytically if we want to avoid arriving at false conclusions about what recognition accomplishes.
58. Honneth, "Recognition as Ideology," 325.
59. Honneth, "Recognition as Ideology," 323.
60. Allen, "Dependency, Subordination, and Recognition," 201–2.
61. Allen, "Recognizing Domination," 26.
62. Allen, "Dependency, Subordination, and Recognition," 200.
63. See Allen, "Recognizing Domination," 26, 30.
64. Butler, *Psychic Life of Power*, 188.
65. Althusser, "Ideology and Ideological State Apparatuses," 269.
66. Allen, "Recognizing Domination," 27.
67. Or should they in fact be called dominating identities?
68. Althusser, "Ideology and Ideological State Apparatuses," 236.
69. Althusser, "Ideology and Ideological State Apparatuses," 269.

70. Althusser, "Ideology and Ideological State Apparatuses," 271.
71. This points back to the discussion at the end of the subsection of this chapter titled "The Ontological Interpretation," concerning what precisely, in Althusser's view, is entailed by the fact that persons who identify as X are not aware that this is the result of a prior subjection.
72. Althusser, "Ideology and Ideological State Apparatuses," 269.
73. Althusser, "Ideology and Ideological State Apparatuses," 269.
74. Althusser, "Ideology and Ideological State Apparatuses," 269.
75. Althusser, "Ideology and Ideological State Apparatuses," 269.
76. Althusser, "Ideology and Ideological State Apparatuses," 269.
77. Althusser, "Ideology and Ideological State Apparatuses," 265.
78. Moreover, it is not even clear whether in the context of his scientific Marxism Althusser is even properly critical of capitalist society, but that is a question for a different occasion.
79. Butler, *Gender* Trouble, 190.
80. Butler, *Gender Trouble*, 24.
81. Butler, *Gender Trouble*, 33.
82. In an article from 2018, I claimed that the naturalization involved in recognition is "the reason why 'the postulation of a true gender identity' . . . persists" (see Lepold, "An Ideology Critique of Recognition," 479). This claim now seems to me to be too strong because there is another reason why the gender binary appears grounded in nature—namely, the simple fact that the gender binary constitutes a social normality that makes it easy to believe that this is how things are, by nature.

REFERENCES

Allen, Amy. "Dependency, Subordination, and Recognition: On Judith Butler's Theory of Subjection." *Continental Philosophy Review* 38 (2006): 199–222.

Allen, Amy. "Recognizing Domination: Recognition and Power in Honneth's Critical Theory." *Journal of Power* 3, no. 1 (2010): 21–32.

Althusser, Louis. "Ideology and Ideological State Apparatuses." In *On the Reproduction of Capitalism*, translated by G. M. Goshgarian. London: Verso, 2014.

Bertram, Georg, and Robin Celikates. "Towards a Conflict Theory of Recognition: On the Constitution of Relations of Recognition in Conflict." *European Journal of Philosophy* 23, no. 4 (2015): 838–61.

Butler, Judith. *Bodies That Matter: On the Discursive Limits of "Sex."* New York: Routledge, 2011.

Butler, Judith. *Excitable Speech: A Politics of the Performative.* New York: Routledge, 1997.

Butler, Judith. *Gender Trouble: Feminism and the Subversion of Identity.* New York: Routledge, 2006.

Butler, Judith. *Giving an Account of Oneself.* New York: Fordham University Press, 2005.

Butler, Judith. "Introduction: Acting in Concert." In *Undoing Gender*, 1–16. New York: Routledge, 2004.

Butler, Judith. *The Psychic Life of Power: Theories in Subjection.* Stanford: Stanford University Press, 1997.

Deines, Stefan. "Verletzende Anerkennung: Über das Verhältnis von Anerkennung, Subjektkonstitution und 'sozialer Gewalt.'" In *Verletzende Worte: Die Grammatik sprachlicher Missachtung*, edited by Steffen Herrmann, Sybille Krämer and Hannes Kuch, 275–94. Bielefeld: Transcript, 2007.

Ferrarese, Estelle. "Judith Butler's 'Not Particularly Postmodern Insight' of Recognition." *Philosophy and Social Criticism* 37, no. 7 (2011): 759–73.

Haslanger, Sally. "Taking a Stand: Second-Order Pathologies or First-Order Critique." In *Debating Critical Theory: Engagements with Axel Honneth*, edited by Julia Christ, Kristina Lepold, Daniel Loick, and Titus Stahl, 35–50. Lanham, MD: Rowman and Littlefield, 2020.

Herrmann, Steffen K. "Anerkennung und Abhängigkeit: Zur Bindungskraft gesellschaftlicher Ungleichheitsverhältnisse nach Hegel." *Deutsche Zeitschrift für Philosophie* 62, no. 2 (2014): 279–96.

Honneth, Axel. "Grounding Recognition: A Rejoinder to Critical Questions." *Inquiry* 45 (2002): 499–520.

Honneth, Axel. "Recognition as Ideology." In *Recognition and Power: Axel Honneth and the Tradition of Critical Social Theory*, edited by Bert van den Brink and David Owen, 323–47. Cambridge: Cambridge University Press, 2007.

Ikäheimo, Heikki, and Arto Laitinen. "Analyzing Recognition: Identification, Acknowledgement, and Recognitive Attitudes Towards Persons."

In *Recognition and Power: Axel Honneth and the Tradition of Critical Social Theory*, edited by Bert van den Brink and David Owen, 33–56. Cambridge: Cambridge University Press, 2007.

Jaeggi, Rahel. "Anerkennung und Unterwerfung: Zum Verhältnis von negative und positiven Theorien der Intersubjektivität." Unpublished manuscript. Goethe University Frankfurt, 2009.

Lepold, Kristina. *Ambivalente Anerkennung*. Frankfurt: Campus, forthcoming in May 2021.

Lepold, Kristina. "An Ideology Critique of Recognition: Judith Butler in the Context of the Contemporary Debate on Recognition." *Constellations* 25, no. 3 (2018): 474–84.

Markell, Patchen. *Bound by Recognition*. Princeton, NJ: Princeton University Press, 2003.

McBride, Cillian. *Recognition*. Cambridge: Polity, 2013.

McQueen, Paddy. "Honneth, Butler and the Ambivalent Effects of Recognition." *Res Publica* 21 (2015): 43–60.

McQueen, Paddy. *Subjectivity, Gender and the Struggle for Recognition*. Basingstoke: Palgrave Macmillan, 2015.

Oliver, Kelly. *Witnessing: Beyond Recognition*. Minneapolis: University of Minnesota Press, 2001.

Petherbridge, Danielle. *The Critical Theory of Axel Honneth*. Lanham, MD: Lexington, 2013.

Stahl, Titus. "Anerkennung, Subjektivität und Gesellschaftskritik." *Deutsche Zeitschrift für Philosophie* 62, no. 2 (2014): 239–59.

8

RECOGNITION, CONSTITUTIVE DOMINATION, AND EMANCIPATION

TITUS STAHL

The claim that recognition is ambivalent is best understood as meaning that social recognition is both a precondition for individual freedom, and a source of freedom-undermining domination. The first part of the claim entails that we can only be truly autonomous, or realize ourselves, once we receive a certain kind of recognition from other people. The second part of the claim—at least on what I view as the dominant reading—entails that recognition (necessarily or at least potentially) constrains our freedom as we need to seek recognition not on our terms, but on those of others. Recognition can therefore also be a source of domination.

The worry about the entanglement of recognition and domination—the second part of the claim—becomes urgent only once we accept its first part, that is, once we assume that recognition is a nonoptional condition of emancipation. The idea that such a link exists has received not only its canonical formulation but also its most subtle analyses in one particular philosophical tradition: that of Hegelian and post-Hegelian continental philosophy. This tradition has historically been read in a way that downplays the ambivalence of recognition. While it is certainly admitted by the positive approach toward recognition that is typical of that tradition that not *all* forms of recognition lead subjects toward autonomy (as becomes obvious in Hegel's famous discussion of recognition in the *Phenomenology of Spirit*), this is taken to be a mere feature of imperfect and deficient forms of recognition. Against this positive view, defenders of the ambivalence claim—as it can be found in authors such as Judith Butler and Louis Althusser—have often held that recognition is not merely *sometimes* entangled with domination but *necessarily so*, and that it is therefore subject to a dialectics which cannot ultimately be resolved.

As I will argue, there are multiple versions of the ambivalence claim. A *simple* version of that claim merely holds that subjects need recognition, but that such recognition is only available on terms defined by others, and that the domination that this implies undermines the freedom that recognition is to secure. As I will show, this simple claim is not enough to make the case for a thoroughgoing ambivalence, as the Hegelian tradition can respond to it by means of a theory of *immanent critique of forms of life*. The resulting idea of ambivalence is not pernicious, but rather an acknowledgment that recognition and freedom are linked by a process which is more complex than one might initially assume.

There are also more nuanced and more threatening versions of the ambivalence claim, however. In particular, in the work of Louis Althusser and Judith Butler we find resources for thinking about the link between recognition and domination in a way that preempts the immanent critique response. These *radical versions* of the ambivalence claim point toward a specific form of domination—which I will term "constitutive domination"—and thereby pose a genuine challenge to the Hegelian tradition. However, I will argue that the Hegelian model of emancipation, once it is suitably extended, can acknowledge the power of these arguments.

The argument will proceed as follows: In "Hegelian Freedom and Its Ambivalence," I briefly introduce the Hegelian model of the link between recognition and autonomy, and the simple ambivalence claim. In "Simple Ambivalence and Immanent Critique," I discuss the idea of immanent critique as a response to this claim. In "Radical Ambivalence and Constitutive Domination," I discuss two models of radical ambivalence and constitutive domination that go beyond the simple ambivalence claim and that seem to undercut the picture of emancipation painted by the Hegelian tradition. In "Emancipation," I examine whether that tradition can nevertheless offer us models of emancipation that acknowledge the possibility of radical ambivalence. I argue that there are resources within the tradition of immanent critique for a broader view of emancipation that can help us to think of resistance against forms of constitutive domination.

HEGELIAN FREEDOM AND ITS AMBIVALENCE

Hegel's work has widely been interpreted as incorporating a social and historical theory of freedom. The social part of the theory is the idea that, for a subject to be free, it must be true that it stands in certain social relationships to other subjects, in particular in relationships of mutual recognition. The historical part is the idea that the nature of freedom—and thus of freedom-constitutive social relations—is not something that we can understand in abstraction from its development, both on the scale of human history as a whole, and on the scale of an individual's development. In other words, freedom is not grounded in static features of individuals, but is an achievement of emancipation.[1]

Among interpreters of Hegel, two strategies have been especially dominant over the past few decades, each adopting a different reading of the link between recognition and emancipation. Some accounts, such as those offered by Charles Taylor and Axel Honneth (who approach the issue from a normative perspective), view recognition as a requirement for subjective self-realization and autonomy.[2] According to their view, due to its intersubjective constitution, our autonomy also always includes dependence on others. By contrast, philosophers such as Robert Brandom use the concept of recognition to answer the constitutive question: how it is possible for our conceptual commitments to have normative significance.[3] On Brandom's account, being free necessarily involves the availability of meaningful choices among different commitments that one can undertake. The availability of such choices presupposes a socially administered structure of norms. Such norms can only exist, however, if the subjects who make up the relevant community ascribe authority to each other to decide on the application of these norms—that is, if they recognize each other. The consequence of both arguments is that one can only become a subject by submitting or subjecting oneself to a web of social norms.[4]

Both traditions sketch a positive picture of the relation between recognition and emancipation: relationships of recognition enable those forms of subjectivity that are capable of governing themselves. Of course, there can always be pathological structures of recognition that damage the ability of individuals to relate critically to their social environment. But such pathologies can only be understood if one compares them to the forms of successful integration through recognition that are the foundations of the possibility of autonomy.

Given this positive picture—which I have merely outlined here—the question emerges whether this approach leaves any room for thinking about the ambivalence of recognition. Clearly, once we acknowledge that freedom is a social achievement, we must accept that our freedom depends not only on concrete others, but on a whole environment of social norms and rules that defines our status as a subject, and that precedes our having it. It seems, then, to be a natural continuation of the argument to say that this network of rules and norms is itself not something that we can freely determine, but rather something which dominates our choices by defining the options available to us. If we want to be judged by others as deserving a certain status, and if we do not want these judgments to be arbitrary and meaningless, then we have to rely on standards of correctness for such judgments which are necessarily outside of our arbitrary control. It thus seems to follow that norms of recognition constitute a limit for our emancipation—we can be emancipated *through* and *within* the social relationships they enable, but we cannot be emancipated *from* these norms, and nor is it up to us to either accept or reject them.

SIMPLE AMBIVALENCE AND IMMANENT CRITIQUE

I would like to begin my discussion of this view by introducing a *simple ambivalence claim*—one which, although it is not actually defended by any of the main contributors to the debate, can nonetheless be easily confused with their views. According to this claim, the dominating potential of the recognition we receive from others flows from the fact that, when we seek to be recognized as subjects, we must make use of concepts or statuses that we take from the discursive or nondiscursive social practices in which we are already embedded and thus, ultimately, from the community from which we seek recognition. If I demand to be recognized as a legal subject or as an autonomous moral agent, I want others to ascribe a status to me the meaning of which is not something that I can determine on my own. If recognition means that others intentionally confer a status upon me, then their intentions will determine (at least to some degree) *what* status they have conferred upon me. This opens up the possibility that I will discover that my interpretation of what the desired status involves diverges from their interpretation, in which case I will realize that the status I desired has a socially determined meaning that I find undesirable.[5]

To put it more simply, the simple ambivalence claim amounts to the idea that any recognition that we can receive by others is framed in terms whose meaning is beyond our control. This can lead to domination in two ways: First, the meaning of those categories in which we could potentially find recognition can be determined by the communicative practices of a community in which we are subordinated, such that our only choice is either to be recognized in terms that support this subordination, or not to be recognized at all. Second, even when people achieve recognition in terms that are acceptable to them, the meaning of these terms is never completely determined for all future cases, and they are always vulnerable to the community from which they seek recognition, which can extend this meaning arbitrarily in a way that disadvantages them.

According to the simple ambivalence claim,

(a) recognition is a necessary condition for subjecthood;

(b) recognition is only possible within an antecedently established normative framework;

(c) subjects cannot choose or control this framework autonomously. It therefore constitutes a limit of, and perhaps an internal undermining factor within, their autonomy.

(d) In particular, it makes them vulnerable to others who can constrain the possibilities of recognition, such that subjects can only gain recognition once they also accept some form of subordination. This can be described as vulnerability to arbitrary exercises of power by others, and thus as domination.

What response to this simple ambivalence claim is available to defenders of the Hegelian framework? It seems relatively obvious that they need not quarrel with (a) and (b). However, a Hegelian critic of the simple ambivalence claim will point out that (c) and therefore (d) are only problematic if we neglect certain core assumptions in Hegel's theory of *Geist*. This is, first, the idea that the set of concepts that forms the range of possibilities for recognition in any given historical society is not only something that the *recognized* subject is unable to arbitrarily determine, but also something that constrains the *recognizers*, that is, the community from which recognition is expected, and which is potentially dominating. On the one hand, this is true in the sense that no individual community member can arbitrarily determine the meaning of the terms by which they and others are recognized. Because the meaning and appropriateness of concepts is socially administered, any particular way of spelling out what a given status means can be criticized by questioning whether the individual doing so conforms to the shared social practice. On the other hand, it is also true in the collective sense that every community as a whole is subject to normative constraints in relation to its conceptual framework. According to Hegel, the totality of the concepts by which a given society formulates its self-understanding is always closely interrelated with standards of justification that determine which concepts can make a claim to objective validity. These frameworks of justification, which ultimately determine the content of both the forms of recognition and the autonomy available in a society, are not static but subject to an internal dynamic. According to Terry Pinkard's reconstruction of the argument of the *Phenomenology of Spirit*,[6] Hegel holds that any given historical form of life is characterized by socially shared concepts and norms, among which are not only norms of recognition, but also standards of justification for claims to objective normative validity. On this interpretation, the narrative that Hegel sketches in the *Phenomenology* is one according to which the norms constitutive of any given form of life will ultimately turn out to be unjustified according to its own criteria for justification, and will therefore be replaced by others.

This dynamic of life-forms is, as Hegel clearly acknowledges, not an automatism; in situations of crisis, individual community members turn critically against their own life-forms and distance themselves from them using the standards of justification provided by those life-forms. According to Hegel, these dynamics play out historically mostly without being recognized as such by the agents—only in modern societies that recognize the historicity of their own life-form, the right of the individual to demand justification for any rule or social practice, and thus also for the concepts under which they are recognized, is also consciously adopted as an essential norm of that life-form. While this reconstruction still holds on to the idea that to be recognized is to submit to and be dependent on norms that are outside of the individual's control, the fact that by doing so one gains contestatory power at the same moment therefore enables the conclusion that the resulting dependence is not one in which the subject is dominated, since it does not enable others to interpret the relevant norms arbitrarily.[7]

Of course, this picture only leads to a rejection of the domination claim once we assume that those who are being recognized by others are, by virtue of being recognized, always also seen as entitled to critically use the justificatory standards linked to the terms under which they are recognized to question the validity of those terms. Domination through a form of recognition which is *normatively unconstrained*, and therefore arbitrary, can only occur when the recognition in question is completely one-sided in the sense that a social status is ascribed to an agent without that agent's thereby being treated as part of the semantic community that determines the meaning of that status.

Hegel seems to assume that such one-sided recognition will not be desirable: If others assign a status to us that just *means* whatever *they take it to mean*, a rational response will be to treat their behavior as unconstrained by *any* norms of consistency, and thus as a "black box," as it were. But if we treat a community that way, we no longer treat its behavior as meaningful at all, and thus its members are no longer potential sources of desirable recognition. All desirable forms of recognition will therefore equip the recognized person with a status that entails contestatory power and thus makes possible for them to engage in an immanent critique of the dominant form of recognition.

It is this model of immanent critique—rather than the more often cited but ultimately social-philosophically dubious passage about the struggle for recognition in the *Phenomenology*—which provides a response to the simple ambivalence claim: if the categories governing subjectivation and recognition are seen not as static, isolated elements of social life, but as historically variable clusters of norms which are constitutively determined by their relation to the totality of all norms of a social life-form, then the internal conflicts characteristic of any life-form will always also enable individuals to question the meaning of the categories under which they are recognized, and thus the conditions of their own subjectivation, thereby enabling them to take up an autonomous stance toward them.

If these premises are accepted, the initial argument is turned on its head: according to the Hegelian view, what it *means to be a subject* is not merely to be *subject to* (and to accept) a given set of norms of recognizability, but also to have the *social status of a being that is entitled to demand justification* and to reject sets of norms that cannot be justified according to the criteria for justification included in them. Being a subject does not therefore entail the *inability*, but the *ability* to distance oneself from the relevant norms and concepts.

RADICAL AMBIVALENCE AND CONSTITUTIVE DOMINATION

So far, I have argued that the fact that recognition must be seen as the social ascription of a desirable status, the meaning of which can never be completely up to the recognized subject, indeed entails the vulnerability of the recognized subject toward the wider community. We can describe these others as having a distinctive form of constitutive power over us. *Constitutive power is the capacity of an agent to determine the conditions under which others can acquire the status of being a subject* (in general, or of some specific kind, as in a legal subject, a gendered subject, and so on). If the members of a community collectively have the power to determine the meaning of norms which govern the ascription of desirable social statuses, that is, recognition, and if to be an autonomous subject is to enjoy having social status of such a kind, this entails that the members of any recognitive community enjoy, collectively, constitutive power over every individual member. There is nothing in the Hegelian story that suggests that such power cannot be distributed unequally: typically, not every member's practical interpretation of the shared meanings carries the same weight, and subordinated groups' challenges to dominant interpretations are typically disregarded or dismissed.

However, what the argument so far also shows is that, within the Hegelian framework, we cannot properly describe this power as *dominating* since all exercises of this power are constrained by the possibility of contestation, and by the need for those supplying the recognition to at least minimally constrain their own interpretations of the categories if their status attribution is to count as meaningful at all.

Those sympathetic to the tradition that claims the ambivalence of recognition, however, will at this point (or perhaps much earlier) object not only that they do not accept the picture of language and meaning sketched so far, but also that the claims about the ambivalence of recognition that one finds in the literature amount to more than an acknowledgment that the terms under which we are recognized acquire their meaning in a social practice over which no individual member has absolute control. Rather, the claim that we find in authors such as Butler and Althusser is that to even enter the "game" of recognition in the first place, that is, to become *recognizable*, one needs to accept certain norms which remain removed from the control of the subject altogether; these norms, by extension, are therefore isolated against critique.

Against the Hegelian view, the respective arguments—which I will review in further detail below—therefore claim that there are forms of recognition which are indispensable to the social status of being a subject (of some kind) and which constitute subjects such as to systematically block them from developing or exercising the capacity to bring forward a specific form of criticism. The relationship of the recognized subject to the norms of recognition is thus viewed not merely as one of dependence, but as one in which a certain sphere of normative behavior isolates itself against a range of challenges by constituting subjects in a way that either excludes, or otherwise disables challenges. This is what I would like to call the *radical ambivalence claim*. In contrast to the simple ambivalence claim, which takes the fact that recognition makes subjects vulnerable to the power of others to be the source of the ambivalence, this claim operates on a *second-order level*: the power it refers to is rooted not in the way others can arbitrarily determine the meaning of the norms in question, but in the way in which subjects' capacities to react to such determination are formed and constituted.[8]

Put briefly, the radical ambivalence claim is the following: there are forms of recognition that are at the same time forms of domination since the subject that results from such recognition is necessarily unable to question or challenge others' interpretations of the normative standards of recognition in the relevant community.

In the works of Butler and Althusser, we can find descriptions of roughly four ways in which the subject's capacity to critically relate to the norms of recognition can be undermined (and with it, the possibility of immanent critique of forms of life on which the Hegelian response to the simple ambivalence claim relies): a social-ontological, a normative, a motivational, and an epistemic relation of dependence, each of which leaves the subject open to domination.[9]

A social-ontological argument is presented in the clearest form by Althusser's analysis of subjectivation in his famous analysis of ideology. Here, it is recognition through interpellation that provides the connection between recognition and domination. To be a subject is to respond in a specific way to one's interpellation as a subject,[10] in particular, by accepting the interpellation and thereby submitting to the categorical framework of subjectivity that interpellation offers. The critique of ideology that Althusser envisages, which most importantly dispenses with the category of the subject, entails that there is no space for the idea of subjectivity without ideological submission—which, in Althusser's terms, means without an interpretation of oneself, and one's social worlds, in the ideological language of subjectivity.[11]

If to be a subject is at the same time a precondition for critique (as at least the Hegelian framework seems to assume), there is thus a seemingly insurmountable dilemma. In order to acquire the status necessary to put forward a critique of social norms, one must have already accepted terms that limit the scope of any such critique. It is thus—in contradistinction to the simple ambivalence claim—not the fact that interpellation offers the subject terms which are not under its control that accounts for its subordination. Rather, the *specific second-order norms* that are constitutive of the very possibility of interpellation from the outset limit the form of any normative structure that could be suggested as an alternative to the existing norms of recognition. To the Hegelian argument regarding immanent critique, the Althusserian must thus respond by allowing for the possibility of critique—the possibility of the subject's questioning and resisting the terms of its recognition—but by simultaneously also emphasizing that the immanent critique in question will necessarily be limited to a critique *within* ideology, a critique that does not and cannot bring the very categories of subjectivation into view.

Althusser represents a relatively simple version of the radical ambivalence thesis. This version has thus faced the objection that Althusser conflates two senses of recognition—a descriptive one in which recognition is merely thought of as identification under some category, and a normative one in which recognition is thought of as the conferral of some sort of normative status. As Axel Honneth argues in his debate with Judith Butler in this volume,[12] it is this conflation that allows for the idea of completely one-sided forms of recognition which the recipient has no power to contest. According to Honneth's argument, this is only possible for recognition in the descriptive sense. Once we move from the descriptive to the normative sense, however, the Hegelian argument suggests that normative recognition must be mutual if it is to be desirable: in order to make sense of why the subject responds to the interpellation, one must assume that what is offered with it is the status of a being whose autonomy is entitled to respect, which in turn allows for critique.

If we make the distinction between the first-order claims of the simple ambivalence thesis and the second-order claims of the radical thesis, however, it becomes clear that this objection is not strong enough. The status of being a subject that is entitled to question and challenge the prevailing norms of its own recognition is perfectly compatible with there being a *limit to the form* these challenges can take.

As Amy Allen masterfully demonstrates,[13] one can read Butler as offering an alternative to the Althusserian formulation of the radical ambivalence claim. Butler's reformulation is especially important because it offers a more nuanced view of the ambivalence in play, allowing, to a considerable degree, for the possibility of resistance—although within the limits of a recognition-critical theory.

The most explicit version of this alternative is certainly to be found in *The Psychic Life of Power*, where Butler connects a reading of Hegel's "struggle for recognition" to Foucault—who, while defending an ambivalence claim about subjectivity and freedom, does not do so with regard to recognition. Butler argues: "But if, following Foucault, we understand power as *forming* the subject as well, as providing the very condition of its existence . . . , then power is not simply what we oppose but also, in a strong sense, what we depend on for our existence and what we harbor and preserve in the beings that we are."[14] She then continues to clearly characterize her view as a version of what I have called a radical ambivalence claim about recognition: "It is not simply that one requires the recognition of the other and that a form of recognition is conferred through subordination, but rather that one is dependent on power for one's very formation, that that formation is impossible without dependency, and that the posture of the adult subject consists precisely in the denial and reenactment of this dependency."[15]

While this might be read as another version of the Althusserian social ontology claim—perhaps liberated from his framework of state apparatuses—Butler makes it very clear that she rejects the social ontological reading.[16] Rather, there are three further versions of the radical ambivalence claim to be found in her work,[17] although she occasionally also formulates the issue as if she endorsed a version of the social ontological claim.[18] A *normative argument* assumes that subjects are normatively inconsistent if they question their dependence on power. A *motivational argument* holds that they cannot want the norms constitutive of their recognition to be put into question due to an affective relation to them, which in itself is necessary for their existence as subjects.[19] This argument starts from the idea that subjects are "passionately attached"[20] to the terms of their recognition. Of course, this must be more than an empirical generalization to play the argumentative role that Butler needs. We must rather assume that such an attachment, which in turn explains the reenactment of the power relations that limit the subject's critical capacities and thereby produce domination, is itself a condition for the subjecthood itself being livable. In that case, to desire to be a subject *and* not to be attached involves a motivational contradiction. An *epistemic* argument, finally, draws on the idea that in order to develop the strategies to criticize the terms of one's recognition, the subject needs to have epistemic access to the way in which it has itself been constituted by a prior subjection to certain terms of recognition.[21] Butler assumes that this is only possible if there is a narrative reconstruction that the subject can give of its emergence—but that such a reconstruction is inaccessible to the subject.

Butler combines these arguments with her highly original idea of emancipation: because the subject is not only a product of power but also a conduit for that power, meaning that the relevant kind of power must be reenacted by the subject to become effective,[22] spaces for subversion open up. While this alternative vision of emancipation will not be the focus of my discussion in what follows, it is clear that the underlying picture of ambivalence challenges the Hegelian point with regard to which the subject is always already capable, due to the status it acquires through recognition, to question the norms that are constitutive of it. Even if there is the possibility of a certain kind of emancipation in the reiteration of the norms, the subject, in Butler's picture, remains inextricably bound to the norms of recognition.

How can we then make sense, in this picture, of the difference between mere dependence on the norms established by others—which is the main focal point of the simple ambivalence claim and which, as we have seen, the Hegelian tradition need not deny—and domination? While Butler and Althusser do not draw this distinction, we can still extract an argument from their writings: in both accounts, it is the limits to their contestatory capacities, that is, the fact that dependence constrains the capacities of subjects to question the conditions of their subjectivation as a whole, that account for the ambivalent character of recognition. *Constitutive domination*, one might therefore say, is a state of dependence on others in the subject's very constitution, where either the social-ontological conditions for becoming a subject, or the normative, motivational, or epistemic implications of this dependence, form a limit to the subject's capacities to contest the norms regulating its recognizability, thus making it vulnerable to the arbitrary power of others.

This account of domination matches the famous but fragmentary reflections on the difference between power and domination that Foucault—on whom Butler also draws extensively—offers in "The Subject and Power."[23] While Foucault does not examine the idea of recognition, he shares with the ambivalence critique the idea that the subject is both partly individuated by, and a relay for, relations of power.[24] The subject's dependence on power does not yet amount to domination for Foucault. Rather, he reserves this term for a situation in which interlocking mechanisms of power achieve a stable and global form, "when an asymmetrical relationship of power has become fixed or irreversible,"[25] which seems to imply that—while strategic resistance is still possible—the possibility of fundamental challenges within that form is systematically ruled out.[26]

EMANCIPATION

The radical ambivalence claim that draws our attention to the possibility of constitutive domination raises the specter of a recognition order which no longer allows for the possibility of immanent critique since it has effectively immunized itself against such critique by restricting the subject's emancipatory capacities from the outset.

Before considering a possible response to this claim by a defender of the Hegelian tradition, it must first be emphasized that there are two possible versions of this idea that differ in terms of how radical they are. The maximally radical version endorses the Hegelian claim that subjective autonomy is a social achievement that is only possible in a community in which people attribute such freedom to each other by recognition. It adds the further claim that any such recognition will *always* come with second-order rules or effects that undermine the capacity of the subjects constituted by it to engage in immanent critique. One can plausibly read Althusser as endorsing this kind of claim. But one can equally well imagine a Nietzschean or Foucauldian reader of Brandom's work who accepts the idea that to be an autonomous subject is to accept responsibility toward one's conceptual commitments, and who combines this with a social theory of responsibility, according to which to submit to the idea of responsibility is to submit to arbitrary social discipline.[27] In both versions, the ambivalence of recognition is thoroughgoing insofar as the autonomy that recognition allows humans to achieve is viewed as inseparable from their being dominated through that very recognition.

There is also a more minimal reading of the radical ambivalence claim, however, which only holds that the link between recognition and subjective autonomy always carries the *risk of enabling* domination. According to this reading, it is not necessarily the case that autonomy-constituting recognition involves second-order limitations of the subject's critical capacities; this is merely a possibility. It must be stressed that even this minimal reading fundamentally changes the original Hegelian narrative: whereas in that narrative of immanent critique it was held that every recognition order *always* contains in itself the resources to overcome dominating recognition, it must now be acknowledged that such orders may immunize themselves against revision, and that the only possible critique is then one that comes "from the outside," as it were. Even though this idea fundamentally complicates the picture, however, there is no general ambivalence when it comes to recognition since it is not recognition in itself, but specific forms of dominating recognition that are ambivalent. Once this idea is introduced, it is quite natural to think of different regimes of recognition as being more or less ambivalent in this sense, and of an ethical imperative to move toward modes of recognition that allow for forms of subjectivity that are less rigid and more easily capable of distancing themselves from the dominant forms. This seems to be the view that Judith Butler ultimately endorses in her later work, even if she does not think that completely nonambivalent forms of recognition are possible.

Having described different versions of the radical ambivalence claim, it must now be asked what remains of the Hegelian story about emancipation. According to this story, any given recognition regime always contains in itself the seeds of its own critique, its crisis, and its eventual replacement by another, less dominating regime. In other words, even those forms of recognition that are in fact implicated in domination also contain the potential for emancipation. According to this line of thought, not only is it impossible to engage in social critique except from a standpoint of subjectivity within a given stage of the development of "spirit," but it is also unnecessary.

It is clear that the first, maximal version of the radical ambivalence claim is incompatible with this story. However, I will attempt to show that on closer inspection it collapses into the more minimal reading of the radical ambivalence claim, which can be responded to by developing a more complex model of immanent critique—one that aims at a broader view of the resources on which such a critique can draw, thus offering a view of emancipation that has yet to be adequately recognized in the classical narrative of Hegelian freedom. I will briefly outline both responses in this section.

I have argued above that the argument that Honneth advances against Butler is not strong enough. This is the argument that normatively significant recognition has to be mutual, and thus always entails that the "recipient" of any given form of recognition is also seen as an equal when it comes to the interpretation of the norms of recognition. It is this argument that needs to be strengthened if one is to show that the maximal version of the radical ambivalence claim is inconsistent. Honneth develops this claim more systematically in a number of articles, for example when he writes: "[T]here can be no ethical sphere, no institutionalized domain of moral action, that is not anchored in relations of reciprocal recognition. This individual empowerment gives each participant the right to cite reasons that in light of a collectively shared norm speak against one person's or several other persons' particular way of putting that norm into practice."[28]

As I have argued, the assumption that the relevant kinds of recognition always involve the entitlement of all parties to criticize each other's interpretation of the recognition norms is compatible with the existence of second-order norms in place that limit the possibility of such critique. It has not yet been shown that such second-order norms are incompatible with mutual recognition. Focusing more narrowly on the issue of emancipation, Honneth provides a more substantial defense of his claim in another article when he writes:

> [T]he norms that enable social integration are by their own nature sufficiently open as to admit recurrent re-interpretation appealing to previously neglected needs or interests. . . . We cannot understand what it even means for such norms to exist except by reference to a reciprocally granted right to object to deviations from them. And we can expand this observation by adding that in guiding themselves by these norms, agents must treat each other as subjects who possess the authority to criticize others' application of those norms. Insofar as social action is possible only on the basis of shared norms, it is always informed by agents' mutual expectations that they are recognized as members of a community in which everyone is licensed to criticize the normatively guided activity of others. These fundamental enabling conditions of social norms explain why we can treat any given interpretation of a social norm as essentially contested or conflictual. It is always possible that someone will offer reasons to doubt that a given norm is applied or interpreted in a way that is consistent with the underlying expectation of mutual recognition.[29]

Is this enough to show that constitutive domination is impossible? This follows only when we assume that any norm—*including* the second-order norms that make subjects recognizable and potential authors of criticism—is always subject to legitimate interpretive conflicts.

Whether this is so, however, is precisely what is at issue in the debate. Althusser seems to assume that there is a clear distinction between answering one's interpellation (and thereby subjecting oneself) and refusing its call (and thereby remaining outside of ideology but also unable to count as a subject of criticism). In this picture, *either* one is always already a subject and has thereby accepted the norms of subjectivation, *or* one is not—and then one cannot be recognized as a challenger. The possibility of refusing to abide by a socially dominant definition of subjectivity, facing exclusion as a result, and *then* challenging this exclusion by putting forward one's behavior as compatible with the shared norms *under a different* interpretation is seen as impossible. To a lesser degree, Butler shares this view as she emphasizes reiteration as a possible source of change of the dominant norms, but not as the source of a normative, argumentative challenge. By contrast, Honneth—who does not consider norms of subjectivation in this context—seems to assume that someone who dissents can always make use, at least provisionally, of the status of a recognized member.

Who is right? I want to suggest two arguments. The first is that there is no answer to be found in a conceptual analysis of normativity. Whether someone who deviates from the norms of recognizability can still be treated as a subject who thereby challenges those norms, or rather will be treated as a nonsubject who has left the game of subjectivity is not a decision to be answered by reflecting on the nature of norms, but a political decision. This argument was first advanced by Sabina Lovibond, who writes:

> We might make use of a pair of familiar terms, "conservative" and "liberal," to denote two contrasting positions. . . . The adherents of these different positions should, I believe, be seen

> as advocates of different policies towards deviant or *unsittlich* behaviour. The liberal commends a policy of toleration—of keeping an open mind as to whether the anomalous way of acting can be brought into connection with established social practices; the conservative, by contrast, calls for a strict policing of *Sittlichkeit* and demands positive disciplinary measures against the author of any anomaly. The relevant discipline consists in a withdrawal of the recognition previously extended to that person as a serious participant in the language-game.[30]

In other words, there is nothing inconsistent about a community's adopting the policy that those who deviate from a given norm of recognizability thereby lose their status as subjects, and thus as potential sources of challenge, effectively isolating the norms of recognizability from criticism. But nor is there anything inconsistent about a community's *not* adopting such a policy and still treating dissenters as potential sources of deviating interpretations. Indeed, it seems as if Butler's own theory of reiteration fundamentally depends on this possibility.

Second, apart from these considerations, what my rendering of the Althusserian argument neglects is the possibility of second-order disagreements *within* society. If we assume that also among those who *do* adhere to the norms of recognizability, there can be disagreements about how to react to others' deviance, the source of criticism need not be the deviant individual, but rather those nondeviant individuals who stand in solidarity with them by advocating a more liberal policy than the rest.

Where does this leave us? Against the initial Hegelian assumption, the possibility of immanent critique turns out to depend on the presence of one of two contingent factors that are not guaranteed to obtain, namely a liberal policy regarding deviations in the social practice in question, and the willingness of group members to stand in solidarity with those threatened by exclusion. Against the Althusserian assumption, however, we can also conclude that the absence of both factors is not something that can be guaranteed by ideology, but will itself be a matter of history and politics.

At this point, the argument converges with one that the Hegelian must make regarding the minimal reading of the radical ambivalence claim: if constitutive domination is always a danger, as it must be acknowledged to be, if conservative policies regarding deviance are followed, then immanent critique in the narrower sense discussed above is not sufficient to help us understand the possibility of emancipation. Instead of assuming that every order of recognition contains in itself the resources for criticizing its dominating aspects, one must look for resources outside a given order of recognition. But that does not necessarily mean giving up the project of immanent critique altogether. Rather, we can envisage a mode of immanent critique that does not merely draw on the standards of justification that are already accepted within a given form of *Geist.* Rather, one can also think of immanent critique—as Marx did—as a mode of critically relating to reality based on the possibilities for solidarity and for shared resistance against a given social order that this order makes available. This does not mean that critique in this sense is without justification; however, it may mean that such justification is not always accessible to those involved in the present and may only be given retrospectively, once—through the inclusion of previously excluded forms of subjectivity—a range of challenges and arguments for reinterpreting the norms of subjectivation have become available.

I have attempted to argue that the Hegelian tradition of thinking about the link between freedom and recognition has thus far failed to produce an adequate response to the claim that recognition is ambivalent in its contribution to human emancipation. Distinguishing between a simple ambivalence claim (a response to which is available in the classic Hegelian idea of immanent critique) and a radical ambivalence claim (where this response fails) helps us to see how the picture of emancipation that is present in this tradition must be extended and revised in order to fully account for the way in which recognition can serve as a vehicle for domination.

NOTES

I am grateful to Kristina Lepold for helpful comments on a draft of this article.

1. For versions of this claim, see Heikki Ikäheimo, "Making the Best of What We Are: Recognition as an Ontological and Ethical Concept," in *The Philosophy of Recognition: Historical and Contemporary Perspectives*, ed. Hans-Christoph Schmidt am Busch and Christopher F. Zurn (Lanham, MD: Rowman and Littlefield, 2010), 343–67; Robert B. Pippin, *Hegel's Practical Philosophy: Rational Agency as Ethical Life* (Cambridge: Cambridge University Press, 2008); Terry P. Pinkard, *Hegel's Phenomenology: The Sociality of Reason* (New York: Cambridge University Press, 1996); Robert B. Brandom, *Reason in Philosophy: Animating Ideas* (Cambridge, MA: Harvard University Press, 2009).
2. Charles Taylor, "The Politics of Recognition," in *Multiculturalism and "The Politics of Recognition,"* ed. Amy Gutmann and Charles Taylor (Princeton, NJ: Princeton University Press, 1992), 25–74; Axel Honneth, *The Struggle for Recognition* (Cambridge: Polity, 1995).
3. Brandom, *Reason in Philosophy*.
4. Robert B. Brandom, "Freedom and Constraint by Norms," *American Philosophical Quarterly* 16, no. 3 (1979): 187–96.
5. Titus Stahl, "Verbrecher, Revolutionäre und Schöne Seelen: Hegel über die Pathologien sozialer Freiheit," *Momente der Freiheit: Beiträge aus den Foren des Internationalen Hegelkongresses 2011*, 2015, 47–69.

6. Pinkard, *Hegel's Phenomenology*; see also Robert B. Brandom, "Sketch of a Program for a Critical Reading of Hegel: Comparing Empirical and Logical Concepts," *Internationales Jahrbuch Des Deutschen Idealismus* 3 (2005): 131–61.
7. The notion of domination that I employ is by and large that of Philip Pettit's republicanism. See Frank Lovett and Philip Pettit, "Neorepublicanism: A Normative and Institutional Research Program," *Annual Review of Political Science* 12, no. 1 (2009): 11–29, https://doi.org/10.1146/annurev.polisci.12.040907.120952.
8. See, for the general structure of such an account, Christopher F. Zurn, "Social Pathologies as Second-Order Disorders," in *Axel Honneth: Critical Essays*, ed. Danielle Petherbridge (Leiden: Brill, 2011), 345–70; Robin Celikates, *Critique as Social Practice: Critical Theory and Social Self-Understanding*, trans. Naomi van Steenbergen (Lanham, MD: Rowman and Littlefield, 2018).
9. The following discussion is closely based on my analysis in Titus Stahl, "Anerkennung, Subjektivität und Gesellschaftskritik," *Deutsche Zeitschrift Für Philosophie* 62, no. 2 (2014): 239–59, https://doi.org/10.1515/dzph-2014-0019.
10. As Lepold argues in chapter 7, the widespread interpretation that recognition-as-interpellation is already an instance of subjectivation is mistaken. According to her analysis, it is rather the uptake that interpellation receives from the individual that accounts for its subjectivation. But even in this case, there is a constitutive link between recognition and subjectivation: being a subject consists in being the object of a form of recognition that has power insofar as the individual confers power on it (and there is no other way to be a subject).
11. Louis Althusser, "Ideology and Ideological State Apparatuses," in *Lenin and Philosophy and Other Essays* (New York: Monthly Review, 2001), 170–75.
12. See chapter 1 for Axel Honneth's first letter to Judith Butler.
13. Amy Allen, *The Politics of Our Selves: Power, Autonomy, and Gender in Contemporary Critical Theory* (New York: Columbia University Press, 2007).
14. Judith Butler, *The Psychic Life of Power: Theories in Subjection* (Stanford: Stanford University Press, 1997), 2.
15. Butler, *Psychic Life of Power*, 9.

16. Butler, *Psychic Life of Power*, 12.
17. This analysis is again taken from Stahl, "Anerkennung, Subjektivität und Gesellschaftskritik."
18. In the extended German version of *Giving an Account of Oneself*, Butler writes, "if one questions the norms of recognition which determine what I can be . . ., then one risks no longer being a recognizable subject with regards to the current regime." Judith Butler, *Kritik der ethischen Gewalt: Adorno-Vorlesungen 2002*, trans. Reiner Ansén and Michael Adrian, 4th ed. (Frankfurt: Suhrkamp, 2007), 35. Translation mine.
19. Butler, *Psychic Life of Power*, 107–9.
20. Butler, *Psychic Life of Power*, 6.
21. "The norms by which I seek to make myself recognizable are not fully mine. They are not born with me; the temporality of their emergence does not coincide with the temporality of my own life." (Judith Butler, *Giving an Account of Oneself*, (New York: Fordham University Press, 2005), 35).
22. Allen, *Politics of Our Selves*, 77.
23. Michel Foucault, "The Subject and Power," *Critical Inquiry* 8, no. 4 (July 1, 1982): 777–95.
24. Allen, *Politics of Our Selves*, 55.
25. Katharine M. McIntyre, "Recognizing Freedom," *Philosophy & Social Criticism*, October 2018, https://doi.org/10.1177/0191453718803419.
26. Foucault, "The Subject and Power," 793–95.
27. Frieder Vogelmann, *The Spell of Responsibility: Labor, Criminality, Philosophy*, trans. Daniel Steuer (Lanham, MD: Rowman and Littlefield, 2017).
28. Axel Honneth, "The Normativity of Ethical Life," trans. Felix Koch, *Philosophy & Social Criticism* 40, no. 8 (October 1, 2014): 823, https://doi.org/10.1177/0191453714541538.
29. Axel Honneth, "Is there an Emancipatory Interest? An Attempt to Answer Critical Theory's Most Fundamental Question," *European Journal of Philosophy* 25, no. 4 (December 1, 2017): 914, https://doi.org/10.1111/ejop.12321.
30. Sabina Lovibond, *Realism and Imagination in Ethics* (Minneapolis: University of Minnesota Press, 1983), 173. See also Titus Stahl, *Immanente Kritik: Elemente Einer Theorie Sozialer Praktiken* (Frankfurt:

Campus, 2013), 385–87. While this argument directly challenges the social-ontological version of the radical ambivalence claim, it also indirectly affects the motivational reading. While it is of course always possible for a nonliberal society to produce nonliberal subjects (this is the premise of much of the psychological work of the early Frankfurt School), it is an open question whether, in any given society, this character form has become so rigid and unambivalent that it does not react at all to the solidarity of others.

BIBLIOGRAPHY

Allen, Amy. *The Politics of Our Selves: Power, Autonomy, and Gender in Contemporary Critical Theory*. New York: Columbia University Press, 2007.

Althusser, Louis. "Ideology and Ideological State Apparatuses." In *Lenin and Philosophy and Other Essays*, 127–86. New York: Monthly Review, 2001.

Brandom, Robert B. "Freedom and Constraint by Norms." *American Philosophical Quarterly* 16, no. 3 (1979): 187–96.

Brandom, Robert B. *Reason in Philosophy: Animating Ideas*. Cambridge, MA: Harvard University Press, 2009.

Brandom, Robert B. "Sketch of a Program for a Critical Reading of Hegel: Comparing Empirical and Logical Concepts." *Internationales Jahrbuch des Deutschen Idealismus* 3 (2005): 131–61.

Butler, Judith. *Giving an Account of Oneself*. New York: Fordham University Press, 2005.

Butler, Judith. *Kritik der ethischen Gewalt: Adorno-Vorlesungen 2002*. Translated by Reiner Ansén and Michael Adrian. 4th ed. Frankfurt: Suhrkamp, 2007.

Butler, Judith. *The Psychic Life of Power: Theories in Subjection*. Stanford: Stanford University Press, 1997.

Celikates, Robin. *Critique as Social Practice: Critical Theory and Social Self-Understanding*. Translated by Naomi van Steenbergen. Lanham, MD: Rowman and Littlefield, 2018.

Foucault, Michel. "The Subject and Power." *Critical Inquiry* 8, no. 4 (July 1, 1982): 777–95.

Honneth, Axel. "Is There an Emancipatory Interest? An Attempt to Answer Critical Theory's Most Fundamental Question." *European Journal of Philosophy* 25, no. 4 (December 1, 2017): 908–20. https://doi.org/10.1111/ejop.12321.

Honneth, Axel. "The Normativity of Ethical Life." Translated by Felix Koch. *Philosophy & Social Criticism* 40, no. 8 (October 1, 2014): 817–26. https://doi.org/10.1177/0191453714541538.

Honneth, Axel. *The Struggle for Recognition*. Cambridge: Polity, 1995.

Ikäheimo, Heikki. "Making the Best of What We Are: Recognition as an Ontological and Ethical Concept." In *The Philosophy of Recognition: Historical and Contemporary Perspectives*, edited by Hans-Christoph Schmidt am Busch and Christopher F. Zurn, 343–67. Lanham, MD: Rowman and Littlefield, 2010.

Lovett, Frank, and Philip Pettit. "Neorepublicanism: A Normative and Institutional Research Program." *Annual Review of Political Science* 12, no. 1 (2009): 11–29. https://doi.org/10.1146/annurev.polisci.12.040907.120952.

Lovibond, Sabina. *Realism and Imagination in Ethics*. Minneapolis: University of Minnesota Press, 1983.

McIntyre, Katharine M. "Recognizing Freedom." *Philosophy & Social Criticism*, October 2018. https://doi.org/10.1177/0191453718803419.

Pinkard, Terry P. *Hegel's Phenomenology: The Sociality of Reason*. New York: Cambridge University Press, 1996.

Pippin, Robert B. *Hegel's Practical Philosophy: Rational Agency as Ethical Life*. Cambridge: Cambridge University Press, 2008.

Stahl, Titus. "Anerkennung, Subjektivität und Gesellschaftskritik." *Deutsche Zeitschrift Für Philosophie* 62, no. 2 (2014): 239–59. https://doi.org/10.1515/dzph-2014-0019.

Stahl, Titus. *Immanente Kritik: Elemente einer Theorie sozialer Praktiken*. Frankfurt: Campus, 2013.

Stahl, Titus. "Verbrecher, Revolutionäre und Schöne Seelen: Hegel über die Pathologien sozialer Freiheit." *Momente der Freiheit: Beiträge aus den Foren des Internationalen Hegelkongresses 2011*, 2015, 47–69.

Taylor, Charles. "The Politics of Recognition." In *Multiculturalism and "The Politics of Recognition,"* edited by Amy Gutmann and Charles Taylor, 25–74. Princeton, NJ: Princeton University Press, 1992.

Vogelmann, Frieder. *The Spell of Responsibility: Labor, Criminality, Philosophy*. Translated by Daniel Steuer. Lanham, MD: Rowman and Littlefield, 2017.

Zurn, Christopher F. "Social Pathologies as Second-Order Disorders." In *Axel Honneth: Critical Essays*, edited by Danielle Petherbridge, 345–70. Leiden: Brill, 2011.

9

RETURN TO REIFICATION

An Attempt at Systematization

HEIKKI IKÄHEIMO

Axel Honneth's book *Reification* is an important attempt at rehabilitating a central concept in the left-Hegelian tradition, an attempt that nevertheless remains curiously left aside in Honneth's subsequent work. Perhaps discouraged by a somewhat negative reception of the book, perhaps by internal problems in it, or perhaps both, Honneth seems to have abandoned the project.[1] In my view there is much to recommend in the book in particular, and in the attempt to rehabilitate reification as a critical concept in social philosophy in general. What I wish to do in this chapter is, first, to provide a conceptual map on issues central to the discussion of reification as a philosophical theme—both for general clarification, and for locating Honneth's particular approach on the map. I will then concentrate on one particular dimension of reification, which is Honneth's main focus—reification of persons—and make further conceptual suggestions for a clarification of this topic. Thirdly, I will concentrate on Honneth's treatment of the theme in *Reification*, focusing especially on an issue that Judith Butler rightly puts her finger on in her critical discussion of Honneth: what exactly it means to "take over" the perspective of the other person, and how exactly such thinking, or refraining from it, relates to the reification of the other person. Like Honneth, I will connect this issue to the concept of recognition; even so, I will do this in a way that differs from Honneth's. Though I will draw on several ideas in Honneth's account of recognition, both in *Reification* and in his pathbreaking *The Struggle for Recognition*, his conceptualization of reification is burdened with certain ambiguities and unresolved tensions which I will try to clarify, working thereby toward a more conceptually controlled and practically useful conception of reification as a tool for immanent social critique. During the course of my discussion, a particular kind of ambivalence will become apparent, one having to do with the uncertainty of what exactly we have in mind when we talk of "recognition": though on a first, rough approximation, recognition of other persons seems the opposite of their reification, there are in fact important phenomena that are cases of "recognition" in a widely accepted sense, yet at the same time they involve something that is, in an intuitive sense, paradigmatically "reifying."[2] To think of this issue clearly and constructively, one needs to operate with concepts of recognition and personhood that are adequately differentiated, both of which I will try to explicate along the way.

PRELIMINARY CLARIFICATIONS

What are we talking about when we talk about reification? Unlike "recognition," "reification" is not part of everyday discourse, and thus we only need to deal with the ways it has been or can be used in philosophy, social theory, and related disciplines. The first thing to do here is to distinguish between *descriptive* and *critical* uses of the term. In a purely descriptive sense, the synthetizing of objects in or for consciousness from the material of sensory inputs is often called, in psychological and philosophical theories of perception, "reification." There is no organized consciousness of the world without reification in this sense, or in other words without sensations being synthetized or organized so that the subject experiences them as being about independently existing entities, of *res*. One can easily generalize this descriptive use of the term from consciousness or perception also to reification or "objectification" of entities as objects by and for subjects in imagination, thought, and discourse. No criticism or evaluation is necessarily involved in using the term in this sense, and to avoid confusion I will call it "objectification," reserving "reification" solely for the critical uses of the term, uses on which it refers to some kind of deficiency, or pathology.[3] As to reification in this critical sense, we need to distinguish then between "subjective" and "objective" senses of it. This terminology, found already in Lukács's classic treatment of the theme,[4] harbors a potential for confusion since what is usually meant by "objective reification" does not refer to a deficient mode of objectification of things in perception, imagination, thought, or discourse, but to a somehow deficient mode of being of things that is independent of, or at least relatively independent of, their objectification. It is "subjective reification," as the term is commonly used, that refers to a deficient way or mode of objectification of things. As what it is that is reified differs in these two cases—things in the first case, and their objectification by a subject or subjects in the second—so must the deficiency that reification involves. In subjective reification this is usually understood in terms of a lack of correspondence of the objectification of things to how the things are "really," "in themselves," or "essentially." There are two classic forms of this in the left-Hegelian tradition, both found (and interconnected) in Lukács: objectifications or representations of entities (in the widest sense, including humans and their relations) as "commodities," and objectifications or representations of the social and institutional world as simply given, "natural," beyond human powers of creation and transformation. Focusing on the latter form, it is thought to be a deficient, "reifying" representation, since in truth institutions are human-made, or to use more contemporary philosophical vocabulary, dependent on their collective "acceptance or ['vertical upwards'][5] recognition,"[6] and thus by their nature *in principle* transformable by humans. In contrast, the deficiency of objective reification is in a failure of the actual constitution of things—as they are in themselves, at least relatively independent of their objectification—to realize an ideal of how they should be. Again, the paradigmatic forms of this in the left-Hegelian tradition are entities in the world becoming commodified, and social life, relations, or institutions becoming rigid, irreplaceable, or difficult to transform. The former is a deficiency, or a "reified" state in light of the ideal of a "rich" world unreduced to one dominant mode of being (that of commodities); the latter is deficient in light of the ideal of transformability *in practice*.

Importantly, such *ideals* can themselves be thought of as either "subjective" or "external," or alternatively as "objective," "real," or "immanent." A subjective or external ideal is something posited, assumed, or experienced by relevant subjects—say, the theoretician, a particular collective, or humanity in general. Reification in this sense means that reality does not correspond to a subjective ideal, or in other words to an objectification or representation of how it should be. In contrast, an immanent ideal is something somehow immanent to the things themselves: their best or most flourishing state, their evaluative essence, or "concept" to use a Hegelian expression. On the latter option, reification means that the actual state of something—its *Dasein* in Hegel's words—does not correspond to or live up to its immanent ideal, evaluative essence, or concept. If the ideal of transformability in practice is subjective or external, this means that the relevant subjects merely *think or assume that* the more open for transformations institutions organizing social life are, the better they are; if it is immanent, this means that they *actually are* better, on immanent standards, the more open to transformation they are.[7] The same goes, *mutatis mutandis*, for commodification as reification: it implies either an external or immanent ideal which a commodified social world does not live up to. What are then the entities or "things," or the various spheres or areas of reality that reification, whether subjective or objective, may concern? A useful and intuitive way is to distinguish here first between (a) persons, (b) the social and institutional world, and (c) nature. As soon as one mentions these three areas of reality as possible instantiations of "reification" in the critical sense, it seems clear that what one means by this term cannot be exactly the same in the three cases. In general, this is so because of the differences in the objective or real constitution of these three areas of reality, or, in other words, because of the differences between them with regard to the features that subjective reification, as a deficient objectification, does not adequately or appropriately reflect, or objective reification, as a deficient actual state, does not adequately instantiate. More precisely, this is so because of the differences between the ways in which objectification and reality are related in the three cases: whereas "realism" on nature, or more exactly on external nature—the view that its basic constitution is robustly independent of its objectification or representation—is, to say the least, a perfectly reasonable position, no reasonable theory can ignore the constitutive dependence of persons as well as of the social and institutional world on their objectification. It is true of both persons and institutions, though in quite different ways, that their objectification is essential to their constitution, or that their being "in themselves" is dependent on their being "for persons." This is also the reason why subjective and objective reification—both of persons and of the social and institutional world—can be closely intertwined with, and strengthen each other.

REIFICATION OF PERSONS

One of the reasons why many readers may have been disappointed and perhaps confused by Honneth's approach to reification is that it involves a shift of focus away from what those who are familiar with the theme through the Marxist tradition, and especially Lukács, would expect. That is, whereas in this tradition the primary focus is on the social and institutional world, or "objective spirit" to put it in Hegel's terms, Honneth's primary focus is on persons, or "subjective spirit." Though it would be obviously wrong to say that reification on the Lukácsian account did not concern persons at all, or that Honneth has no interest in the social and institutional world, there is undeniably a shift in focus, to do with Honneth's embrace of the intersubjective turn in Frankfurt School critical theory instigated by Habermas. In what follows, I will focus on the reification of persons, abstracting from the connections that it has to reification of the social and institutional world, or of nature. In my discussion of the first issue, I will argue that there are aspects of interhuman relations that are "purely intersubjective" in an important way, namely in that they are not a response to norms, whether institutional or informal. One only needs to be very precise about what these purely intersubjective aspects are, and how exactly they relate to the institutional aspects of social life.

Let me start with a simple idea that draws on what I said in the previous section: subjective reification of persons means their deficient objectification, in the sense of objectification or representation that does not appropriately reflect, or is not appropriate to, the real constitution of persons. What we are dealing with here are essential or "person-making" features of persons, and objectifications that are deficient in the sense of not appropriately reflecting such features. In the extreme case, subjective reification of persons means their objectification as nonpersons, or, to put things preliminarily in a very rough and ready way, as "mere things."[8] (Let me say this already: one should not be misled by this common expression into thinking that reification does not allow for degrees.) Much then hangs upon what exactly one thinks it is to be a person, or, in other words, what exactly one thinks are the person-making features that are not appropriately reflected in reifying objectifications. "Personhood" is a notoriously contested concept, but the most important issue for our purposes is to distinguish between two concepts of personhood, which I suggest grasp two "layers of full-fledged personhood": the psychological, and the juridical or institutional.[9] On the first concept, being a person is having psychological features or structures that distinguish one as a person from psychological nonpersons such as simpler animals.[10] On the second concept, being a person is having rights and/or other deontic statuses that distinguish one as a person from juridical nonpersons, such as slaves.

Corresponding to these, we thus have two forms of subjective reification as deficient objectification of persons, one that does not appropriately or adequately reflect the psychological person-making features—whether actual or potential—of someone or some people, and another one that does not appropriately or adequately reflect her or their juridical person-making features—whether these are something they actually have, or something they ought to have according to a subjective or objective ideal or norm. To put this in terms of recognition: whereas in the first case reification is objectification of someone without recognition, or with inadequate recognition of her as a psychological person, in the second case it is the objectification of someone without recognition, or with inadequate recognition of her as a person in the juridical or institutional sense. Neither one of these two cases clearly has to be a matter of either/or, as in both cases there can be degrees and thus different mixtures of reification and recognition. Also, just like the two layers of full-fledged personhood, the psychological and the institutional, the two corresponding kinds or layers of recognition and reification are also partly independent of each other. For example, though being a slave means paradigmatically being denied fundamental person-making rights and being reified as property, this is perfectly compatible with their being objects of varying degrees of recognition as psychological persons (say, simply by being linguistically addressed). On the other hand, though, in capitalism, the capitalist and the worker recognize each other as juridical persons; this is perfectly compatible with varying degrees of mutual or one-sided intersubjective reification between them in a sense or senses which,[11] I will argue, can be understood as deficient or inadequate objectification of the other as a psychological person.[12]

Though the idea of "objective reification" has mostly figured in thinking about reification of the social and institutional world, it is a useful concept also in thinking about reification of persons, such as in reflecting on Honneth's discussion of "self-reification."[13] One of the fundamental premises in Honneth's thought since *The Struggle for Recognition*—a premise widely accepted in philosophical and psychological thought on human subjectivity, "the I," "the self," or as I prefer to say, psychological personhood—is that certain kinds of psychological *self-relations* are somehow essential to being a psychological person.[14] This is just to say that in the case of psychological persons, their being "for themselves" is partly constitutive of their being "in themselves." Put in other words, one cannot be psychologically a person without objectifying oneself, or, that is, without having various kinds of theoretical and practical attitudes toward oneself. Another fundamental premise of Honneth's is that the quality of a person's self-objectifications or attitudes toward herself is partly dependent on how others objectify her, or, that is, on the attitudes they have toward her. Put in recognitive terms, the thought is that experienced recognition by others supports one's "positive self-relations," or attitudes of recognition toward oneself, and that these are an essential ingredient in the psychological resources required for a satisfying kind of, or flourishing, self-realization in the world. In a nutshell, one can only flourish as a person if one's self-objectifications involve enough recognition for oneself, and this is likely to be the case only if one has experienced enough recognition-involving objectification of oneself by others.

Though Honneth does not develop this particular aspect of the theme in *Reification*, I suggest that roughly the same model of thought can be usefully applied, *mutatis mutandis*, to reification. Subjective reification of a person in the sense of reification-involving objectifications or attitudes toward her by others may clearly "support" her subjective self-reification in the sense of a reifying set of self-attitudes, and since self-attitudes are essential to being a person, this is intimately intertwined with—even if it is not simply the same thing as—"objective reification" of a person in the sense of impediments to full realization of her psychological person-making capacities. (Think of incapacity to form balanced judgments, lack of courage to act on them, fear of voicing one's views to others, pathological forms of dependence on, or avoidance of, others, overly rigid personality, debilitating depression, and so on.) Understanding the connections or intertwinements of reifying self-attitudes and "actually being reified" of course requires much more than these armchair-philosophical suggestions, but the general idea of a connection between subjective (self-) reification of a person as a reifying set of self-attitudes on the one hand, and objective reification of the person as hindered actualization of psychological person-making capacities on the other, should already be of some illumination.

In terms of the distinction between psychological personhood and juridical or institutional personhood, the specific way in which subjective and objective reification of persons are related in the latter case is a fairly simple matter in comparison to how they are related in the former. Juridical or institutional personhood is an institutional status that exists only within an institutionalized system of rights and duties. Institutions, or, in other words, institutionalized systems of rights and duties or entitlements and responsibilities, only exist to the extent that they are accepted or "vertically upwards" recognized by the relevant collective, or, in other words, are "objectified" by them in supportive ways; and anyone only has particular rights and duties, such as the fundamental ones that make up the status of a juridical person, to the degree that she is "recognized" as having them by the relevant collective. Hence, with regard to juridical personhood there is no difference between subjective reification—being objectified as a nonperson by the relevant authoritative others—and objective reification—actually being a nonperson in the juridical or institutional sense.[15]

As we can already see, there are both similarities and differences between the two issues of subjective and objective reification of the social and institutional world on the one hand, and subjective and objective reification of persons on the other. How exactly these issues are related is something that I will have to leave for another occasion, continuing here solely on reification of persons. More exactly, I will only discuss reification of persons in the first mentioned sense concerning psychological personhood, as this is what Honneth's account of reification focuses on.

HONNETH ON (SUBJECTIVE) REIFICATION OF (OTHER) PERSONS

After these clarifications, let me now take up a fundamental issue in Honneth's *Reification*, one that Judith Butler rightly focuses on in her critical discussion of the text.[16] It is what I consider as perhaps the most innovative and fruitful aspect of Honneth's elaborations: the way in which he connects the concept of recognition to the notion of "taking over [the other's] perspective,"[17] or "triangulation,"[18] something that is fundamental to the structure of intentionality distinctive of psychological persons. Honneth's idea is that below or before the three forms or dimensions of recognition he distinguished in *The Struggle for Recognition*,[19] there is a more "elementary" form of intersubjective recognition. By this he means an emotional attunement to the other, which in early infancy opens the infant's perspective to the perspective of its mother or caretaker, or makes it possible for the infant to place herself "in the perspective of another," and thereby enter a world of shared meanings.[20] It is from the perspective of relevant others that she is attuned with that the infant learns to grasp "the abundance of existential significance that situational circumstances can have for people," becoming thus aware of "a world of meaningful qualities" in which one must involve oneself practically.[21] In other words, the helpless infant must learn the practical meanings of things, qualities, events, and circumstances from the perspective of the adult, and the elementary form of recognizing the adult, an emotional attunement to her, enables the infant to enter her perspective.

Honneth's idea is further that a "forgetting" or repression of this original emotional attunement is at the heart of relating to others in emotionally cold, purely "observing," or "reifying" ways, ways in which they appear as mere objects or things, rather than as subjects or persons. Furthermore, Honneth suggests that forgetting or somehow losing sight of the emotional and practical significances that things, facts, and events in the world have for other people is "reification" of the former—an idea that resonates with Adorno's reflections on the meanings of everyday objects, as well as with Heidegger's elaborations on *Vorhandenheit* as a forgetting or obfuscation of the practical significance, or *Zuhandenheit*, of objects, only giving both an explicitly intersubjectivist twist. Given this triangular structure of human intentionality, "reification" of other persons in the sense of a loss of attunement with their perspectives is hence bound up with "reification" of the lifeworld in the sense of "forgetting" or losing from sight the practical significances of objects, facts, and events for them. Honneth's original idea is that, unlike on the default account I sketched above, a reifying objectification of things in the external world is not a matter of misrepresenting how the things are "in themselves," independently of their objectification, but rather of not including their practical significances for the respective, reified other persons, into one's own objectifications of those things. In other words, reifying other persons means not triangulating one's perspective with theirs, or not having one's objectifications appropriately mediated with theirs. Honneth does not develop this idea further in terms of the decisively important difference between "things," or entities, facts and events of nature on the one hand and those of the social or institutional reality on the other hand, which means that if one wants to follow the basic idea, there are many further details in terms of which it needs to be elaborated.

At this point, there is, however, another issue in Honneth's model that I want to turn to. Honneth's critics have suspected that his is an overly optimistic anthropology as it depicts the first human relation of the infant as one of harmonious immersion in the perspective of the other, without conflict or anxiety. This leads Jonathan Lear to describe Honneth's account as a "secularized version of the fall,"[22] one that builds "too much goodness in the original position."[23] Judith Butler, partly in a similar vein, queries Honneth regarding the role of negative emotions, of need, aggression, separation, and sadism, suggesting that without accounting for them Honneth's reflections on the "genuine bond" between the infant and its mother, which in reification is "forgotten," are a sort of Arcadian myth of presocial innocence, something supposed to function both as a foundation for other social relations and as an ideal for them—an ideal which, one might add, they cannot but fail to live up to.[24] In his reply to Lear and Butler, Honneth is at pains to argue that his description of the infant's immersion in the mother's or caretaker's perspective does not imply a naïvely optimistic or romantic picture of human infancy, that it does not imply an "overly optimistic anthropology," or read "too much intersubjective sympathy into the initial situation."[25] What he meant, Honneth explains, is "a necessary prerequisite of all human communication, one which consists in experiencing the other in a way that is not connected with normative implications or even positive attitudes."[26] This form of recognition is, according to him, "not intended to contain any norms of positive concern or respect," nor "positive, benevolent feelings."[27] Honneth goes as far as to claim that "[l]ove and hate, ambivalence and coldness, can all be expressions of this elementary recognition as long as they can be seen to be modes of existential affectedness."[28] According to Honneth's response to his critics, what he was actually talking about is thus something completely neutral in morally evaluative terms, a precondition of human life beyond, or below, good and evil.

There are a number of problems in this response. Firstly, it is actually at odds with many points in Honneth's text where he talks of the phenomenon in question in terms of clearly positive attitudes;[29] and as far as I can see, there is no place in it where he talks of it in terms of negative ones. Thus, Honneth seems to have in fact revised his position in this regard in addressing his critics; but since he merely claims that this is what he meant all along, instead of explicitly reflecting on and revising the passages in the text where this seems not to be the case, there remains an air of ambivalence or indecision. But secondly, and more importantly, if one accepts Honneth's revised view that the phenomenon in question is actually morally neutral, this seems to seriously compromise the usefulness of his conception of reification for the purposes of immanent social critique. For even if one accepts—as most would and in my view should—Honneth's view that (subjective) reification of other persons is *not merely* a moral failure, or not a moral failure in any simple or straightforward way, conceiving of reification as a lack of, or "forgetting" something, that is morally *completely* neutral seems to make reification itself a morally neutral or amoral phenomenon. On this line of thought, the difference between nonreifying hate or coldness on the one hand, and reifying coldness and hate on the other, becomes not only intricate in ways that Honneth nowhere explains, but also morally neutral and thus of dubious utility for his brand of immanent social critique that wants to tap into *moral experiences*.

Given this awkward position, it is perhaps not surprising that Honneth finally ends up in his response giving up on the project for all practical purposes, by depicting reification as such an extreme and rare phenomenon,[30] that its relevance for social critique becomes indeed highly questionable. My view is that this is a theoretical impasse which in practical terms abandons important lived experiences, experiences which are everything other than marginal or rare; that have a clear moral quality which, in favorable circumstances, can turn into moral motivation for emancipatory action; and that it makes much sense to conceptualize as cases of "reification of persons." That it is a *theoretical* impasse means that it is a result of theorizing not quite having found its way, and thus something that can be overcome by further philosophical work.

Working toward a solution then, it is useful to thematize a further, closely related problem in Honneth's conceptualization in *Reification*: the unclear relation between the "elementary" form of recognition on the one hand, and the three forms of recognition Honneth distinguished in *The Struggle for Recognition* on the other—as well as a related ambivalence concerning the exact nature of these three forms. By suggesting that the "elementary" or "existential" form of recognition provides the "foundation for all other, more substantial forms of recognition,"[31] by which Honneth apparently means the three forms of love, respect, and esteem that he distinguished in *The Struggle for Recognition*,

Honneth raises the expectation that he is thinking of the latter as "more substantial" ways of taking the other's perspective, ways that are morally nonneutral.[32] After all, Honneth has always emphasized that expectations for these forms of recognition are moral expectations. I think this is exactly the right way to look at recognition between individuals as an appropriate, "personifying" objectification, or as "taking the other as a person."[33] Or, more exactly, it is the right way to look at a particular form of it which I call "purely intersubjective recognition" in distinction to "norm-mediated" recognition.[34] Whereas by "norm-mediated" recognition between individuals I mean recognition that responds to the object's *right or entitlement* to be "recognized," where the entitlement or right stems from prevailing *norms*, whether informal or institutionalized (as in recognizing in the sense of treating someone as a juridical person), by "purely intersubjective" recognition I mean recognition between individuals that is not governed by norms in this way, or in other words is not a response to the other's right or entitlement to be recognized. Honneth's description of the "elementary" form of recognition is a case in point: even though the relationship of the infant and the mother is embedded in a normatively governed social world, and though the mother's thoughts, emotions, and actions are—as those of a socialized person—in innumerable ways guided or governed by social norms, there are decisively important elements of the infant–mother relationship that are not so governed. As the infant is, on Honneth's account, only capable of entering a world of shared meanings and—so one must assume—norms by entering the mother's or caretaker's perspective, this entering itself cannot yet be, from the infant's perspective governed by norms. It makes no sense to think of the phenomenon in question as the infant obeying or responding to norms, or duties and rights that these prescribe, since it has no grasp of anything like norms, duties, or rights before triangulation with the perspectives of the relevant others.

But, more importantly for my purposes, I believe there are three "substantial" forms of interhuman recognition that are "purely intersubjective" in the sense of not being required responses to norms, and thus to duties/responsibilities or rights/entitlements—namely love, respect, and gratitude, in the relevant senses of these terms. The first two of these are furthermore "personifying" objectifications of the other that essentially involve a triangulation with her perspective. Loving as the simple attitude of caring about the other's happiness or well-being for her own sake is, I want to argue, best understood as having the world in view, or objectifying it and "situational circumstances" in it, to borrow Honneth—including oneself and one's actions—in a motivationally effective way in light of the other's concern for her own happiness or well-being. It is in this sense that the loving person becomes "another self" to the loved person, to use Aristotle's famous expression:[35] the former is concerned about or moved in an unmediated way by what (or by what he believes) advances or is contrary to the latter's happiness or well-being, without mediation by norms (or by prudential considerations). The simple attitude of loving someone is not mediated by norms in the sense of being a required response to norms, or duties and rights; it is not something "for the sake of" duty or rights, nor for the sake of prudential considerations or anything else—this is exactly what the "for her own sake" expresses.[36] (This is compatible with the loving person disagreeing with the loved person about *what* actually advances the latter's happiness or well-being, as it concerns only the *mode* or *perspective* of caring about her happiness or well-being.)

The same holds for respect in the purely intersubjective sense of experiencing the other as having authority on the norms or terms of coexistence: it is not a required response to norms regulating the relationship, and thus to the other's rights or one's corresponding duties. Experiencing some others as having unmediated authority on shared life and thus on oneself is what makes social norms "normative" for a person in the first place. Or, to put this in another way: the normative force of norms on me is that of the others I respect, and thus respect in this foundational sense too is a "purely intersubjective" phenomenon not mediated by norms in the described way.[37] Similar to love in the abovementioned sense, it too is furthermore a way of objectifying the world and "situational circumstances" in it—including oneself and one's actions—in a motivationally effective way from the viewpoint of the other. However, unlike love, respect is not a way of objectifying something in light of the other's concerns, and thus happiness or well-being, but rather in light of her normative authority.

Finally, gratitude is a response to actions by others that one believes to be motivated by love (or to loving motivation, as gratitude can be appropriate even if an action thus motivated fails).[38] Like love and respect, it too is unmediated by norms (as well as by prudential considerations): feeling gratitude out of duty is an oxymoron, just as loving or respecting someone in the purely intersubjective sense out of such motives is.[39] Yet gratitude is more difficult (if at all possible) to conceive as a form of triangulation, and thus in what follows I will mostly concentrate on love and respect.

What I am proposing is thinking of love and respect in the senses just explained as "substantial" ways of taking up the other's perspective—as "axiological" and "deontological" triangulation respectively, where the world and the "situational circumstances" in it are revealed in light of axiological determinations (good and bad) that stem from the other's concerns, or of deontological determinations (right and wrong, obligatory, permitted, prohibited, etc.) that stem from the other's authority, respectively. Though they are still relatively indefinite as to their content, the attitudes of love and respects are by no means morally neutral or "unsubstantial." The experience of love or respect, or lack of them, by relevant others, if anything, is a morally or ethically fundamental intersubjective experience.

Returning to Honneth, this would provide a way of reconstructing his idea of more and less "substantial" ways of taking over the other's perspective; yet an important feature of Honneth's writing militates against it: unlike his conception of the "elementary form," Honneth does not consistently conceive of the "more substantial" forms of recognition as "purely intersubjective." Already in his debate with Nancy Fraser published in 2003, Honneth conceived of all interindividual recognition as governed by historically and culturally specific "recognition-orders," or, in other words, by sets of norms, and thus as a normatively or (since the "recognition-orders" are, on Honneth's account institutionalized) "institutionally" mediated phenomena. More relevantly, even in *Reification*, where Honneth refocuses on the purely intersubjective dynamics of early interaction, he actually does not conceive of the "more substantial" form of perspective taking as purely intersubjective, but rather as mediated by "culturally specific norms of recognition," which "regulate how subjects deal with each other legitimately in various social relations" and what "duties" they have toward each other.[40] On this view, recognition is an expected or prescribed response to given norms.

It remains thus unclear how exactly Honneth thought the purely intersubjective phenomenon of taking over the other's perspective, or intersubjective triangulation that is, could function as a foundation for living by norms which prescribe legitimate ways of relating to the other, or "recognizing" the other. For sure, without intersubjective triangulation, an infant does not enter a world shared with other persons at all. But acting toward you according to norms does not need to involve taking up your perspective, at least in any deep or "substantial" way.[41] The connection between these two different kinds of "recognition" remains unthematized and unclear in *Reification*.[42] It can be grasped by utilizing the view I introduced above of love and respect as axiological and deontological triangulation.

RECOGNITION, REIFICATION, AND PERSONHOOD

As already mentioned, a central point in Butler's criticism of Honneth's allegedly idealizing view of the infant–mother relation is that it is not at all obvious that all ways of taking up the other's perspective are morally or ethically positive.[43] In his response, Honneth shirks this critique, since he claims that the phenomenon he was after is prior to the distinction between good and bad, a necessary condition of both good and bad, or good and evil forms of intersubjectivity. But this means that Honneth cannot have very much left to say about this topic, exactly because he frames his discussion of reification at this undifferentiated level. What I want to show in the following is that, by framing it at the more "substantial" level of the abovementioned forms of axiological and deontological triangulation, we gain a more differentiated and more useful grasp of important phenomena which can be considered as forms of purely intersubjective recognition, but which are by no means clearly morally or ethically positive. In fact, they are also paradigmatic phenomena to be conceived of as interhuman reification—a case of the "ambivalence" or recognition which is important for Butler's own work, yet, arguably, is not treated in it in a way that is sufficiently conceptually differentiated.[44]

What I have in mind are ways of seeing the world in light of the other's concerns or authority—ways of axiological and deontological triangulation—but in a particular way. Think of inspecting actual and possible circumstances in light of what promotes the other's happiness or well-being, but doing this in order to gain profit, or in order to be able to manipulate the other efficiently. Such could be a capitalist's or an advertising agent's, or even an extortionist's or torturer's way of taking up the axiological perspective of the relevant other or others. Or think of inspecting actual or possible circumstances in light of what the other judges as right and wrong, but doing this out of mortal fear for him, or since one wants to make the other feel respected and thus to be off their guard. Such could be a slave's way of taking up the deontological perspective of a tyrannical slave owner, or that of a con artist of his victim.[45] In such cases, in order to be maximally successful, the objectifying person has to really "put herself in the shoes of" the objectified person, or to really see things "from her point of view."[46]

What exactly is then the difference between these forms of axiological and deontological triangulation on the one hand, and the more clearly positive attitudes of love and respect on the other? It is the difference between the *conditionality* and *unconditionality* of taking up the other's practical perspective. Whereas love, as described above, is an unconditional mode of concern for the happiness or well-being of the other, there is also a conditional mode of the same: concern for the other's well-being out of prudential reasons, because, or to the extent that, it seems positively or negatively instrumental for one's own goals, happiness, or well-being. The conditional mode of recognition is a normal part of life, but once it predominates over the unconditional mode in one's objectifications of someone or some people, this is rightly considered morally or ethically problematic, and in extreme cases—think of the extortionist or torturer—deemed evil.

Things are similar with the deontological dimension: in contrast to an unconditional mode of being moved by the other as having authority on one, an attitude that is naturally termed "respect," there is also a conditional mode of the same, namely being moved by the other's authority, or taking his judgments or will into account, out of fear or other prudential motives. Again, the latter is a normal part of life, but when it becomes the predominant way in which the authority of the other matters in a relationship, the relationship is hardly ethically or morally ideal, and when it is the only way, there is thought to be something morally seriously wrong with the relationship, and rightly so. Think of slavery,[47] or the relationship of the con artist to his victims.

In my view, one of the unhelpful and unintuitive features of Honneth's account of reification is his Heidegger- and Lukács-inspired way of understanding the distinction between recognitive objectification on the one hand, and reifying objectification on the other, as a distinction between involvement that is emotional or affective, and "observation" that is disengaged, disinterested, or motivationally neutral.[48] Another such feature is his rather artificial rejection of instrumentalization as a form of reification.[49] Honneth is committed to this rejection for two reasons: firstly, since instrumentalization is clearly a phenomenon of a "more substantial" level than the level where Honneth locates reification. And secondly, since instrumentalization is clearly not something disinterested or disengaged. Whereas the idea of disinterested observation makes sense in the context of Lukács's discussion of subjective reification as a "naturalization" of the social and institutional world—an attitude toward institutions guided by the assumption of their naturality or unchangeability, and thus lacking interest in changing what cannot be changed—it is misleading when applied to subjective reification of other persons.[50]

On the model I am proposing, the difference between (purely intersubjective) recognition and reification of other persons is not a difference between interestedness and disinterestedness, but rather between *modes* of the interest or motivation involved. This difference affects the precise determinations of the space of axiological and deontological significances in light of which the world appears in triangulation. It is only in the *unconditional* mode of axiological and deontological recognition/triangulation that the other's concerns, and thus what is good or bad (or evil) from her perspective, or her authority, and thus what is right and wrong from her perspective, have the same unconditional importance for one as one's own happiness or well-being, or one's own will or claim to sharing authority with others do. (This is assuming that one's own self-attitudes are adequately recognitive, or adequately nonreifying.) In contrast, in the conditional or prudential mode of axiological and deontological recognition/triangulation, the importance of the other's concerns and authority is conditional on one's own concerns.

This is to say that only in the unconditional mode does the other fully appear to me as an irreducibly other person with a perspective irreducible to mine, hence making myself for myself one person among many. It is exactly not being seen, and thus treated by others as a fully independent other person whose life has unconditional or irreducible importance, and/or who has an unconditional or irreducible claim for authority, that is paradigmatically experienced as being "treated like a thing"—or, in other words, being reified.[51] And while gratitude may not be another way or dimension of triangulation, it, too, is the unconditional mode of a dimension of purely intersubjective recognition, one which also has a conditional mode that is paradigmatically experienced by its objects as being treated like a thing, or, in other words, being reified. The general form here is appreciation for contributions to something one values, and the conditional mode is instrumental valuing, or instrumentalization in short. Whereas in instrumental valuing the other is reduced to her functionality to my ends, in gratitude she is taken as a genuinely other free being with her own ends, a free person who is free to contribute and chooses to do so out of (at least partly) unselfish motivation, or, in other words, out of love.

I have suggested that all forms of reification of other persons are deficient or inadequate objectifications of the other as a psychological person, but in what way exactly is this true of conditional, and thus reifying recognition? The answer is, I suggest, that the conditional mode does not mirror the attitudes of self-recognition that are required for flourishing, or fully actualized psychological personhood. If one is to flourish as a (psychological) person, one's set of recognitive attitudes toward oneself clearly cannot be merely conditional: Firstly, one cannot take one's life, happiness, or well-being as having merely instrumental importance (for something or someone else). Secondly, one cannot take one's claim to sharing authority on the norms or terms of a shared life to be strictly conditional on the judgments or interests of others. Nor can one take oneself as a contributor to the good of others merely in the sense of an instrument to their goals, rather than a free being worthy of their gratitude.

Merely conditional *self*-recognition is subjective reification of oneself, and, as I explained above, it contributes to one's objective or "real" reification as a psychological person, that is, to a failure to realize an ideal of psychological personhood, or an important part of it. Hence, merely conditional recognition *by others* does not reflect the mode of self-recognition that is constitutive of a flourishing psychological personhood of the recognizee—the unconditional mode, that is. Put in other terms, it does not reveal the recognizee in light of significances that a flourishing psychological person needs to have in her own eyes—someone whose life, well-being, or happiness has intrinsic importance, someone who has unconditional claim to coauthority on the norms or terms of shared life, and a gratitude-worthy contributor to the good of some others. Seeing the other in light of these significances is recognizing her as a psychological person in the full sense of the term, as an irreducibly "other" center of concerns and authority.[52] Depending on whether one thinks of this conception of flourishing psychological personhood either as (A) a subjective, perhaps culturally specific (western) ideal, or alternatively as (B) a "real" or "immanent" ideal of psychological personhood (in general), one will conceive of the conception of "objective" reification of psychological personhood at stake in terms of failing to realize either (A) or (B). Those attracted by cultural relativism will gravitate toward the first option; those attracted by anthropological universalism toward the second.

I have presented above some general outlines of a conceptualization of various phenomena that have been thought of as "reification" in critical social philosophy, and concentrated on one of them: the reification of other persons. Part of what I hope to have shown is that what we can meaningfully call interhuman reification comes in various forms that are, in part, mutually independent. Reification in its many forms also comes in degrees, ranging from everyday inconsiderateness or coldness, through degrees of instrumentalization, to psychopathic or genocidal inhumanity. Contrary to Honneth's conclusion, interhuman reification is not something extremely rare, however rare its extreme forms may be. One obvious implication of this is that the milder forms may, in suitable circumstances, function as preparation for the more extreme forms, and it is for critical social philosophers to discern it already in its milder and apparently harmless forms and quantities. As for normative social theory, I take it that the basic idea of Honneth's book *The Struggle for Recognition* still stands: societies and forms of interhuman coexistence can be evaluated and criticized in terms of the extent to which, and the ways in which, they facilitate or encourage genuine recognition—or its negations, most importantly the different forms of interhuman reification.

NOTES

I thank Cinzia Ferrini, John Ganz, Vuokko Jarva, Christopher Yeomans, and the other participants of an academia.edu session on the draft version of this chapter for helpful questions and comments.

1. In Honneth's own words: "now, having written the book, I have come to the conclusion that perhaps the concept of reification does not add too much to our understanding of the world and capitalism." Daniel Gamper, "Interview with Axel Honneth," *Barcelona Metropolis*, Spring (April–June 2010), https://www.academia.edu/30326708/Interview_with_Axel_Honneth.
2. In writing this paper I have learned enormously from Titus Stahl, *Immanente Kritik: Elemente einer Theorie sozialer Praktiken* (Frankfurt: Campus, 2013), chapter 8, which is perhaps the single most useful text on reification I know of.

3. The unfortunately common tendency to use "objectification" more or less synonymously with "reification" in the critical sense can lead to serious theoretical confusion, or a secularized version of the "original sin" figure, on which simply being conscious of something as an object is already somehow normatively dubious. In distinguishing these terms I take my lead from Testa, who criticizes both the early Frankfurt school and John Searle's social ontology for a lack of proper distinction between objectification and reification. Italo Testa, "Ontology of the False State—On the Relation Between Critical Theory, Social Philosophy, and Social Ontology," *Journal of Social Ontology* 1, no. 2 (2015): 271–300.
4. See György Lukács, *History and Class Consciousness* (Cambridge, MA: MIT Press, 1971).
5. See Heikki Ikäheimo, "Recognition, Identity and Subjectivity," in *The Palgrave Handbook of Critical Theory*, ed. M. J. Thompson (Basingstoke: Palgrave, 2017), 569.
6. John Searle, *Making the Social World: The Structure of Human Civilization* (Oxford: Oxford University Press, 2010), 13.
7. Needless to say, one needs to subscribe to a particular kind of realism to think that there are objective ideals irreducible to subjective ones. And obviously, "better" can refer here to different kinds of goodness.
8. Purely terminologically, it is thus with regard to persons that the term reification, or "thingification" is at its most appropriate.
9. See Heikki Ikäheimo, "Recognizing Persons," *Journal of Consciousness Studies* 14, no. 5–6 (2007): 224–47.
10. Note that there is no need to think of psychological personhood as a matter of either/or, as all psychological capacities allow for degrees.
11. There is a temptation to respond to the alleged romanticism of the young Marx and those following him by pointing out to rights (or "abstract right" in Hegel's wording) as ameliorating interhuman reification. This, I am arguing, is a mistake.
12. The usefulness of the concept of "objectification" as I use it here is that it covers both "theoretical" and "practical" forms of subjective reification. In other words, it covers both reifying representations—be they aesthetic images, discursive descriptions, or theoretical conceptualizations—and practical reifications—including

practical attitudes, and ways of treating. To (subjectively) reify a person is thus to objectify her either theoretically, or practically, or both, in a way that does not reflect or is not appropriate to her being a person, either in the psychological sense, or in the juridical sense, or both.

13. Axel Honneth, *Reification* (Oxford: Oxford University Press, 2008), 63–74.
14. Axel Honneth, *The Struggle for Recognition*, trans. Joel Anderson (Cambridge: Polity, 1995).
15. It is of course possible for *nonauthoritative* others to objectify or treat someone who is a juridical person as a nonperson in this sense, in which case what we have is a violation of an existing status, and thus objectification not being appropriate to reality. In the more serious case of subjective reification by authoritative others (such as a political community reifying newcomers as slaves), the deficiency of subjective reification is not a discrepancy with reality (the slaves are actually slaves, not juridical persons if those with authority objectify them as such), but must be sought in a (subjective or objective) ideal or principle according to which they *ought* to be objectified as juridical persons and thus be such.
16. Honneth, *Reification*, 97–119.
17. Honneth, *Reification*, 40–52.
18. Honneth, *Reification*, 42.
19. See Honneth, *Reification*, 37–38, 90n70.
20. Honneth, *Reification*, 45.
21. Honneth, *Reification*, 45.
22. Honneth, *Reification*, 131.
23. Honneth, *Reification*, 132.
24. Honneth, *Reification*, 108.
25. Honneth, *Reification*, 147.
26. Honneth, *Reification*, 148.
27. Honneth, *Reification*, 151.
28. Honneth, *Reification*, 152.
29. See, for example, Honneth, *Reification*, 45: "The act of placing oneself in the perspective of a second person requires an antecedent form of recognition that cannot be grasped in purely cognitive or epistemic

concepts, as it always and necessarily contains an element of involuntary openness, devotedness, or love."

30. Honneth, *Reification*, 157: "these brief remarks demonstrate how improbable true cases of reification are for the social lifeworld as a whole."
31. Honneth, *Reification*, 90n70.
32. A further ambivalence concerns the exact nature of the "elementary form." On the one hand, Honneth says it is merely a precondition of taking up the other's perspective; on the other hand, he sometimes gives the impression that it is already a "less substantial" form of doing it.
33. See Heikki Ikäheimo, "On the Genus and Species of Recognition," *Inquiry* 45, no. 4 (2002): 447–62.
34. See Ikäheimo, "Recognition, Identity and Subjectivity."
35. On love as a form of recognition, see Heikki Ikäheimo, "Globalizing Love: On the Nature and Scope of Love as a Form of Recognition," *Res Publica* 18 (2012): 11–24.
36. Note that this only holds for the attitude in question and that it is perfectly compatible with the loving person having other attitudes and emotions toward the loved person that are mediated by norms, self-interest, and what not. It is a commonplace that the attitudinal complexes people have toward each other are complicated and often fraught with internal tensions. Even more importantly, that something is not *mediated* by norms in the sense that I mean—by being a response required by a norm—does not rule out that it is *affected* by norms. For example, in a racist society there are typically informal norms restricting interaction between the majority and the minority color individuals in such a way that individuals belonging to the first group tend not to see individuals belonging to the latter in ways that would move the former to having (unconditional) purely intersubjective recognition for the latter. This is an aspect of what Judith Butler conceives of as norms of recognizability: they affect the likelihood of different kinds of recognition, some of which are in my sense "purely intersubjective," between individuals or groups (See Judith Butler, *Undoing Gender* (New York: Routledge, 2004), 2; Judith Butler, *Giving an Account of Oneself* (New York: Fordham University Press, 2005), 22–30; and Ikäheimo, "Recognition, Identity and Subjectivity," 578–81).

37. Can there be norms prescribing who ought to be "respected" as an authority in particular issues? Yes indeed, but the normative grounding must have a rock bottom, and there is nothing else this could be (on a secular worldview) than the experienced authority of other persons. On the details of how this works, see Dave Elder-Vass, *The Causal Power of Social Structures: Emergence, Structure and Agency* (Cambridge: Cambridge University Press, 2010).
38. See Ikäheimo, "Recognition, Identity and Subjectivity."
39. To be exact: valuing or appreciating someone for his beneficial actions or motivations is of course mediated by interest, but that the appreciation is gratitude rather than instrumental valuing is not grounded on norms, self-interest, or any other consideration.
40. Honneth, *Reification*, 153. For a more extended discussion of this problematic in Honneth, see Heikki Ikäheimo, *Anerkennung* (Berlin: De Gruyter, 2014), chapter 6.
41. For example, A may treat B according to the rights B has thanks to the prevailing system of law, and thus "recognize" B as a bearer of rights, without caring about B's own views on these rights, and thus without respecting her as having authority on them.
42. For the same problem in Fichte's pioneering *Foundations of Natural Right*, see Ikäheimo, *Anerkennung*, chapter 3.
43. Honneth, *Reification*, 97–119.
44. See Ikäheimo, "Recognition, Identity and Subjectivity," 578–81.
45. I borrow the con artist example from Jonathan Lear in Honneth, *Reification*, 134.
46. Similar points are made by Raymond Geuss, 127, and Lear, 134–35, in Honneth, *Reification*.
47. Perhaps needless to say, the main problem is not that the slave has merely prudential concern for the master's authority, but that the relationship is pathological in a way that makes this likely to be the case.
48. See, e.g., Honneth, *Reification*, 24–25, 56, 60.
49. Honneth, *Reification*, 148–49.
50. As Butler's writes, "instrumental reason and modes of reification can themselves become forms of passion, modes of attachment, sites of emotional investment and excitation"—they are "not exclusively detached and dry and scientific" (Honneth, *Reification*, 105).

51. Butler grasps the axiological side of this in terms of "grievability," and emphasizes the framings in terms of which the lives of some individuals and groups appear as grievable and those of others do not (see Judith Butler, *Frames of War: When Is Life Grievable?* (London: Verso, 2009)). Conceiving of love (or respect) as "purely intersubjective" phenomena in my sense is compatible with their being affected by frames in Butler's sense.
52. This is how I propose to spell out Dewey's important idea that the significance "man" (or "human") is a moral significance. See Honneth, *Reification*, 39–40.

REFERENCES

Butler, Judith. *Frames of War: When Is Life Grievable?* London: Verso, 2009.

Butler, Judith. *Giving an Account of Oneself.* New York: Fordham University Press, 2005.

Butler, Judith. *Undoing Gender.* New York: Routledge, 2004.

Elder-Vass, Dave. *The Causal Power of Social Structures: Emergence, Structure and Agency.* Cambridge: Cambridge University Press, 2010.

Gamper, Daniel. "Interview with Axel Honneth." *Barcelona Metropolis* Spring (April–June), 2010. https://www.academia.edu/30326708/Interview_with_Axel_Honneth.

Honneth, Axel. *Reification.* Oxford: Oxford University Press, 2008.

Honneth, Axel. *The Struggle for Recognition.* Translated by Joel Anderson. Cambridge: Polity, 1995.

Ikäheimo, Heikki. *Anerkennung.* Berlin: De Gruyter, 2014.

Ikäheimo, Heikki. "Globalizing Love: On the Nature and Scope of Love as a Form of Recognition." *Res Publica* 18 (2012): 11–24.

Ikäheimo, Heikki. "On the Genus and Species of Recognition." *Inquiry* 45, no. 4 (2002): 447–62.

Ikäheimo, Heikki. "Recognition, Identity and Subjectivity." In *The Palgrave Handbook of Critical Theory*, edited by M. J. Thompson. Basingstoke: Palgrave, 2017.

Ikäheimo, Heikki. "Recognizing Persons." *Journal of Consciousness Studies* 14, nos. 5–6 (2007): 224–47.

Lukács, György. *History and Class Consciousness*. Cambridge, MA: MIT Press, 1971. First published in 1923.

Searle, John. *Making the Social World: The Structure of Human Civilization*. Oxford: Oxford University Press, 2010.

Stahl, Titus. *Immanente Kritik: Elemente einer Theorie sozialer Praktiken*. Frankfurt: Campus, 2013.

Testa, Italo. "Ontology of the False State: On the Relation Between Critical Theory, Social Philosophy, and Social Ontology." *Journal of Social Ontology* 1, no. 2 (2015): 271–300.

10

NEGATIVITY IN RECOGNITION

Post-Freudian Legacies in Contemporary Critical Theory

JEAN-PHILIPPE DERANTY

This chapter aims to address the ambivalence of recognition by focusing on the problems surrounding the different possible ways to account for *negativity in recognition*.

By recognition, I mean an aspect of social relations through which the identity of a person is established or confirmed, or indeed, is denied, in some of its features, as a result of the attitudes of other persons toward that person. Three main dimensions of recognitive relations immediately emerge from this basic characterization. First, recognitive relationships have a deep impact on the *subject* involved in recognition. In the Hegelian tradition in particular, the one that is commonly mobilized to discuss issues of recognition, human persons are largely defined by their involvement in processes of recognition, in terms of their very sense of self and the worth they attach to their existence and features of their identity.[1] Secondly, the notion of recognition helps to focus on particular dimensions of *social relations*, notably those dimensions that establish the *value frameworks* within which individual existences unfold. Thirdly, because of the impact of recognitive relations on the lives of subjects, there is a *political* dimension to recognition. If forms of injustice or suffering or forms of social violence against individuals can be traced back to the structure of particular relations of recognition, to the way in which particular individuals are recognized by others, then addressing those forms of injustice or suffering requires changing the existing structures of recognition; it involves struggles *of* recognition. And in cases where individuals are not even acknowledged in their existence or in some significant features of their identity, then addressing injustice or suffering involves struggles *for* recognition. These are all *political* considerations.

The variegated interplays between subjective experience, and the social and political processes in which subjects are caught up, form the heart of the debates on recognition. Within those debates, one of the more specific lenses through which discussions unfold centers around the issue of "negativity." Authors debate as to whether a particular model of recognition makes sufficient room for, or accounts accurately enough for, negative phenomena at the level of subjective life, social relations, or politics. These negative phenomena can be *empirical* in kind, for instance in cases where a particular historical formation can be shown to harbor specific forms of misrecognition, or denial of recognition, that produce specific forms of injustice or suffering. Debates are also conducted at a conceptual level with many authors arguing that recognition understood as a structural dimension of social relations harbors forms of negation, in the relations that subjects have to themselves, or to the collective. In this case, negation, "the negative," is taken in an *ontological* sense, as essential elements in the structure of subjectivity, or social relations, or politics. And many authors make the methodological case that recognition is not an adequate *normative* concept to use for social and political theory.

This chapter's first aim is to shed light on the manifold issues that arise in debates on recognition when they are discussed through the lens of "the negative." I consider only those theories that accept that recognition is a valid concept for social critical analysis. Critiques of the recognition paradigm *as such* have been formulated in particular by Patchen Markell,[2] Kelly Oliver,[3] and Alexander Garcia Düttmann.[4] For these critiques, the conceptual framework that centers on recognition is too rigid; it is not adapted to the diversity and contingency that characterizes ethical encounters and political situations. It leads to a theoretical reification and simplification of identities and relationships. For these authors, then, employing a theoretical approach guided by the concept of recognition is negative in the basic sense of being inadequate. Whilst the criticisms emphasize important dimensions and objections that recognition theorists ought to consider, they won't be part of the inquiry here. I focus on the negativity of recognition on the assumption that the concept itself is valid at some level of analysis.

In the first section, I focus on a first set of recognition models, developed by philosophers such as Habermas, Fraser, and Tully, who all approach negative forms of recognition from a strictly normative point of view (section 1). For these authors, negative instances of recognition relate only to the social and political dimensions of the concept. They name forms of injustice arising from social structures and political struggles against them. This demarcates their approaches from a broad field, in which the concept of recognition and the negativity of recognition are taken not just in a normative sense, but also in a thick psychological sense, in relation to the subject of recognition. In order to navigate the large field of authors who also use recognition in such a thick sense, I suggest that a useful heuristic tool is to begin by distinguishing between two basic ways of using post-Freudian tropes. The first type of approach leans on the writings of Lacan, and makes negativity a structural feature of relations of selves to themselves and to others. The second approach focuses on object relations and argues that relational experiences at the core of recognitive relations are structurally ambivalent, and have both negative and positive facets, but that this does not warrant a negative appraisal of recognition as a norm. Over against these two ways of linking subject theory and recognition, I highlight an alternative, less well known, but in my mind more promising third way: a generalized theory of object relations, for which we find the most developed model in the writings of Stéphane Haber, and which is in fact already anticipated in Hegel's theory of subjective spirit, and a number of authors in Hegel's wake.

In the remainder of the chapter I try to identify different meanings of negativity in recognition, and their conceptual stakes, depending on which of the three approaches is taken to the three dimensions highlighted above. Section 2 is dedicated to discussions around the subject model itself: what does negativity mean for each of the approaches at this level? Section 3 asks similar questions at the level of social relations. And Section 4 is dedicated to negative recognition at the level of politics. At each of those levels, I present the generalized model of object relations as the more robust approach for contemporary critical theory. I thus use the "passage through the negative" first as an object of intrinsic interest to clarify issues in contemporary critical theory, but also at the same time as a way to advocate an alternative general approach in this field.

STRICTLY NORMATIVE NEGATIVITY

As a first step to clarify the issues related to negativity in recognition, once the concept has been fully embraced, we can note that a number of important authors use the concept of recognition in a strictly normative way, that is, without making the normative value of the concept dependent on any thick psychological or sociological theory of the subject. This is the case, for example, for Habermas. Whilst Habermas has proposed his own version of ontogenesis in a number of texts,[5] these texts do not carry the normative weight of his critical diagnoses. Rather, it is his general theory of communicative rationality and his theory of modernity that ground social criticism for him. Subject theory complements, on the psychological side, a model that is developed independently of it. Recognition is one of the names for the kind of reciprocal normative expectations between agents that structure modern social relations.[6] A comparable approach is adopted by Nancy Fraser, since she makes recognition one of the ways in which to flesh out the fundamental norm of participatory parity.[7]

In models that make strictly normative uses of the vocabulary of recognition, negative forms of recognition designate forms of social relations in which subjects fail to receive what they are entitled to on the basis of their status as equal members of the polity. These failures of recognition can be negative either because the way in which the individuals are recognized is negatively loaded (for instance, in modes of social perception that prejudicially emphasize sexual or racial features), or individuals are simply not recognized in some morally relevant capacity (for instance, their interests or even their voices do not count in a democratic process).

Interesting in this respect is the work of James Tully. Tully uses the concept of recognition only at the level of political theory, as a concept by which we can capture one of the normative claims raised by individuals and groups in democratic struggles.[8] The negativity of recognition, for him, lies first of all in its possible negative normative valence, the fact that it points to particular forms of injustice. Even though recognition for Tully is directly related to individuals' and groups' identities, its import is not psychological. The negativity of recognition has other meanings for him, to the extent that recognition also designates the quality of social bonds, describes a structure of the polity, both as a society made up of shared territorial, symbolic, and historical resources, and as a political collective. In these other senses, the negativity of recognition characterizes forms of social relation in which unjust distribution of material and symbolic goods is prevalent; in turn, these social relations demand forms of struggle for recognition. These struggles then make up a third sense of negative recognition, as political forms of redress.

Over against these strictly normative uses of recognition, for many other authors in contemporary critical theory, the appeal of the notion is its ontological richness, the fact that its normative force and critical potential are directly connected to substantive descriptive dimensions, especially psychological and sociological ones. It is here that the debates about the exact meaning and place of negativity in relation to recognition has the highest theoretical stakes, since it determines much of the overall shape of the theoretical model.

NEGATIVITY IN THE SUBJECT OF RECOGNITION

For a number of influential approaches in contemporary critical theory, the problematic nature of recognition is not limited to issues of injustice, but also to the fact that negativity can designate an aspect of the relation of the self to itself, as a result of socialization. This explains why many authors in critical theory continue to believe that substantial reference to psychoanalysis is indispensable for the purposes of critical theory.[9]

Indeed, one useful way to find one's bearings in contemporary critical theory in relation to issues of recognition, particularly to the treatment of its negative forms, is by looking at how the Freudian heritage is assumed and further developed in that field. A major point of differentiation between theorists is whether one adopts a Lacanian route, or whether one prefers a different way to articulate some key Freudian concepts and arguments.[10] On one end of the spectrum, we find a way of discussing the link between recognition and subjectivity that, very broadly speaking, adopts a Lacanian air. I use this vague expression to signal that this is to be understood in a very general sense, in terms of general theoretical gestures that define a common language, or a common set of approaches, in one section of contemporary critical theory. These basic assumptions can be cashed out in different ways. For example, they vary enormously between Butler and Žižek, and indeed throughout these thinkers' respective *oeuvres*.

A first significant feature in those approaches relates to the idea that the specificity of an individual subjective formation comes down to the particular way in which individuals construct their "desire," that is, their own psychic ways of relating to and longing for constitutive objects. A defining insight in this field is that the relation of the self to itself is mediated by the desire for an object that remains inherently inaccessible to the self. The self constitutes itself around its own void, structures itself by desiring an object that will forever remain lost.

A key second feature is: what makes this object inaccessible is that it is captured by a law that forbids it to the subject. A "third" intervenes in dyadic relationships, and is responsible for the turn of the primary longing for the object into a mediated desire for the desire of the Other. As that Other captures the desired object, the mediation via the Other is also what makes the object inaccessible. This "third," which embodies the symbolic realm, becomes the placeholder for suprasubjective forms of power and domination on which the subject remains utterly dependent, since the subject owes her identity to the place she takes within these power relations.

These two features (the constitutive object as intrinsically lacking, and the capture of the subject in the nets of symbolic power) give negativity a very specific meaning and function in such an approach. First, negativity becomes the structural law of subjective formation itself, in an absolute, unresolvable sense. Identity becomes synonymous with absolute self-loss or radical splitting. Recognition is negative here first of all in the sense that relationships with significant others, rather than starting a process of subjective formation at the end of which the self might be minimally in touch with itself, or might be able to "appropriate" itself, in fact lead to a radical "misrecognition" of the self by itself. Relations of recognition on that model produce a wholly negative form of self-recognition, or *méconnaissance*.[11]

Secondly, the indefinite longing for an impossible object is accompanied by modes of aggression that are directed against the absent object, or against Others whom the self thinks have captured the object. Or, indeed, violence is directed against the self itself, to the extent that the loss of the object is imputed to the self itself, in forms of guilt and melancholy.[12] On such a model, negativity therefore implies aggression. Aggression in this version of subjective negativity is not just a consequence of recognition, it is inherent in the structure of recognition.[13]

Other theorists, like Cornelius Castoriadis, Axel Honneth, or Amy Allen, do not follow this Lacanian approach. Instead, the key insight in these alternative appropriations of the Freudian heritage is the ambiguity of the human subject's reliance on object relations, that is, the fact that object dependence can lead either to pathological formations, possibly to aggression, but is also the condition for access to both the self and the other.[14] In this kind of approach, negativity is also unavoidable. Recognition as seen from the perspective of object-relations theories is articulated in terms of inter- and intrasubjective struggles.[15] The basic idea is that experiences of symbiosis, of fusion, or of monadological plenitude in Castoriadis's case,[16] lead to frustration and aggression when they are broken, when the other asserts its independence.[17] These negative moments, however, are only the negatives of the constitutive, founding experiences in which the self learns that it can have its needs fulfilled, its helplessness can be answered, and when the longed-for object or a substitute is present again.[18]

The difference between the two positions is that in the first, Lacanian, approach, negativity is intrinsic, whereas in the second, the negativity of recognition is negative in relation to a positive. From the "Lacanian" perspective, it is naive to think that the negativity at the heart of subjectivity is the negativity of a positivity. The subject is just pure self-negativity. This Lacanian approach can draw not just on Hegel's analysis of the struggle for recognition in the *Phenomenology of Spirit*, but can also claim to give an "empirical," psychological sense to Hegel's definition of subjectivity as absolute negativity. In object-relations models, negativity is just as inherent. But recognition in these models is truly ambivalent, and can turn from positive to negative and vice versa.

If one thinks in the wake of Lacan, the only way in which the subject can find peace in its own self-alienation is by deliberately owning it, or, as in Butler's early writings, by playing with it, by turning the discourse of the Other against itself. We might say that recognizing one's essential misrecognition is the path to autonomy on that model. But then the question of where the urge to exit self-alienation comes from, and whether it even makes sense to seek such exit, becomes tricky to articulate within the terms of that framework. In object-relations theory, by contrast, the subject needs to "work through" negativity to develop "positive" forms of self- and other-relations that are based on the ideal of free communication, that is, free letting go of self and other within the relationship.

However, these two basic methodological ways to think about the place and valence of negativity in subjectivity as a result of constitutive object relations do not exhaust the options. Already in Hegel, especially in the *Encyclopedia*'s theory of subjective spirit, object relations are not restricted to the love bonds through which the subject attaches to significant persons.[19] The "objects" to which the self attaches in processes of internalization and externalization also include "symbolic," cultural, and social objects (language, collective ethos, representations of the polis as a whole), both in their meanings and in their material instantiations, as well as material and natural objects, things, and forms of the environment, which frame and fill up interpersonal and symbolic worlds. These latter objects matter not only in indirect ways: as vehicles for the erotic or symbolic bonds they can represent or materially mediate. They also present direct opportunities for the subject to engage in the world and "find itself at home" in it, either through processes in which external objects are shaped according to inner beliefs or desires, or through processes in which external objects impact and shape inner life. This generalized version of object relations finds important theoretical support in some of Freud's late texts, following the shift to his second topic. In "The Ego and the Id" or "Inhibition, Symptom, Anxiety," Freud reemphasizes the role of the ego in its role as a mediator seeking to accommodate the requests stemming from the subconscious inner drives with the requests stemming from the external world.[20] Indeed, in a text directly applying the topic presented in "The Ego and the Id," negation as a modal part of a subject's judgment is reconstructed by Freud as the process allowing the subject to mediate between internal and external demands, by simultaneously acknowledging and repressing the objects pushing to be recognised.[21] Following the impressive reconstruction proposed by Stéphane Haber, we can take these later texts as the theoretical birthplace of currents in post-Freudian psychoanalysis (notably in Harold Searles and André Green, following Bowlby and Winnicott), which propound a generalized model of object relations.[22]

On this model, the formation of the subject involves the creation and deployment of dynamic relations with objects that make it possible for the self to develop in his or her own vitality (rather than as just positive psychological self-relations). These objects are not restricted to internal, fantasized figures as in Lacan, or to real/fantasized others as in interpersonalist models. Rather, they are objects that belong to three different worlds that overlap but are irreducible to each other: the inner world of conscious and subconscious life; the natural, material world in which vital forces can be expanded or find the mediations necessary for the fixation or expression or development of subjective formations; and the intersubjective world, in which the subject finds essential poles of reference for its constitution.[23] On this generalized model of object relations, recognition is only one type of object relation.[24]

Negativity here denotes first of all the structural experience of the "not-self," to which the self might attach, or which the self might repel, or from which it might withdraw. It also denotes the empirical forms of diminished, warped, or even destroyed relations to objects, which immediately impact on subjective life since the latter depends on the series of bonds it has created with its objects. Some of these damaged object relations are relations of recognition, but not all of them are. Relations of recognition have primacy in socializing the subject, and this generalized model can overlap largely with the restricted model propounded by Honneth and Benjamin. But it reframes relations of recognition within a larger conceptual scheme, so that the structural negativity at the heart of the subject is not limited to that which stems from recognitive relations.

NEGATIVE SOCIALITY

Recognition as it is discussed in the previous section relates to primary socialization. The issue of negative recognition at the level of social relations relates first of all to the effects that particular structures of society have on the subjective life that begins to emerge with primary socialization. To further examine the possible options at this level of social relations, it is useful to continue to use the rough divide between Lacanian and non-Lacanian post-Freudian positions.

One key feature that roughly unifies a particular section of critical theory is thinking of subject-constitutive bonds as being framed and "overdetermined" by their taking place under the authority, the law, of a "third." This conceptual scheme provides a powerful way to understand the "psychic life of power," the way in which the social order, with its inherent logic of hierarchical division and exclusion (between the high and the low, the normal and the abnormal, the noble and the ignoble, the in and the out, and so on), seeps into subjective lives and shapes identities. Historically speaking, such a scheme was developed and became popular in contemporary critical theory in reference to two combined references: Lacan's tripartite Imaginary/Symbolic/Real topic, and Althusser's famous text on ideology and state apparatuses.[25] Particularly influential was Althusser's claim, explicitly related to Lacan's teaching, that the modes of "interpellation" of individuals by state institutions in the course of social life, as they subject individuals to the norms making up the content of ideological reproduction, also performatively produce them as social subjects, "normalizing" them into the required social order. This, we might say, provided something like a structuralist version of the "individuation through socialization" thesis. Althusser's proposal provides a powerful social-theoretical translation of the Lacanian idea, according to which the subject is constituted by identifying with its imaginary position in a symbolic order, and that this order thereby structures subjectivity through the internalization of its discursively mediated, underlying normative assumptions. The outcome of this conceptual combination is a way of thinking that allows one to account for the way in which social life, as it is organized in specific institutions, and as it is reproduced in everyday forms of interaction, can shape individual subjectivities despite the latter's utter diversity; how homogeneous symbolic patterns can be instilled into the myriad of individual psyches, and therefore how power functions and is reproduced by the subjects themselves through the very mechanisms of their psychic lives. Foucault's analysis of the constitutive function of disciplinary practices in modern society, in his writings of the mid-1970s, could provide a powerful additional reference for this way of thinking.[26]

From the perspective offered by such a model of socialization, it is naive to discuss relations of recognition as though they merely involve subjects facing each other, horizontally as it were, and to believe that such "horizontal," dyadic relations provide all the necessary theoretical vocabulary to model the social framing of psychic formation. Instead, the psychoanalytic insight into the radical gap between conscious self-representation and unconscious psychic reality, combined with the insight into the structural overdetermination of the individual psyche by its inscription in the symbolic order, leads to the conclusion that relations of recognition in fact produce an irreducible "misrecognition" of the subject: a misrecognition of the subject by itself, and a misrecognition of the Other: of its power over us, and of its very reality. Hegel's struggle for recognition can be read from this perspective no longer as the genetic precursor to a successful integration of multiple Is into a We, but rather as highlighting already the internal splitting that structures the consciousness involved in that struggle and its outcomes.[27]

In particular, emphasis can be put on the forms of inner splitting and self-loss that are reproduced in various forms in the conceptual schemes following the famous master/slave relationship. Indeed, the accent can be placed on the fact that recognition in that text involves an unfurling of death and violence, in action and in thought, against the Other *and* against oneself, to produce the normalized, particular-universal individual who has to live its life in the We.[28]

For critical theorists writing in that vein, the negativity of recognition, understood as condition of sociality, therefore involves: subjection to power, in such a way that the subject reproduces its own subjection to the existing norms in living its subjective life; internalization of the structure of domination underpinning society; and a process in which psychic life is submitted to intense violence since it is forced to split itself through the process of "misrecognition"; a process which can also produce externalized, other-directed violence, as the law of exclusion is held up not only to oneself but also to others. In that approach, self-directed aggression can be projected outwards, notably toward those who fall on the wrong side of the symbolic law, the ones who are "othered" within the normalizing logic of the big Other.

Through the psychoanalytical cure, the subject caught up in the endless pursuit for an inaccessible object can "traverse the fantasy" and realize that "the Other doesn't exist."[29] The subjected can talk back to interpellating subjection and problematize and shake in its foundations the gendered performativity of social power.[30] The dominated can challenge ideology by placing themselves outside of it in realizing their place in class struggle. Violence toward oneself and violence toward others can be remediated once one acknowledges the joint condition of relational and reciprocal vulnerability and mortality.[31] These are all indications, summarizing positions taken by Žižek and Butler, to show that the possibility of something like "positive" recognition remains even within the Lacanian/Althusserian model, that is, a form of self- and other-acknowledgment which is no longer destructive, whether or not it is an outcome of struggle.

Object-relation theorists also emphasize vulnerability as an intrinsic dimension of "individuation through socialization." They agree that the subject is "produced" through the internalization of external normative patterns, and conclude from this that "pathological" norms produce subjective suffering precisely because subjects owe their psychic identity to the socializing process. Indeed, the account of psychic suffering induced by negative relations of recognition includes the whole array of physical, psychic pathologies that "Lacanian" models entertain.[32]

The fundamental difference between the two kinds of approaches stems from the fact that, for the philosophers who do not operate within the Althusserian/Lacanian background, recognition is normative in and of itself, in the strong, moral, and not just in the descriptive sense of the term "normative," as synonymous with "normalizing." That is, negative forms of recognition are negative precisely because they are "wrong" or "pathological" or misshapen forms of recognition. The standard allowing us to call them bad or wrong is implicit in the idea of *recognition itself*. Recognition is an inherently normative concept, in the strong, moral, we might say Kantian, sense of the term, that is, as a necessary condition of just and nondistorted intersubjective practices, as a norm that helps distinguish between those relations that are good, or those that are bad, for human individuals as beings that are intrinsically vulnerable to their social environment. So these theorists of recognition can make room for negative recognition, for the negativity of recognition, and of course they do, and in fact the whole point of using a normative concept of recognition for critical theory is to be able to diagnose and condemn negative forms of recognition for the damage they do to individuals and communities, and indeed to society at large. But the negativity is not the negativity *of* recognition, but the negativity of *particular forms* of recognition. Or, to say it differently, recognition is *not structurally* negative; rather, the point of recognition is to diagnose *empirical* forms of negative relations of recognition.

Another important difference between the two approaches concerns the possibility of historicization in the critical diagnosis. The Lacanian/Althusserian model of subjection can be applied to a variety of social contexts but is independent, in its structure, from history. It is true, broadly speaking, of all social situations within modern, disciplinary, capitalistic societies. Whatever shape the "big Other" takes, its most relevant function in the critical story is its oppressive normativism, and the fact that it is imposed on individuals to make subjects of them. By contrast, whereas the normative model of "individuation through socialization" is just as formal to begin with,[33] in its negative application, that is, in its application to empirical pathologies or injustices of recognition, it is more intimately related, *in its very content*, to the specificity of social contexts. The general norm of mutual recognition can be specified when one considers the precise dimensions of identities and practices that are negatively evaluated or suffer from invisibility in particular social contexts. In other words, it appears more historically sensitive, not just because it can be applied to different historical contexts, but also because changes in the very structures of relations of recognition is part of the program.[34]

If we turn our attention to the alternative model that was sketched at the end of the previous section, we can see that it overlaps with the normative view of recognition but reframes it within a broader background, with important consequences for thinking about negative social relations. The two models overlap to the extent that the generalized object-relations model includes intersubjective dependency as a key form of vulnerability. But on this more general model of dependency, the subject is made vulnerable *not just* in terms of intersubjective relations. A generalized model of vulnerable relationality also focuses on the ways in which the self inhabits its own bodily life, and how this vitality in turn expresses itself and realizes itself (or not) in the material, objectual realms, notably the material realities involved in the worlds of production and consumption. The main issue this broadening of the framework raises is not just the descriptive issue of whether recognition theory is sufficient by itself to account for all the pathologies of contemporary society, although that is definitely a valid concern. The main issue raised by this alternative model of object relations concerns recognition itself, and how to conceptualize its negative manifestations. If the subject of recognition is also a subject who is constituted through attachments to nonhuman worlds, if her life is not just psychosocially vulnerable but also somatically and sensuously, then the valence of particular recognitive relations will be intrinsically linked to those extrapersonal dimensions. It will become difficult to disentangle other than in analytical fashion the intersubjective from the nonsubjective dimensions. To take an example, important aspects of the experiences of precarization and alienation caused by changes in conditions of employment and the organization of labor processes are related to the spatial and somatic dimensions of subjective experience. These are not just by-products or extrinsic dimensions of particular working relations which could be analyzed in the last instance as particular states in capitalistic relations of recognition. The impact of new information technologies and the management strategies they serve, for instance, or the ways in which work spaces are set up, require a perspective that goes beyond the analysis of unequal power relations and issues of recognition of the working activity; the pathologies they create require a broader view of the subject. As Marx stated already, capitalism attacks the worker "at the very roots of his life."[35] The exploitation of the worker's life, including his or her inner, mental, and affective life, cannot be fully accounted for in terms of recognition, at least not descriptively.[36]

NEGATIVE POLITICS

Negative recognition at the political level relates to questions that fall on two different sides.

On the one side, negativity can relate to actions and reactions to the social facts associated with structures of misrecognition, or denial of recognition, by the individuals subjected to them.

Very schematically, we can distinguish between two ideal-typical forms of such actions and reactions: either forms of refusal and resistance; or forms of internalization of negative recognition. The internalization of stigma or of exclusionary social logics becomes a political problem, a problem of negative politics we might say, when it makes those subjected to it unwittingly contribute to the very collective that demeans or excludes them.

On the other side, negativity in the political can point to what we might term "pathological politics," that is, the forms of collective and institutional action that enact negative social recognition. These forms of action are pathological when they contravene basic rights of the persons, in a very minimal sense of rights, as something due to them given the conditions of modern societies, from their right to participate in democratic process, to their rights to personal safety. As with the first aspect, the boundary between the social and the political is also very thin at this level. Social contempt, for instance, is a form of social relation, but can also have performative, enacted aspects, which make it also a form of "politics" when these translate into real consequences in the organization of collective life. Inflated nationalism is based on a perception of self and other, and as such is a form of social relation, but can also lead to forms of collective action, whether they are institutionalized, as in the case of police violence and administrative discrimination, or not, as in the case of mob violence or violence directed at individuals on the basis of social prejudices.

"Lacanian" positions face difficulties in relation to the first dimension of negative politics, given the internalization model of power they operate with. Such a model of power leads to two conclusions: either that there is no agency for dominated subjects, or that any apparent form of resistance is only an effect of the power structure. Given the deep level at which forms of "misrecognition" are supposed to be entrenched within subjectivities, such theories seem to back themselves into a corner in relation to the very possibility of emancipatory politics.[37]

Furthermore, these positions tend to favor strong forms of social constructivism, which leads them to reject the language of normativity in any external, transcending sense of the term. But that in turn robs them of any consistent ground from which to criticize particular social or political formations, or from which to evaluate the moral or political significance of a social movement.

By contrast, normative approaches to recognition can deal with these issues more consistently. The language of recognition allows them to establish an internally consistent link between the diagnosis of injustice and the analysis of politics. Injustice or suffering resulting from misrecognition or denial of recognition does not always trigger a struggle of or for recognition.[38] In these cases, theory has to ponder what the obstacles to the rejection of negative recognition are. Recognition theories usually recognize the need for a theory of ideology, which accounts for the internalization of negative recognition, and, on the political level, to forms of voluntary servitude. However, on their accounts, when the social and cultural conditions are right, the groups suffering injustice or socially caused suffering can reject the negative recognitive order they are subjected to, and engage in struggles of or struggles for recognition. In cases such as these, the normativity of recognition provides the internal link between social injustice, social suffering, and social anger, and the normativity of negative politics. By normativity of politics, I mean the answers to the following questions: whether the aims of a movement are justified or not (what kind of new recognition they aim for, and whether it itself contains forms of negative recognition); whether the means the movement employs for their ends are justified (are their political tactics and strategies themselves based on forms of misrecognition, or denial of recognition?).[39]

Discussions of these issues regarding the normative basis of social criticism makes up a significant portion of the contemporary debates in critical theory.[40] However, whilst the "Lacanian" approaches seem to have difficulties escaping the suspicion that they simply give themselves with the left hand the normative language their right hand has rejected, they seem to be much more apt when it comes to the second, descriptive dimension of negative politics, the one that deals with "pathological politics."

This is because the use of a model of the Lacanian/Althusserian kind helps theory to give due place to the cruelty and violence inherent in socialization. One criterion for a successful critical theory is whether it rises to the challenge presented to it by social and political reality. This is not merely about empirical validity, but also about the disclosive force of theory. A critical theory model might be useful even if it is empirically shaky or normatively confused, or logically inconsistent in the final analysis, simply if it provides a language and a perspective that allow one to catch a glimpse of the full extent of social pathologies.[41] Even if one is skeptical of the full normative, or logical, or empirical validity of the models propounded by, for example, Butler or Žižek, their analyses of ideological effects on subjects and communities seem to be located, at least rhetorically, at the right level of severity and seriousness, one that does justice to the phenomena their models are about. They disclose something of the enormous violence against subjects that is harbored in mechanisms of heterosexist imposition, or of the violence that "liberal" societies can display toward their others, internally or indeed in colonial and postcolonial wars, as a result of the rejection of otherness. Critical theory needs to speak a language that does justice to the incredible potentials for violence, cruelty, and destruction that the contemporary world still entails. In a sense, one of the tasks of critical theory today might be precisely to give a full account of the negativity of recognition, the way in which, in its pathological dimensions, it triggers forms of savagery that polite discussions in academic political philosophy don't seem willing or able to capture.

This is one possible way to look at the tasks of critical theory in relation to negative politics: its disclosive duty, we might say. In the course of his response to Joel Whitebook's criticism, Honneth has in effect argued for the opposite position.[42] In showing that his theory of recognition does have the potential to make room for "the work of the negative," that is, the capacity for subjects to object to aspects of their socialization, Honneth also made the point, implicitly, that the language in which a theoretical model is developed need not display a similar tone as the descriptive language in which the model is put to use in social criticism. The dispassionate language of theory can therefore always lend itself to more vivid descriptions when applied to particular phenomena. A model of subject formation premised upon object-relations theory, like the one upon which Honneth's theory of recognition is built, rejects the idea of an innate drive for aggression, and instead analyzes the capacity for aggression as a derivative consequence of the frustration felt in experiencing the independence of the author. But nothing in that theoretical account excludes the possibility that the frustration felt toward the independence of the other can take extreme forms. Indeed, other object-theoretical models, like those developed by Castoriadis and more recently by Amy Allen in reference to Melanie Klein, seek precisely to make the questions of violence and cruelty central in the general project of social criticism, by focusing on their subjective roots, namely the inherent ambivalence of primitive, constitutive relational experiences.[43] Their psychoanalytical models differ significantly from Honneth's, but share with him the decisive idea of the intrinsic ambivalence of constitutive relational experiences.

On the issue of pathological politics, the alternative object-theoretical approach I have been canvassing has much to contribute as well, the details of which cannot fit here.[44] Let me just highlight a key methodological point of difference as a way to conclude this short study of negative forms of recognition. The characteristic aim of this alternative approach is to define a generalized normative framework, in terms of the avenues social life ought to provide in order for individuals to be in a position to establish life-sustaining attachments to different kinds of objects (internal; intersubjective; and material). From this generalized point of view, pathological politics are not limited to direct forms of interpersonal injustice or violence, and they do not arise solely from the fraught nature of I–thou relationships and the strain particular social formations can put those under. Pathological politics can also include self-directed violence. This is the case, for example, when the competition between social agents is part of a broader culture of performance and universal evaluation, as in contemporary neoliberal capitalism. Such social logics might also be related to predatory and recklessly destructive attitudes to external objects (whether human or nonhuman), in the name again of heightened performance and competition. In scenarios of this kind, the political project that would be adapted to respond to such negative politics would not be limited to a struggle for the recognition of particular attributes of misrecognized subjects. It would have to target the social set up as a whole, in which negative forms of recognition might be at play, but only as one axis amongst other, life-threatening social conditions.

As this study has attempted to show, negativity is a concept that appears at different levels and in a variety of meanings and usages within debates on recognition. The term arises in discussions about models of subjectivity, social relations, and political structures. It is used in debates regarding the critical analysis of empirical phenomena, and in choosing between theoretical options, and between methodological approaches. The term is often discussed in ontological terms, as a structure of subjectivity or sociality, but also in normative terms, as an ideal of social relations, or on the contrary as a deleterious ideal to aim for. The outcome of this conceptual survey is paradoxical. For beyond this great multiplicity of uses and of levels of analysis, the focus on "the negative" in recognition, by making us return to the Hegelian and Freudian roots of the problem, leads us to discover (or so I have tried to argue) that relations of recognition, however essential they are to functioning subjectivities and social bonds, do not exhaust the range of relations through which a subject constitutes itself. Subjects attach to other kinds of objects, and the normativity of social life therefore encompasses more than just relations of recognition.

NOTES

1. See Heikki Ikäheimo for a particularly lucid exposition of all the conceptual and normative dimensions entailed in this fundamental claim, "Holism and Normative Essentialism in Hegel's Social Ontology," in *Recognition and Social Ontology*, ed. H. Ikäheimo and A. Laitinen (Leiden: Brill, 2011), 145–210.

2. Patchen Markell, *Bound by Recognition* (Princeton, NJ: Princeton University Press, 2003).
3. Kelly Oliver, *Witnessing: Beyond Recognition* (Minneapolis: University of Minnesota Press, 2001).
4. Alexander Garcia Düttmann, *Between Cultures: Tensions in the Struggle for Recognition* (London: Verso, 2000). In *Against Recognition*, Lois McNay does not perform an external critique of the paradigm. She acknowledges that the language of recognition is indispensable today as a sociological and political descriptor. Her criticism is internal; it targets the conceptualization of power by recognition theorists. Lois McNay, *Against Recognition* (Cambridge: Polity, 2008).
5. Notably at the start of Jürgen Habermas, *The Theory of Communicative Action*, vol. 2, *Lifeworld and System: A Critique of Functionalist Reason* (Boston: Beacon, 1985), 22–42; in *Moral Consciousness and Communicative Action* (Oxford: Polity, 1992), as well as in "Individuation Through Socialization," in *Postmetaphysical Thinking* (Cambridge, MA: MIT Press, 1992), 149–203.
6. This is clearly the sense of "mutual recognition" in the texts gathered in *Moral Consciousness and Communicative Action*. See also Kenneth Baynes, "Freedom and Recognition in Hegel and Habermas," *Philosophy Social Criticism* 28, no. 1 (2002): 1–17.
7. See for instance her contributions in Nancy Fraser and Axel Honneth, *Redistribution or Recognition? A Political-Philosophical Exchange* (London: Verso, 2003).
8. James Tully, "Struggles Over Distribution and Recognition," *Constellations* 7, no. 4 (2000): 469–82; "Recognition and Dialogue: The Emergence of a New Field," *Critical Review of International Social and Political Philosophy* 7, no. 3 (2004): 84–106. See also David Owen, "Foucault, Tully and Agonistic Struggles Over Recognition," in M. Bankovsky and A. Le Goff, *Recognition Theory and Contemporary French Moral and Political Philosophy* (Manchester: Manchester University Press, 2012), 88–108.
9. See, for instance, Axel Honneth, "The Work of Negativity: A Recognition-Theoretical Revision of Psychoanalysis," in *The I in We: Studies in the Theory of Recognition* (Cambridge: Polity, 2012), 193–96; as well as Amy Allen, "Are We Driven? Critical Theory and

Psychoanalysis Reexamined," *Critical Horizons* 16, no. 4 (2015): 311–28. Indeed, this also explains why Hegel remains a decisive reference within critical theory, from Butler to Žižek to Honneth, we might say. On the side of philosophy, see in particular Rebecca Comay, *Mourning Sickness* (Stanford: Stanford University Press, 2011), and on the side of psychoanalytical practice, see André Green, *Le Travail du Négatif* (Paris: Minuit, 2011) for the strong conceptual links still being explored between Hegel and Freud. It is not only the *Phenomenology of Spirit*, and its historical influence on French thought, culminating in Lacan's specular theory of identity, that warrants these links. Hegel's theory of subjective spirit in the *Encyclopedia* substantially anticipated some of the core insights developed a century later by Freud. Hegel's theory of ontogenesis in that part of the *Encyclopedia* already conceives of the process of subjective formation as a difficult "work" facing the threat of splitting, potentially leading to denials of reality principle, life disgust, loss of object, repression, and so on.

10. Amy Allen and Maria Ruti in their *Critical Theory Between Klein and Lacan: A Dialogue* (London: Bloomsbury, 2019) highlight many possible rapprochements between a Lacanian and an object-theoretical, Kleinian approach. However, it remains heuristically interesting to approach the post-Freudian heritage and its legacy in critical theory from this initial distinction.
11. Jacques Lacan, *Écrits: The First Complete Edition in English* (London: Norton, 2007), in particular page 80.
12. See, in particular Lacan, *Écrits*, chapter 6, "Aggressiveness in Psychoanalysis." See also Judith Butler, *The Psychic Life of Power*, notably chapter 5.
13. See, for instance, Judith Butler, "Longing for Recognition," in *Hegel's Philosophy and Feminist Thought: Beyond Antigone?*, ed. Kimberly Hutchings and Tuija Pulkkinen (New York: Palgrave Macmillan, 2010), 109–29. Or Žižek, *The Sublime Object of Ideology* (London: Verso, 1989).
14. A major reference here is provided by Jessica Benjamin's work, which brings together object-relations psychoanalysis and arguments from the tradition of the Frankfurt School, including its Hegelian heritage. See in particular *The Bonds of Love: Psychoanalysis, Feminism, and the Problem of Domination* (New York: Pantheon, 1988). More recently, see

Transitional Subjects: Critical Theory and Object Relations, ed. Amy Allen and Brian O'Connor (New York: Columbia University Press, 2019).

15. The classical appropriation of object-relations theory is now of course Axel Honneth's in *Struggle for Recognition* (in particular, 95–107), and subsequent texts in the second half of the 1990s. See a recent proposal for a shift in Honneth's object-relations theory by Richard Ganis, "Insecure Attachment and Narcissistic Vulnerability: Implications for Honneth's Recognition-Theoretic Reconstruction of Psychoanalysis," *Critical Horizons* 16, no. 4 (2015): 329–51.
16. See, for instance, Cornelius Castoriadis, *The Imaginary Institution of Society* (Cambridge, MA: MIT Press, 1997), 294–301.
17. See Axel Honneth, *The I in We*, 229.
18. Axel Honneth, "Appropriating Freedom: Freud's Conception of Individual Self-Relation," in *Pathologies of Reason: On the Legacy of Critical Theory* (New York: Columbia University Press, 2009), 126–45.
19. G. W. F. Hegel, *Philosophy of Mind*, trans. W. Wallace & A. V. Miller, revised with an introduction by Michael Inwood (Oxford: Clarendon, 2007), 96: "the world throws its threads so far into the subject that what the subject is for itself in truth only consists of these very threads."
20. S. Freud, "The Ego and the Id," in *Standard Edition*, vol. 19 (London: Hogarth, 1961), 3–69; Sigmund Freud, *Inhibition, Symptom and Anxiety* (New York: Norton, 1959).
21. S. Freud, "Negation" (1925), *Standard Edition*, vol. 19, 235–39: "Judging is a continuation, along lines of expediency, of the original process by which the ego took things into itself or expelled them from itself, according to the pleasure principle. The polarity of judgment appears to correspond to the opposition of the two groups of instincts which we have supposed to exist."
22. See in particular Harold Searles, *The Nonhuman Environment in Normal Development and in Schizophrenia* (New York: International Universities Press, 1960); and André Green, *Propédeutique: La métapsychologie revisitée* (Paris: Champ Vallon, 1995) and *Key Ideas for a Contemporary Psychoanalysis: Recognition and Misrecognition of the Unconscious* (London: Routledge, 2005), notably 119–22.
23. Stéphane Haber, *Freud et la Théorie sociale* (Paris: La Dispute, 2012), 68–115. See also *L'Aliénation: Vie sociale et expérience de la dépossession*

(Paris: PUF, 2007), in which a first version of this generalized model of relationality articulated on the three worlds of self, other (society), and nature is presented. See *L'Homme dépossédé: Une tradition critique de Marx à Honneth* (Paris: CNRS Editions, 2009), for a first application of this model to critical theory.

24. I have attempted to show how this generalized model of object relations was adopted by major post-Hegelian philosophers, with Feuerbach the first key episode, in Jean-Philippe Deranty, "Feuerbach's Theory of Object-Relations and Its Legacy in 20th Century Post-Hegelian philosophy," *Southern Journal of Philosophy*, 53, no. 3 (2015): 286–310. A major source of inspiration for this general model is the psychodynamic model developed by Christophe Dejours, notably in *Le Corps, d'abord* (Paris: Payot, 2003) and *Travail Vivant* (Paris: Payot, 2010).
25. Louis Althusser, "Ideology and Ideological State Apparatuses," in *Lenin and Philosophy and Other Essays* (New York: Monthly Review, 1971), 121–76.
26. In particular Michel Foucault, *Discipline and Punish: The Birth of the Prison* (London: Penguin, 1991).
27. Catherine Malabou, "Impossible Recognition: Lacan, Butler, Zizek," in M. Bankovsky and A. Le Goff, eds., *Recognition Theory and Contemporary French Moral and Political Philosophy* (Manchester: Manchester University Press, 2012), 41–53.
28. See Judith Butler, *The Psychic Life of Power* (Stanford: Stanford University Press, 1997).
29. Žižek, *The Sublime Object of Ideology*.
30. Judith Butler, *Excitable Speech: The Politics of Performativity* (New York: Routledge, 1996).
31. Judith Butler, *Giving an Account of Oneself* (New York: Fordham University Press, 2005); Butler, "Longing for Recognition," 126.
32. Estelle Ferrarese, "Judith Butler's 'Not Particularly Postmodern Insight' of Recognition," *Philosophy and Social Criticism* 37, no. 7 (2011): 759–73.
33. Honneth, *Struggle for Recognition*, 171–80.
34. See Nancy Fraser's critique of Butler in "Heterosexism, Misrecognition and Capitalism: A Response to Judith Butler," *Social Text* 15, no. 3/4 (1997): 279–89.
35. Karl Marx, *Capital*, vol. 1 (London: Penguin, 1990), 484.

36. See a similar kind of criticism by Hartmut Rosa in relation to the acceleration thesis: recognition is certainly a central conceptual and normative concern for a critique of contemporary society, but it has to be complemented by a consideration of the frames of experience in which demands for recognition are formulated, which significantly alter their meaning and structure. *Weltbeziehungen im Zeitalter der Beschleunigung* (Berlin: Suhrkamp, 2013), 279–83.
37. Matthew Sharpe and Geoff Boucher, *Žižek and Politics: A Critical Introduction*, (Edinburgh: Edinburgh University Press, 2010).
38. Honneth, *Struggle for Recognition*, 163–64.
39. Emmanuel Renault, *L'Expérience de l'Injustice: Reconnaissance et Clinique de l'Injustice* (Paris: La Découverte, 2004); Jean-Philippe Deranty and Emmanuel Renault, "Politicizing Honneth's Ethics of Recognition," *Thesis Eleven* 88, no. 1 (2007): 92–111.
40. See in particular Amy Allen, *The Politics of Our Selves: Power, Autonomy, and Gender in Contemporary Critical Theory* (New York: Columbia University Press, 2008), as well as Seyla Benhabib, Judith Butler, Drucilla Cornell, and Nancy Fraser, *Feminist Contentions: A Philosophical Exchange* (New York: Routledge, 1992).
41. Axel Honneth, "The Possibility of a Disclosing Critique of Society: The Dialectic of Enlightenment in Light of Current Debates in Social Criticism," in *Disrespect: The Normative Foundations of Critical Theory* (Cambridge: Polity, 2007), 49–62.
42. Axel Honneth, "Facets of the Presocial Self: A Rejoinder to Joel Whitebook," in *The I in We*, 217–31.
43. Cornelius Castoriadis, "The Psychical and Social Roots of Hatred," in *Figures of the Thinkable* (Stanford: Stanford University Press, 2007), chapter 6. Amy Allen, "Are We Driven?"
44. See Stéphane Haber, *Penser le néocapitalisme: Vie, capital et aliénation*, (Paris: Les Prairies Ordinaires, 2013).

BIBLIOGRAPHY

Allen, Amy. "Are We Driven? Critical Theory and Psychoanalysis Reexamined." *Critical Horizons* 16, no. 4 (2015): 311–28.

Allen, Amy. *The Politics of Our Selves: Power, Autonomy, and Gender in Contemporary Critical* Theory. New York: Columbia University Press, 2008.

Allen, Amy, and Maria Ruti. *Critical Theory between Klein and Lacan: A Dialogue.* London: Bloomsbury, 2019.

Althusser, Louis. "Ideology and Ideological State Apparatuses." In *Lenin and Philosophy and Other Essays*, 121–76. New York: Monthly Review, 1971.

Baynes, Kenneth. "Freedom and Recognition in Hegel and Habermas." *Philosophy Social Criticism* 28, no. 1 (2002): 1–17.

Benhabib, Seyla, Judith Butler, Drucilla Cornell, and Nancy Fraser. *Feminist Contentions: A Philosophical* Exchange. New York: Routledge, 1992.

Benjamin, Jessica. *The Bonds of Love: Psychoanalysis, Feminism, and the Problem of Domination.* New York: Pantheon, 1988.

Benjamin, Jessica. *Transitional Subjects: Critical Theory and Object Relations*, edited by A. Allen and B. O'Connor. New York: Columbia University Press, 2019.

Boucher, Geoff, and Matthew Sharpe. *Žižek and Politics: A Critical Introduction.* Edinburgh: Edinburgh University Press, 2010.

Butler, Judith. *Excitable Speech: The Politics of Performativity.* New York: Routledge, 1996.

Butler, Judith. *Giving an Account of Oneself.* New York: Fordham University Press, 2005.

Butler, Judith. "Longing for Recognition." In *Hegel's Philosophy and Feminist Thought. Beyond Antigone?*, edited by Kimberly Hutchings and Tuija Pulkkinen, 109–29. New York: Palgrave Macmillan, 2010.

Butler, Judith. *The Psychic Life of Power.* Stanford: Stanford University Press, 1997.

Castoriadis, Cornelius. *The Imaginary Institution of Society.* Cambridge, MA: MIT Press, 1997.

Castoriadis, Cornelius. "The Psychical and Social Roots of Hatred." In *Figures of the Thinkable*, chapter 6. Stanford: Stanford University Press, 2007.

Comay, Rebecca. *Mourning Sickness.* Stanford: Stanford University Press, 2011.

Dejours, Christophe. *Le Corps, d'abord.* Paris: Payot, 2003.

Dejours, Christophe. *Travail Vivant.* Paris: Payot, 2010.

Deranty, Jean-Philippe. "Feuerbach's Theory of Object-Relations and Its Legacy in 20th Century Post-Hegelian Philosophy." *Southern Journal of Philosophy* 53, no. 3 (2015): 286–310.

Deranty, Jean-Philippe, and Emmanuel Renault. "Politicizing Honneth's Ethics of Recognition." *Thesis Eleven* 88, no. 1 (2007): 92–111.

Düttmann, Alexander Garcia. *Between Cultures: Tensions in the Struggle for Recognition*. London: Verso, 2000.

Ferrarese, Estelle. "Judith Butler's 'Not Particularly Postmodern Insight' of Recognition." *Philosophy and Social Criticism* 37, no. 7 (2011): 759–73.

Foucault, Michel. *Discipline and Punish: The Birth of the Prison*. London: Penguin, 1991.

Fraser, Nancy. "Heterosexism, Misrecognition and Capitalism: A Response to Judith Butler." *Social Text* 15, no. 3/4 (1997): 279–89.

Fraser, Nancy, and Axel Honneth. *Redistribution or Recognition? A Political-Philosophical Exchange*. London: Verso, 2000.

Freud, Sigmund. "The Ego and the Id." In *Standard Edition*, vol.19, 3–69. London: Hogarth, 1961.

Freud, Sigmund. *Inhibition, Symptom and Anxiety*. New York: Norton, 1959.

Freud, Sigmund. "Negation [1925]." In *Standard Edition*, vol. 19, 235–39. London: Hogarth, 1961.

Ganis, Richard. "Insecure Attachment and Narcissistic Vulnerability: Implications for Honneth's Recognition-Theoretic Reconstruction of Psychoanalysis." *Critical Horizons* 16, no. 4 (2015): 329–51.

Green, André. *Key Ideas for a Contemporary Psychoanalysis: Recognition and Misrecognition of the Unconscious*. London: Routledge, 2005.

Green, André. *Le Travail du Négatif*. Paris: Editions de Minuit, 2011.

Green, André. *Propédeutique: La métapsychologie revisitée*. Paris: Champ Vallon, 1995.

Haber, Stéphane. *Freud et la Théorie sociale*. Paris: La Dispute, 2012.

Haber, Stéphane. *L'Aliénation: Vie sociale et expérience de la dépossession*. Paris: PUF, 2007.

Haber, Stéphane. *L'Homme dépossédé: Une tradition critique de Marx à Honneth*. Paris: CNRS Editions, 2009.

Haber, Stéphane. *Penser le néocapitalisme: Vie, capital et aliénation*. Paris: Les Prairies Ordinaires, 2013.

Habermas, Jürgen. "Individuation through Socialization." In *Postmetaphysical Thinking*, 149–203. Cambridge, MA: MIT Press, 1992.

Habermas, Jürgen. *Moral Consciousness and Communicative Action*. Oxford: Polity, 1992.

Habermas, Jürgen. *The Theory of Communicative Action*. Vol. 2, *Lifeworld and System: A Critique of Functionalist Reason*. Boston: Beacon, 1985.

Hegel, Georg Wilhelm Friedrich. *Philosophy of Mind*. Translated by W. Wallace & A. V. Miller. Revised with an introduction by Michael Inwood. Oxford: Clarendon, 2007.

Honneth, Axel. "Appropriating Freedom: Freud's Conception of Individual Self-Relation." In *Pathologies of Reason: On the Legacy of Critical Theory*, 126–45. New York: Columbia University Press, 2009.

Honneth, Axel. "The Possibility of a Disclosing Critique of Society: The Dialectic of Enlightenment in Light of Current Debates in Social Criticism." In *Disrespect: The Normative Foundations of Critical Theory*, S. 49–62. Cambridge: Polity, 2007.

Honneth, Axel. "The Work of Negativity: A Recognition-Theoretical Revision of Psychoanalysis." In *The I in We: Studies in the Theory of Recognition*, S. 193–96. Cambridge: Polity, 2012.

Ikäheimo, Heikki. "Holism and Normative Essentialism in Hegel's Social Ontology." In *Recognition and Social Ontology*, edited by H. Ikäheimo and A. Laitinen, 145–210. Leiden: Brill, 2011.

Lacan, Jacques. *Écrits: The First Complete Edition in English*. London: Norton, 2007.

Malabou, Catherine. "Impossible Recognition: Lacan, Butler, Zizek." In *Recognition Theory and Contemporary French Moral and Political Philosophy*, edited by M. Bankovsky and A. Le Goff, 41–53. Manchester: Manchester University Press, 2012.

Markell, Patchen. *Bound by Recognition*. Princeton, NJ: Princeton University Press, 2003.

Marx, Karl. *Capital*. Vol. 1. London: Penguin, 1990.

McNay, Lois. *Against Recognition*. Cambridge: Polity, 2008.

Oliver, Kelly. *Witnessing: Beyond Recognition*. Minneapolis: University of Minnesota Press, 2001.

Owen, David. "Foucault, Tully and Agonistic Struggles Over Recognition." In *Recognition Theory and Contemporary French Moral and Political*

Philosophy, edited by M. Bankovsky and A. Le Goff., 88–108. Manchester: Manchester University Press, 2012.

Renault, Emmanuel. *L'Expérience de l'Injustice: Reconnaissance et Clinique de l'Injustice*. Paris: La Découverte, 2004.

Rosa, Hartmut. *Weltbeziehungen im Zeitalter der Beschleunigung*. Berlin: Suhrkamp, 2013.

Searles, Harold. *The Nonhuman Environment in Normal Development and in Schizophrenia*. New York: International Universities Press, 1960.

Tully, James. "Recognition and Dialogue: The Emergence of a New Field." *Critical Review of International Social and Political Philosophy* 7, no. 3 (2004): 84–106.

Tully, James. "Struggles Over Distribution and Recognition." *Constellations* 7, no. 4 (2000): 469–82.

Žižek, Slavoj. *The Sublime Object of Ideology*. London: Verso, 1989.

11

BEYOND NEEDS

Recognition, Conflict, and the Limits of Institutionalization

ROBIN CELIKATES

The claim that individuals need recognition seems intuitively plausible and has acquired the character of a commonplace in recent philosophical discussions. For example, it is often argued, in a broadly Hegelian spirit, that agency—being an agent—has to be understood not as a given, but as a status or an achievement, in any case as something that depends (in both its social-ontological and normative dimensions) on social conditions of possibility among which relations of recognition take pride of place.

In the existing literature on both recognition and needs, however, the claim that there is a basic need for recognition is rarely explicitly spelled out and defended. In what follows, I address some of the problems that contemporary theories of recognition face in explaining the link between needs and recognition in terms of conditions of agency. The chapter has three parts: I will first sketch how this link can be conceived of, and discuss the extent to which recognition itself can be understood as a basic human need. Starting from an idea that is prominent in the work of Charles Taylor and Axel Honneth, namely that recognition is a basic human need in the sense that it is something that it is necessary for human beings to have, I will then discuss the implications of this anthropological claim about recognition as a condition of agency. After having pointed out some of the problems such an understanding of recognition has to confront, I will, in the last step, argue for a negative, minimalist, and proceduralist approach that focuses on misrecognition, and conceives of recognition as primarily directed at the status of agents as parties in struggles for and over recognition. Rather than providing a full-blown alternative to Honneth's account—the most prominent and systematic theory of recognition yet—I understand this approach as emphasizing and spelling out those aspects of his account that highlight the role of struggles rather than needs, and thereby allow for a more systematic acknowledgment of the ambivalence of actually existing forms of recognition.

WHAT IS THE 'NEED FOR RECOGNITION' A NEED FOR?

In his influential 1992 essay, "The Politics of Recognition," Charles Taylor makes the following claim: "Due recognition is not just a courtesy we owe people. It is a vital human need. . . . What has come about with the modern age is not the need for recognition but the conditions in which the attempt to be recognized can fail. That is why the need is now acknowledged for the first time."[1] The claim that recognition is a "vital human need" sounds intuitively appealing—but Taylor more or less relies on this intuitive appeal without giving it much further thought. Instead of spelling out how to understand it, he addresses the changing circumstances under which this apparently ahistorical need has, in his view, become so politically pertinent. In what follows, I am not directly interested in the politics of recognition. Instead, I would like to take a step back and ask, "What is the 'need for recognition' a need for?"[2]

In order to give an initial answer to this question, I will quickly and very schematically sketch some of the main theses of the theory of recognition as developed primarily by Honneth in his attempt to renew the tradition of Frankfurt School critical theory.[3] As we will see, individual needs play a somewhat ambivalent role in this theoretical framework, one that stands in a relation of tension with its claim of being grounded in contemporary struggles for recognition.

Honneth distinguishes three modes of recognition that correspond to three aspects of being a person or an agent: Every person has, firstly, concrete needs and desires she seeks to realize in the intimate relationships of friendship, love, and family; secondly, every person has a claim to moral and legal respect, more precisely to equal status as a citizen that can only be realized in legal relations between bearers of rights that are expressing moral and legal respect for each other; and thirdly, every person has distinct abilities and achievements that earn her, if all goes well, social esteem and integrate her into communal webs of solidarity. These three modes of recognition make possible three basic practical self-relations that are seen as constitutive for being an autonomous agent, namely self-confidence, self-respect, and self-esteem. Following Hegel, Honneth claims that in modern societies these relations of recognition are institutionalized in three social spheres of recognition, namely the family; law and the state; and civil society and the market economy. They make up what, in his more recent work and in characteristically Hegelian terminology, Honneth calls "democratic ethical life" (*demokratische Sittlichkeit*), that is, that set of dynamic practices and institutions which both already realizes recognition and freedom, and enables its own transformation from a partial realization toward a more comprehensive realization of recognition and freedom, thus making moral and social progress possible.[4]

In order to achieve a clearer understanding of the link between needs, recognition, and agency, we should now quickly look in more detail at the three modes of recognition one by one. First, there is *love* and the relation of *self-confidence* that it enables. In a sense, love is the most fundamental form of recognition, since it is, as Honneth puts it, "conceptually and genetically prior to every other form of reciprocal recognition."[5] We develop the corresponding kind of self-relation as infants, but we also have to continually renew it once we are grown up, so that parent–child relations, intimate relationships, and friendships can be seen as playing a functionally equivalent role in establishing and upholding the ability of the individual to express her needs and desires without anxiety. These kinds of relationships are constitutive of a very basic form of trust and center on being recognized as an individual with specific physical and affective needs. They are most fundamentally threatened by disrespect and misrecognition in the form of abuse and rape that will, in most cases, shatter the kind of self-confidence that can only thrive in relations of recognition.

There seem to be at least two problems here that are worth mentioning. Honneth tends to treat the love of parents for their children as structurally similar to relations of love and friendship among adults (or among parents and their older children), apparently ignoring or underestimating the degree to which the former is characterized by a necessarily asymmetrical relation of dependence and authority, which seems to leave insufficient room for the complexities of individuality and agency in the strong sense. Additionally, while care and love imply the recognition of the *neediness* of the child, and, following from this recognition, the motivation to satisfy the child's needs, it is not clear whether they constitute a *personal* recognition of the child as an individual in the strong sense (as in the case of love and friendship involving older children and adults), that is, as an individual with a complex and internally structured set of individual needs that are inseparably tied to how that individual articulates them. Rather, care and love in the case of small infants seem to involve what, following a distinction introduced by Andreas Wildt, we can call a kind of *propositional* recognition of the fact that the child is needy.[6] This type of recognition is not merely propositional, as it usually involves the motivation to act in ways that respond to the child's needs, but, again, this motivation seems to be rooted in a recognition of the child's neediness rather than in the recognition of the child as an individual with individual needs in the more demanding sense. This is the first way in which the relation between needs, recognition, and agency proves to be ambivalent: It is simply not clear whether what Honneth conceives of as the need for recognition in the form of love is stable across the different intersubjective relations he subsumes under this label, and the (different) role(s) individual agency plays in these relations.

Second, there is *respect* and the relation of *self-respect* that it enables. Here, the focus is on moral and legal relations (established within the institutional contexts provided by the law and the state) that make it possible for individuals to achieve recognition as persons with dignity, as free and equal subjects on a par with others, and as beings with a moral and legal status whose claims count and cannot simply be ignored or dismissed. This kind of recognition is primarily threatened by disrespect and misrecognition in the form of a denial of rights and of exclusion from the legal community. One of the problems to be mentioned here is the apparent tension between the universal moral principle of equal respect, and its particularistic legal institutionalization in the form of national citizenship, which gives a certain communitarian twist to Honneth's theory of recognition, in turn posing difficulties concerning the status of migrants and minorities in multicultural societies.[7]

Third, there is *social esteem* and the relation of *self-esteem* that it makes possible. The institutional framework for this kind of recognition, which focuses on what the person does, not on what she is, is provided by civil society and the market economy in which, respectively, contributions to cooperative social life and individual achievements are valued and (symbolically or materially) rewarded. This form of recognition is threatened by disrespect and misrecognition in the form of denigration and stigmatization, which devalues individual contributions to society (some of the most pertinent examples obviously involve the gendered division of labor and the lack of recognition for care work that structurally goes along with it). This third set of claims also runs into several problems, the most obvious of which is whether the market economy can really be understood as institutionalizing the achievement principle, and whether that principle can be operationalized at all—given the difficulties in separating what are ultimately undeserved talents (marketable skills that are the results of the morally arbitrary "lottery of nature" or of social privilege) and truly individual achievements due to the subject's own efforts.[8]

The most relevant points regarding these three modes of recognition are nicely summed up in the following quote from Honneth's contribution to the exchange with Nancy Fraser: "In intimate relationships, marked by practices of mutual affection and concern, they [subjects] are able to understand themselves as individuals with their own needs; in legal relations, which unfold according to the model of mutually granted equal rights (and duties), they learn to understand themselves as legal persons owed the same autonomy as all other members of society; and, finally, in loose-knit social relations—in which, dominated by a one-sided interpretation of the achievement principle, there is competition for professional status—they in principle learn to understand themselves as subjects possessing capabilities and talents that are valuable for society."[9]

In order to make sense of what Honneth often refers to as the developmental and progressive potential of the different modes of recognition, they have to be understood as internally conflictual and dynamic (not static or stable). Recognition is therefore not to be thought of as a state that could be achieved once and for all, on an individual or social level, and then just enjoyed. The internally conflictual, and dynamic or progressive structure of recognition can be traced back to two ways in which recognition is linked to conflict. First, the differentiation of the abovementioned institutionalized spheres of recognition—the family, the state, and civil society—is itself not an ahistorical given, but the outcome of a historical process which is driven by struggles for recognition. Second, within these three spheres, the extension and reinterpretation of the principles of recognition—love, respect, and esteem—is again the outcome of a dynamic of progress that leads to more inclusive (in terms of the subjects who are recognized) and more differentiated (in terms of the qualities of these subjects that are recognized) forms of recognition, and is driven by struggles for recognition as well. Accordingly, the degree of inclusivity and individualization of relations of recognition can serve as the immanent standard for their critical evaluation.[10]

This last point can be spelled out as follows for the three modes of recognition.[11] With regard to *love*, progress can be understood as the inclusion of newly developed or previously ignored or marginalized individual needs by appeal to mutually attested love, demanding a different or expanded form of care (think of the needs of children with disabilities). With regard to moral and legal *respect*, it would require showing how previously excluded individuals and groups deserve legal recognition, or how facts that have been unduly neglected call for a differentiation of legal principles on the basis of the idea of equality (think of irregularized migrants or, again, people with disabilities). And with regard to *social esteem* it consists in demanding greater social esteem, and at the same time a redistribution of (material) resources for unduly neglected or underappreciated activities and individual capacities by appeal to the achievement principle (think of care work at home or in the family).

This analysis raises at least two fundamental questions, the first concerning the source of this conflictual dynamic, and the second the role of needs.[12] Let us first turn to the question of the source of conflicts: How should we understand the kind of conflict that leads to the extension and reinterpretation of the principles of recognition in the direction of greater inclusivity and individualization? Honneth's approach provides two conflicting answers, both of which seem to run into problems. A first possibility, which he takes from psychoanalysis, is that "one might be able to trace the fact that relations of recognition are permanently marked by the possibility of conflict back to the need to rebel against all forms of 'recognized' independence of the other, in order to recreate the original situation of guaranteed, secure symbiosis."[13] But the assumption that there is such a pre- and antisocial need, a longing for an original state of fusion, anchored in human nature, that generates the agonistic or conflictual character of relations of recognition, seems too speculative and psychological to be entirely convincing given the intersubjectivist framework—a problem Honneth himself points to in his critical exchange with Joel Whitebook.[14] Another possibility, more openly embraced by Honneth, is to point to the gap between the normative content of the principles of recognition and their always deficient social institutionalization, and to argue that "the demand for social recognition always possesses a surplus of validity and therefore in the long run brings about an increase in the quality of social integration."[15] Again, however, this claim seems rather speculative and too teleological for an approach that claims social-theoretical plausibility: as if the *telos* of reciprocal recognition was already part of every order of recognition, somehow unfolding a normative dynamic that sets in motion a historical process of moral progress. One problem with this picture is that it tends to leave little room for the agency of those who are struggling for recognition and thus risks missing important features of the struggle for and over recognition that Honneth set out to conceptualize—a problem to which I will return in the last section. Furthermore, even if one acknowledges that such a gap exists and opens up the possibility of struggles for recognition,[16] one might still wonder where the motivation for engaging in such struggles comes from, and how exactly the moral experience of misrecognition in combination with an awareness of this gap comes to fuel those struggles. It seems that the theory of recognition stands in need of a more systematic account of how the experience of misrecognition is translated into collectively shared interpretations and claims, and of how these claims are translated into more or less organized social movements—but also of how structural obstacles can come to block this process of translation from being effective or getting off the ground in the first place.[17]

Whichever answer to the question about the source of the conflictual dynamic will turn out to be most convincing, the theory of recognition is also ambivalent when it comes to the role of needs. Needs play a role on two levels. As we saw, need is the object of one kind of recognition, namely love, and, at the same time, there seems to be a need for recognition in all three dimensions, but the relation between these two ways of using the concept of need is not immediately clear. In addition, there is the question of the historical variability and plasticity of needs. Needs do not seem to be historically invariant anthropological features, just waiting to be discovered and attended to.[18] As Honneth acknowledges, even with regard to the most basic, and most directly needs-centered dimension of love, historical research has shown how the marking off of childhood and the emergence of "bourgeois" love marriage shaped and transformed what it means to receive care as an infant or a partner.[19] Similarly, what it means to be respected as a moral subject and agent, or to be esteemed as a member of society with socially valuable traits and abilities, has changed as well (and in a variety of ways that cannot be neatly assigned to the two dimensions of inclusion and individualization). Rather than understanding this historical process as a process of the discovery of needs earlier epochs failed to attend to, it might more plausibly be construed as a process in which human beings, on the basis of historically specific experiences, came to understand themselves in a certain way (for example, as aspiring to a certain kind of individuality). Even though one might still argue that individuals invariantly depend on, and in this sense need, recognition, the historical (and cultural) variability of the concrete form these needs assume imposes a heavy theoretical burden on such general claims. Furthermore, this emphasis on the historicity of needs seems to be in line with the historicist turn—a turn away from a more anthropologically grounded understanding of recognition—characterizing Honneth's more recent work.[20]

Against this background the following question arises: what specifically is the need for recognition supposed to be a need for, or, to put it in other terms, what is recognition a necessary condition for? There are several familiar candidates that one finds in the literature (all of them also make their appearance in Honneth's work), among them subjectivity/personhood, practical identity/personal integrity/self-realization, human flourishing, a specifically human way of life, and autonomous agency. Whichever of these one accords fundamental relevance to, it is important to note that recognition is always (although by no means always explicitly) seen as a condition in a double sense: as a condition for *developing* this kind of self-relation, and the set of capacities that go along with it; and as a condition for *maintaining* it (once one has acquired it). For example, subjects do not only have to acquire the capacity for leading an autonomous life (or the relevant set of capacities), they also have to be able to maintain and to exercise this capacity over time—and recognition is a condition for both.[21] Accordingly, there is a need for recognition not just during the period of the formation of these capacities (infancy and childhood), but also during the whole course of one's life. In the next section, I will turn to the understanding of recognition as a condition for autonomous agency, because this tends to be seen as a particularly clear case often focused on in the literature.

THE NEED FOR RECOGNITION AND THE CONDITIONS OF AGENCY

According to a common understanding of "basic needs," if there is a basic need for recognition, individuals experience serious harm in case that need is not satisfied. As David Wiggins puts it in an influential formulation, "a person needs x [absolutely] if and only if, whatever morally and socially acceptable variation it is (economically, technologically, politically, historically . . . etc.) possible to envisage occurring within the relevant time span, he will be harmed if he goes without x," and "y's need for x is *basic* just if what excludes futures in which y remains unharmed despite his not having x are laws of nature, unalterable and invariable environmental facts, or facts about human constitution."[22] Accordingly, if an individual is misrecognized in one or more of the three dimensions of recognition (love, respect, esteem) she will suffer a lack of self-confidence, self-respect, or self-esteem, since these constitutive features of being a person depend upon the corresponding intersubjective relations. Furthermore, if recognition is an "agency need," a necessary condition for individual agency,[23] misrecognition will damage individuality and agency.

How damaging the lack of recognition or the suffering from misrecognition will be, obviously depends on its severity. Also, the connections just indicated should not be understood as describing a causal mechanism that necessarily occurs in each single case; rather, this is what normally happens if people are misrecognized, and what normally happens is partly relative to social context. Recognition is here understood to be a basic need in the sense that individuals need it in order to become and/or to sustain themselves as individual agents. It is important to note that the reference to needs is not to be understood in a narrowly instrumentalist sense, as if recognition was a detachable means to the separate end of being an individual agent. Rather, the link should be understood as a constitutive one: Being recognized in these various dimensions is an essential aspect or part of being an individual agent.[24] On the one hand, this idea undeniably has intuitive plausibility because it seems that, if we are not recognized in certain ways, this undermines our capacity to become and sustain ourselves as individual agents (at least in the usual case). In addition, there also seems to be some empirical support for this claim, for example, from child psychology, although the findings will probably not be decisive.[25] On the other hand, however, there is also a series of problems that such an understanding of recognition runs into. Taken together, these problems suggest that it might be more promising to uncouple recognition from substantial notions of basic human needs.

First, it is not entirely clear how strong the claim that recognition is a basic need is supposed to be. Do the different modes of recognition merely facilitate the development of the corresponding self-relations that are seen as constitutive for individual agency, or are they really necessary conditions in the strict sense? It is one thing to claim that these forms of recognition *facilitate or enhance* being an autonomous individual, it is quite another to claim that they are *necessary* for both the development and maintenance or exercise of the relevant capacities. It could of course also be that they are conditional as far as the development of the capacities in question is concerned, and merely facilitating when it comes to their actualization or exercise (or they might be necessary for a threshold level, but facilitating for more demanding forms of agency). In any case, a distinction should be made between facilitative and necessary conditions, between what is regarded as functionally facilitating and what is regarded as conceptually required. In the absence of such a distinction, referring to the need for recognition as a condition of agency will remain ambivalent.[26] Here, I only indicate that such a distinction is called for, without developing it myself, as this task is best left to those who wish to continue to conceptualize recognition in terms of basic human needs.

Secondly, it is an obvious fact that members of marginalized and subaltern groups have been, and often still are, systematically denied recognition, and that this is not necessarily damaging to their individual and collective agency—an agency that is actualized in their struggles for and over recognition. What is more, talking of a need for recognition, on the strong understanding that implies that recognition is a necessary condition of agency, seems to have a paradoxical effect. As Patchen Markell notes, "if the absence of recognition by definition leaves its victims stunted and undeveloped—potential persons *only*—then it would seem, ironically, that to have a justifiable claim to recognition is also to be unable to demonstrate it, at least without the assistance of those who have already actualized their powers, and so can testify to your equal personhood with unequalled confidence and maturity."[27]

This last implication would seem empirically problematic, since if recognition is a condition for individual agency in the strong sense, then how can we understand the manifold struggles for and over recognition in which the victims of misrecognition are actually engaged in? At least more attention would have to be paid to the question of how much recognition by whom is needed and whether, and, if so, how, recognition by some (e.g., members of a dominated group) can offset misrecognition by others (e.g., members of a dominant group).[28] In addition, the conditionality claim also seems normatively problematic because it opens up what Veit Bader calls "the incapacitation trap": it runs the danger of further restricting actors' capacities by way of theoretically diagnosing their structural incapacitation.[29] This gives rise to a certain danger of "victimizing the victims," of describing them, as a consequence of one's theoretical commitments, as even more powerless than they actually are. In an additional step—not taken by

Honneth—this way of framing the effects of misrecognition could even justify resorting to a paternalistic attitude, since if the capacities necessary for individual agency are lacking, there at best seems to be room for paternalistic interaction ("we," then, might have to liberate "them"). It is precisely this assumption that Ralph Ellison exposes as just another form of misrecognition in his novel *Invisible Man*, when he lets I.M., the protagonist, slowly realize the white paternalism of "Brother Jack," whose "Brotherhood" is supposedly aimed at emancipating African Americans while it really locks them into their subordinate position. The urge to call for an avant-garde because those suffering from misrecognition lack agency thus conflicts precisely with the recognition of those affected and their claims to, and manifestations of, agency on both the individual and the collective level.

MISRECOGNITION: TOWARD A NEGATIVE, MINIMALIST, AND PROCEDURALIST APPROACH

The argument thus far is not supposed to deny the intuitive appeal of the idea that individuals need recognition in the sense that, under normal circumstances, recognition plays a constitutive role in making it possible to live a life as an individual agent—it is simply meant to highlight some of the difficulties one will encounter if one tries to spell out this intuition in a positive way. In this last section, I want to at least indicate why it might make sense to follow a negative (or negativistic) approach that focuses on misrecognition, and that is at the same time minimalist and proceduralist in order to avoid some of these difficulties. As I indicated at the outset, this approach is not intended as an alternative to Honneth's theory of recognition, as it builds on one of its central themes—struggles and conflicts in response to misrecognition—while jettisoning substantial anthropological or psychological assumptions about supposedly basic needs for recognition.

A first line of argument in favor of a negativistic approach can start from the observation that, while most would probably agree that severe violence (like child beating) will almost certainly damage the development of individual agency, it is far less clear what individual agency (or autonomy, psychic "health," etc.) requires in more positive terms.[30] These further claims are usually contested both empirically and theoretically—it is simply unclear how much and what kind of recognition (love, respect, and esteem) is (positively or optimally) needed for individual agency or for self-confidence, self-respect, and self-esteem. What seems clear, in contrast, is that the absence or denial of such recognition can, and in most cases will, albeit to very different degrees, constitute a harm and can thus be understood to frustrate, again to very different degrees, basic human needs. Whether other forms of misrecognition would also have such consequences is much less certain: "Above [quite minimal] thresholds, people eventually achieve the minimally needed psychic capacities for agency and judgment, however 'damaged' they may be declared by psychologists, therapists, and other experts."[31]

This raises the question whether we really need an ideal theory of positive recognition, spelling out how a society would look like that realizes full reciprocal recognition, in order to know, detect, and evaluate what misrecognition is, or whether a rough notion of minimal recognition that starts from the experience of social suffering is enough.[32] A negative, minimalist, and proceduralist approach that focuses on misrecognition takes this second route.

Such a view can initially be characterized by two features: its emphasis on context dependence and contestability (or contestedness). First, on such a view, what the need for recognition consists of, should be seen as essentially depending on context (except for the most basic cases), since the form(s) of recognition required in any given case depend(s) on the form(s) of *misrecognition* to be redressed. As Nancy Fraser observes, "everything depends on precisely what currently misrecognized people need in order to be able to participate as peers in social life. And there is no reason to assume that all of them need the same thing in every context. . . . Which people need which kind(s) of recognition in which contexts depends on the nature of the obstacles they face. . . . That, however, cannot be determined by an abstract philosophical argument."[33] Second, the focus on contestability and contestedness emphasizes that how exactly the link between misrecognition and recognition is to be construed will already be part of the conflict, the struggle for and over recognition in which individuals claim a voice.

These two assumptions fit well with the perspective of critical theory, which has always insisted on the socially mediated nature of all but the most basic needs (whose invocation will be, in most circumstances, politically trivial). Recall Adorno's insistence that "[n]eed is a social category," that the "distinction between superficial and basic needs is a socially produced illusion," and that critical theory must proceed "by recognizing each and every question of need in its concrete interrelation with the whole of the social process, as opposed to appealing to need in general."[34] On this view, we should start from the fact that the identification, ascription, and interpretation of needs are rarely self-evident and beyond dispute, and usually politically contestable and contested precisely because needs underdetermine what we are supposed to make of them. They are the objects of struggles over legitimate interpretations and authoritative definitions of individual and social needs, and this includes the distinctions between "mere" preferences or desires and "true" needs (e.g., the preference people might have for an iPhone and their need to communicate), instrumental and categorical needs, etc. As Nancy Fraser argues in two of her early essays that exemplify these characteristics of critical theory,[35] needs are constructed "according to certain specific—and, in principle, contestable—interpretations, even as they lend those interpretations an aura of facticity that discourages contestation."[36] The politics of need interpretation may be particularly visible in conflicts between social movements and needs "experts" (Fraser herself is mainly thinking of the feminist movement and its struggle against welfare-state bureaucrats' preconceptions of "what women need" and "what is good for them"), but it is also at play in more mundane and less openly political forms of needs talk that individuals are engaged in on an everyday basis (e.g., in families or among friends and colleagues).

In order to take this problematic into account, Fraser suggests a distinction between the juridical, administrative, and therapeutic management of *need satisfaction* and the politics of *need interpretation*.[37] Whereas the former tends to resort to monological and administrative processes of need *definition*, which are in principle independent from the affected individuals' points of view, the latter should be understood as striving for dialogical and participatory processes of need *interpretation* in which individuals can have a say. Once we acknowledge that the politics of needs does not only pertain to the distribution of satisfactions (specific goods), and take into account that recognition cannot be understood along the lines of a good to be distributed in that way, this has immediate procedural implications: most importantly, the possibility of effective participation in the interpretation of needs and their political contestation is a minimal condition for the legitimacy of these interpretations.[38]

For a critical perspective, it is essential to be able to distinguish better from worse interpretations of people's needs. To say that needs are culturally constructed and discursively interpreted should therefore not be understood as saying that any need interpretation is as good as any other—that would amount to a problematic form of relativism. "Ordinary" agents as well as theorists can and should ask how these interpretations come about: How exclusive or inclusive are the relevant needs discourses? How hierarchical or egalitarian are the relations among the participants? What opportunities of contestation are open to them, and is the possibility taken into account that individuals sometimes lack an appropriate vocabulary for interpreting their needs or the means to make their interpretations heard? The corresponding restrictions and constraints can take many forms. For an example, think of what Miranda Fricker calls "testimonial injustice" and "hermeneutical injustice," referring to (a) cases in which members of socially salient groups suffer from credibility deficits due to socially mediated and shared stereotypes as they fail to be recognized as full participants in epistemic, and more specifically, testimonial practices; and (b) cases in which members of socially salient groups can articulate significant aspects of their social experience only in inadequate ways or not at all, given the hermeneutical resources (vocabularies, concepts, etc.) at their disposal.[39] Another, related example is provided by Honneth's early analysis of processes of cultural exclusion that can lead to "desymbolization" and "individualization," where desymbolization results in weakening the ability to articulate one's experience, which is the basis of the successful thematization of social injustice, and individualization, which reduces the likelihood of communicative agreement about group- and class-specific experiences of injustice by either directly requiring or structurally privileging individualistic action orientations and self-understandings.[40] These are the kinds of obstacles that can be understood as being at stake in struggles for and over recognition—and they are the focus of a proceduralist approach that concentrates on identifying and removing such obstacles instead of spelling out a positive or ideal aim.

This shift from substance to procedure also has implications for critical theory's traditional talk of "false needs": instead of criticizing socially mediated needs on the basis of some privileged insight into human nature and society's distorting influences—that is, their "false content" (think of Herbert Marcuse's substantialist critique of capitalist consumerism in *One-Dimensional Man*)—critical theory should focus on the false naturalization, and dominating ascription, of needs. What is problematic, from this point of view, is not so much the substantial incompatibility of felt ("superficial") needs with presumably "real" ("basic") needs—the identification of which relies on epistemologically demanding claims critical theorists have until now had difficulty redeeming. Rather, critical theorists should worry about how "the social mediation of needs"[41] goes wrong, and how it is structured by socially produced misunderstandings and distortions of the status of needs as given, natural, beyond politics, and not open to interpretation, contestation, and transformation—that is, misunderstandings and distortions that keep agents from engaging in the politics of need interpretation that is inseparably conflictual and dialogical.[42]

Against this background, however, one kind of recognition still seems to be presupposed by conflicts regarding recognition, namely recognition as a (legitimate) party of a conflict. This kind of recognition refers to agents' capacity to individually and collectively enter into and take part in a conflict. Agents have to be understood as being able to, and as having the (moral or political, if not legal) right or standing to, contest and put into question claims to recognition that affect them.[43] On this basis we can introduce an analytic distinction between two kinds of recognition: what we can (for lack of a better term) call recognition$_1$ refers to the recognition of agents as sources of potentially valid claims and reasons, that is, as participants in the reflexive thematization and problematization of relations of recognition, including the "norms that govern recognizability,"[44] whereas recognition$_2$ consists of the recognition of agents' specific properties, needs, achievements, etc. Recognition$_1$ is more fundamental in that it is necessary in order to account for the difference between a mere "collision" between competing claims and a conflict or a struggle for and about recognition that is always already structured in a normative way, although these normative structures can themselves become the object and aim of these conflicts and struggles.[45]

Two clarifications are in order. On the one hand, to put it simply, as a matter of empirical fact, conflicts over recognition often get started when the oppressed can credibly threaten violent unrest; in such cases, the privileged often respond in ways not motivated by the tacit recognition of the oppressed as being able to enter into a conflict, but by their aim to secure their position of power. However, once a genuine conflict in contrast to a mere collision evolves, some recognition of the other side as a party to that conflict—and not merely as an enemy force to be crushed by all means—seems to become unavoidable. Conflicts have their own normative structure and unfold their own normative dynamic. From this point of view, and in line with the analysis put forth by Georg Simmel, conflicts appear not as dysfunctional threats to social relations but as particular types of social relation, interaction, and even integration.[46] Struggles and conflicts, then, are not to be understood as mere reactions to perceived deficits in the social realization of the ideal of recognition. Rather, relations of recognition are intertwined with individual and collective capacities for conflict, as well as constituted and maintained in conflicts.

On the other hand, the possibilities of institutionalizing these conflicts or struggles for and about recognition appear to be limited. As Lawrence Hamilton argues, the "inter-subjective power to identify, express and evaluate needs, interests and their formative practices and institutions," that is, the "power to determine needs" can only be realized in institutional contexts.[47] At the same time, it is important to realize that its institutionalization will always have to be accompanied by informal and extra- or anti-institutional forms of political action (such as, prominently, social movements and civil disobedience) that allow agents to voice their claims, to protest and to participate, when—as is often the case in existing institutions—the official and regular institutional channels of action and communication are closed to them or are ineffective in getting their objections and claims across.[48] At least two features of both the struggles for and about recognition, and the institutions that grow out of, or respond to them, are responsible for this situation: On the one hand, struggles for recognition lead to attempts at institutionalization and to institutions in which the "power to determine needs" is individually and collectively exercised. On the other hand, these very institutions can easily turn into obstacles that block or neutralize the contestation of existing relations of recognition, because of an intrainstitutional dynamics of becoming autonomous in relation to the struggles from which they arose, and on which they depend both in terms of their functioning (which is usually not exclusively due to their internal structure but also to external pressures) and their stabilization (which is usually assured not just through practices and habits, but also through struggles and movements). In this way, institutions can end up masking their own contingency and undermining their own functioning through ossification.[49]

While acknowledging the needs of others as normatively significant, and responding to them accordingly, are indeed important aspects of recognition, this still falls short of recognition in an important sense, if it does not include recognition$_r$, that is, the recognition of the status of the agent as a party with her own voice in struggles for and over recognition not only within but also outside of institutions. It seems that Honneth has something similar in mind when he characterizes social visibility as the elementary form of recognition and social invisibility as the elementary form of misrecognition,[50] but also when, following Joel Feinberg, he stresses the importance of procedural rights that protect and institutionalize "the recognizable capacity to assert claims."[51] What is recognized, in this sense, are not specific properties or needs or the value of an individual, but her status as a potential source of reasons and valid claims (as what John Rawls calls a "self-authenticating source of valid claims"[52])—her capacity to engage in normative conflicts. However, Honneth articulates this insight only partially because he understands this status as just another property that demands recognition.

On this basis, it might also become possible to address a criticism that is often leveled against needs discourse, for example by Jeremy Waldron. For Waldron, "[t]here seems to be something *passive* about needs-talk; a person with needs addresses others as a potential recipient of their concern and assistance." In Waldron's view: "A person has needs in the same sense as an automobile does . . . A mechanic can be an authority on a car's needs (much more than the car or the owner can be) and similarly a nutritionist, a social scientist or a therapist can be an authority on people's human needs. . . . The point is that she does not have to defer to the subject's conscious articulation of his needs; she can do all she has to do with an understanding of how a person works (or how *this* person works) and what is the proper condition of human flourishing."[53]

Bracketing the relatively simple understanding of needs that seems to underlie Waldron's formulations, we can still acknowledge that worries like these have their source in the very logic of needs-talk, since sentences like "*P* needs *X*" and "*X* is necessary as a minimum condition for *P's* survival, human functioning, etc." aspire to an objectivity that is, at least in principle, wholly independent from *P's* self-understanding. One way to take these worries seriously is to put more emphasis on the contextuality and contestability of needs claims and to acknowledge, in accordance with this emphasis, the fundamental importance of recognition$_{I}$ in both theory and practice.

So, to come back to the fundamental question I started with: Do we need recognition in this latter sense? As I have tried to show, the claim that we need recognition in the sense that our survival depends on it, or that without it no agency is possible at all, is difficult to spell out, but we seem to need it at least in the sense that being recognized as a potential source of valid claims, a legitimate party to a conflict, is a constitutive aspect of enacting one's agency in social and political practices and institutions.

In this way, the need for recognition points beyond the realm of needs since the ability to participate in social and political practices in which needs are attributed, articulated, and interpreted, and these attributions, articulations, and interpretations are contested, is essential to recognition$_I$.

Relations of recognition turn ideological if they deny their essentially conflictual character, for instance in claiming to respond to, or realize, presumably ahistorically given needs. For this reason, it is often precisely the denial of their conflictual character that struggles for and over recognition have to target in the first place. These conflicts, in turn, play an important heuristic and epistemic role in that they can serve as the starting point for a critical theory that is not formulated in the name of a substantial account of human needs. They can also serve as a reminder that the struggle for recognition should not come to a premature end, a false reconciliation—indeed, in Jim Tully's words, "struggles over recognition, like struggles over distribution, are not amenable to definitive solutions beyond further democratic disagreement, dispute, negotiation, amendment, implementation, review, and further disagreement. Recognition in theory and practice should not be seen as a telos or end state, but as a partial, provisional, mutual, and human-all-too-human part of continuous processes of democratic activity in which citizens struggle to change their rules of mutual recognition as they change themselves."[54]

NOTES

I presented earlier versions of this chapter at talks and conferences in Basel, Évian-les-Bains, Budapest, Dublin, Strasbourg, Lund, Copenhagen, Frankfurt, Beijing, Rotterdam, and Amsterdam;

thanks to all participants, and especially to Joel Anderson, Georg Bertram, Estelle Ferrarese, and Brian O'Connor, as well as the editors of this volume, for their comments and questions. An earlier and shorter version of this text has appeared in French as "Reconnaissance, conflit, et la politique des besoins," in *Qu'est-ce que lutter pour la reconnaissance?*, ed. Estelle Ferrarese (Lormont: Le Bord de l'eau, 2013), 110–32.

1. Charles Taylor, "The Politics of Recognition," in *Multiculturalism: Examining the Politics of Recognition*, ed. A. Gutmann (Princeton, NJ: Princeton University Press, 1994), 26.
2. See also Arto Laitinen, "Recognition, Needs and Wrongness," and Heikki Ikäheimo, "A Vital Human Need," *European Journal of Political Theory* 8 (2009): 13–30 and 31–45.
3. See especially Axel Honneth, *The Struggle for Recognition: The Moral Grammar of Social Conflicts* (Cambridge: Polity, 1995); Nancy Fraser and Axel Honneth, *Redistribution or Recognition?* (London: Verso, 2003), and Axel Honneth, *Freedom's Right: The Social Foundations of Democratic Life* (New York: Columbia University Press, 2014); for the topic of this chapter, see also Joel Anderson and Axel Honneth, "Autonomy, Vulnerability, Recognition, and Justice," in *Autonomy and the Challenges to Liberalism*, ed. J. Christman and J. Anderson (Cambridge: Cambridge University Press, 2005), 127–49.
4. See Honneth, *Freedom's Right*, and Robin Celikates (ed.), "A Debate with Axel Honneth on His Book *Das Recht der Freiheit*," *Krisis* 1 (2013), https://archive.krisis.eu/wp-content/uploads/2016/12/krisis-2013-1-01-celikates.pdf. Clearly, recognition is here construed as a positive or enabling condition, and it should at least be mentioned that there is also a well-known tradition of negative theories in which—to simplify—recognition is seen as a source of unfreedom and conformity, as dominating, normalizing, reifying, and alienating (this tradition includes, among others, Jean-Paul Sartre, Louis Althusser, and Judith Butler). See, for example, Thomas Bedorf, *Verkennende Anerkennung* (Berlin: Suhrkamp, 2010); Rahel Jaeggi, "Anerkennung und Unterwerfung," unpublished MS, https://www.philosophie.hu-berlin.de/de/lehrbereiche/jaeggi/mitarbeiter

/jaeggi_rahel/anerkennungunterwerfung; and Kristina Lepold, "An Ideology Critique of Recognition: Judith Butler in the Context of the Contemporary Debate on Recognition," *Constellations* 25, no. 3 (2018): 474–84.

5. Honneth, *The Struggle for Recognition*, 107.
6. See Andreas Wildt, "Recognition in Psychoanalysis," in *The Philosophy of Recognition*, ed. H.-C. Schmidt am Busch and C. Zurn (Lanham, MD: Lexington, 2010), 189–210. Wildt, however, is more interested in the kind of recognition the young child is engaging in.
7. This tendency might also be seen at work in the narrative of Honneth's *Freedom's Right*, which presents the nation-state as the successful realization of the "democratic we"—a "we" that he takes to be the presupposition of the democratic process rather than its contested outcome, or preliminary effect.
8. See, however, Honneth's attempt to separate the market from capitalism and to revive the idea of a socialist market economy in *The Idea of Socialism* (Cambridge: Polity, 2017), chapter 3.
9. Honneth, *Redistribution or Recognition?*, 142.
10. See Axel Honneth and Titus Stahl, "Wandel der Anerkennung: Überlegungen aus gerechtigkeitstheoretischer Perspektive," in *Strukturwandel der Anerkennung: Paradoxien sozialer Integration in der Gegenwart*, ed. Axel Honneth, Ophelia Lindemann, and Stephan Voswinkel (Frankfurt: Campus, 2013), 294–98.
11. See Honneth, *Redistribution or Recognition?*, 144–45.
12. For a critical discussion of the underlying notion of progress, see Lois McNay's contribution to this volume, and Amy Allen, *The End of Progress: Decolonizing the Normative Foundations of Critical Theory* (New York: Columbia University Press, 2016), chapter 3.
13. Axel Honneth, "Grounding Recognition," *Inquiry* 45, no. 4 (2002): 504.
14. See Axel Honneth, "Facets of the Presocial Self: A Rejoinder to Joel Whitebook," in *The I in We: Studies in the Theory of Recognition* (Cambridge: Polity, 2012), 217–31; "Omnipotence or Fusion? A Conversation between Axel Honneth and Joel Whitebook," *Constellations* 23, no. 2 (June 2016): 170–79.; and Amy Allen's contribution to this volume.

15. Honneth, *Redistribution or Recognition?*, 174–75. In *Freedom's Right*, Honneth understands the set of dynamic practices and institutions that already realizes recognition and freedom as, at the same time, enabling its own transformation from a partial toward a more comprehensive realization of recognition and freedom.
16. See Christopher F. Zurn, *Axel Honneth: A Critical Theory of the Social* (Cambridge: Polity, 2015), chapter 3.2.2.
17. See Emmanuel Renault, *The Experience of Injustice: A Theory of Recognition* (New York: Columbia University Press, 2019).
18. See Honneth, *Grounding Recognition*, 515.
19. See Honneth, *Redistribution or Recognition?*, 138–39. For a critical discussion of the idealizing tendencies in Honneth's account of love and the family, see McNay's contribution to this volume.
20. While Honneth's early work explicitly takes an anthropological perspective, his later works seem to be marked by a historicist and institutionalist turn to the development of social institutions and practices over time. Claims about philosophical anthropology or individual psychology are almost completely absent from the picture emerging from his two recent books, *Freedom's Right* and *The Idea of Socialism*. This is in principle good news from the perspective elaborated in this chapter, but in parts of his more recent work, Honneth tends to sideline conflict and struggle, making them seem secondary with regard to the unfolding of institutionalized achievements and incremental learning processes. For an antidote, see Axel Honneth, "Is there an Emancipatory Interest?," *European Journal of Philosophy* 25, no. 4 (2017): 908–20.
21. On the link between becoming an autonomous agent and sustaining oneself as such an agent, see David Copp, "Rationality, Autonomy, and Basic Needs," in *Being Humans*, ed. Neil Roughley (Berlin: de Gruyter, 2001), 341.
22. David Wiggins, "Claims of Need," in *Needs, Values, Truth* (Oxford: Oxford University Press, 1998), 14–15.
23. See Lawrence Hamilton, *The Political Philosophy of Needs* (Cambridge: Cambridge University Press, 2003), chapter 1.4.
24. See Laitinen, "Recognition, Needs and Wrongness," and Ikäheimo, "A Vital Human Need."

25. For a discussion of related problems, see José Brunner, *Die Politik des Traumas: Gewalt, Gesellschaft und psychisches Leid in den USA, in Deutschland und im Israel/Palästina-Konflikt* (Frankfurt: Suhrkamp, 2014); and Robin Celikates and Daniel Loick, "Die Diagnose als Symptom: Zu José Brunner's Frankfurter Adorno-Vorlesungen 2009," in *WestEnd: Neue Zeitschrift für Sozialforschung* 7, no. 1 (2010): 171–74.
26. This ambivalence is also present in the otherwise clarifying discussion in Anderson and Honneth, "Autonomy, Vulnerability, Recognition, and Justice."
27. Patchen Markell, "The Potential and the Actual: Mead, Honneth, and the 'I,'" in *Recognition and Power*, ed. Bert van den Brink and David Owen (Cambridge: Cambridge University Press, 2007), 105–6.
28. On the compensatory function of recognition provided by certain countercultures to those who suffer from misrecognition by society at large, see the remarks in Axel Honneth, "Brutalization of the Social Conflict: Struggles for Recognition in the Early 21st Century," *Distinktion: Scandinavian Journal of Social Theory* 13, no. 1 (2012): 16–17. This compensatory function, however, is not necessarily politically empowering.
29. Veit Bader, "Misrecognition, Power, and Democracy," in *Recognition and Power*, 259n60. On this trap and how agents can avoid it, see also Estelle Ferrarese, "'Gabba-Gabba We Accept You, One of Us': Vulnerability and Power in the Relationship of Recognition," *Constellations* 16 (2009): 604–15.
30. See Bader, "Misrecognition, Power, and Democracy."
31. Bader, "Misrecognition, Power, and Democracy," 260.
32. See Emmanuel Renault, "A Critical Theory of Social Suffering," *Critical Horizons* 11 (2010): 221–41.
33. Fraser, *Redistribution or Recognition?*, 45.
34. Theodor W. Adorno, "Theses on Need," *Adorno Studies* 1, no. 1 (2017): 102–3.
35. Nancy Fraser, *Unruly Practices* (Minneapolis: University of Minnesota Press, 1989), chapters 7 and 8.
36. Fraser, *Unruly Practices*, 146.

37. Fraser, *Unruly Practices*, 156. On the centrality of the interpretation and political evaluation of needs, see also Hamilton, *The Political Philosophy of Needs*, chapters 2–3.
38. Obviously, the less one agrees that needs claims are usually disputed, the less one will think their contestability should be centrally acknowledged in both theory and practice. For the position according to which needs claims are self-evident, see Gillian Brock and Soran Reader, "Needs-Centered Ethical Theory," *Journal of Value Inquiry* 36 (2002): 425–34.
39. See Miranda Fricker, *Epistemic Injustice* (Oxford: Oxford University Press, 2007), chapters 1 and 7.
40. See Axel Honneth, "Moral Consciousness and Class Domination," *Praxis International*, 2 (1982): 12–24.
41. Adorno, "Theses on Need," 102.
42. On such an interpretation of the tasks of critical theory, also see Robin Celikates, "Systematic Misrecognition and the Practice of Critique: Bourdieu, Boltanski, and the Role of Critical Theory," in *Recognition Theory and Contemporary French Moral and Political Philosophy*, ed. Miriam Bankovsky and Alice Le Goff (Manchester: Manchester University Press, 2012), 160–72; as well as *Critique as Social Practice* (London: Rowman and Littlefield, 2018).
43. See Georg W. Bertram and Robin Celikates, "Towards a Conflict Theory of Recognition: On the Constitution of Relations of Recognition in Conflict," *European Journal of Philosophy* 23 (2015): 838–61.
44. Judith Butler, *Giving an Account of Oneself* (New York: Fordham University Press, 2005), 25.
45. Hegel can be interpreted as making a similar point in his analysis of the tragedy of ethical life in the *Phenomenology of Spirit*: it is not just that Creon and Antigone cannot mutually recognize each other; they cannot even, in general, in the proper sense, recognize *anyone*, because in their doing they are immediately attached to certain values and conceptions of achievements—they are therefore also unable to enter into a proper conflict, and thus end up in a mere "collision" that cannot be worked through.
46. See Georg Simmel, *Sociology: Inquiries Into the Construction of Social Forms* (Leiden: Brill, 2009), vol. 1, chapter 4; and Robin Celikates,

"Nicht versöhnt: Wo bleibt der Kampf im Kampf um Anerkennung?," in *Socialité et reconnaissance*, ed. Georg W. Bertram et al. (Paris: L'Harmattan, 2007), 213–28.

47. Lawrence Hamilton, "Power, Domination and Human Needs," *Thesis Eleven* 119, no. 1 (2013): 57–58.
48. See Robin Celikates, "Democratizing Disobedience," *Philosophy & Social Criticism* 42 (2016): 982–94.
49. See Rahel Jaeggi, "What Is a (Good) Institution?," unpublished MS. Hamilton ("Power, Domination and Human Needs") is more optimistic with regard to the possibilities of institutionalization.
50. See Axel Honneth, "Invisibility: On the Epistemology of 'Recognition,'" *Proceedings of the Aristotelian Society* Supplementary Volume 75 (2001): 111–26.
51. Honneth, *The Struggle for Recognition*, 120. On the importance of the corresponding democratic institutions, see Honneth, *Freedom's Right*, chapter 6.3. One might argue that the full spectrum of rights to political communication and association is minimally required as it allows those who claim to be misrecognized to have the full freedom to raise their claims.
52. John Rawls, *Political Liberalism* (New York: Columbia University Press, 1996), 32.
53. Jeremy Waldron, "The Role of Rights in Practical Reasoning: 'Rights' Versus 'Needs,'" *Journal of Ethics* 4 (2000): 129–30.
54. James Tully, "Struggles Over Recognition and Distribution," *Constellations* 7 (2000): 477. This implies that struggles for recognition cannot exclusively be understood on the model of the interpretation and reinterpretation of (hegemonic or institutionalized) norms of recognition as they often seek to establish alternative norms (think of how Frantz Fanon, Glen Coulthard, or Audra Simpson theorize the political struggles of the subaltern or the First Nations who turn their back on the existing normative order).

BIBLIOGRAPHY

Adorno, Theodor W. "Theses on Need." *Adorno Studies* 1, no. 1 (2017): 101–4.

Allen, Amy. *The End of Progress: Decolonizing the Normative Foundations of Critical Theory*. New York: Columbia University Press, 2016.

Anderson, Joel, and Axel Honneth. "Autonomy, Vulnerability, Recognition, and Justice." In *Autonomy and the Challenges to Liberalism*, edited by J. Christman and J. Anderson, 127–49. Cambridge: Cambridge University Press, 2005.

Bader, Veit. "Misrecognition, Power, and Democracy." In *Recognition and Power*, edited by B. van den Brink and D. Owen, 238–69. Cambridge: Cambridge University Press, 2007.

Bedorf, Thomas. *Verkennende Anerkennung*. Berlin: Suhrkamp, 2010.

Bertram, Georg W., and Robin Celikates. "Towards a Conflict Theory of Recognition: On the Constitution of Relations of Recognition in Conflict." *European Journal of Philosophy* 23 (2015): 838–61.

Brock, Gillian, and Soran Reader. "Needs-Centered Ethical Theory." *Journal of Value Inquiry* 36 (2002): 425–34.

Brunner, José. *Die Politik des Traumas: Gewalt, Gesellschaft und psychisches Leid in den USA, in Deutschland und im Israel/Palästina-Konflikt*. Frankfurt: Suhrkamp, 2014.

Butler, Judith. *Giving an Account of Oneself*. New York: Fordham University Press, 2005.

Celikates, Robin. *Critique as Social Practice*. London: Rowman and Littlefield, 2018.

Celikates, Robin, ed. "A Debate with Axel Honneth on His Book *Das Recht der Freiheit*." *Krisis* 1 (2013).

Celikates, Robin. "Democratizing Disobedience." *Philosophy & Social Criticism* 42 (2016), 982–94.

Celikates, Robin. "Nicht versöhnt: Wo bleibt der Kampf im Kampf um Anerkennung?" In *Socialité et reconnaissance*, edited by Georg W. Bertram et al., 213–28. Paris: L'Harmattan, 2007.

Celikates, Robin. "Reconnaissance, conflit, et la politique des besoins." In *Qu'est-ce que lutter pour la reconnaissance?*, edited by Estelle Ferrarese, 110–32. Lormont: Le Bord de l'eau, 2013.

Celikates, Robin. "Systematic Misrecognition and the Practice of Critique: Bourdieu, Boltanski and the Role of Critical Theory." In *Recognition Theory and Contemporary French Moral and Political Philosophy*, edited by Miriam Bankovsky and Alice Le Goff, 160–72. Manchester: Manchester University Press, 2012.

Celikates, Robin, and Daniel Loick. "Die Diagnose als Symptom: Zu José Brunner's Frankfurter Adorno-Vorlesungen 2009." *WestEnd: Neue Zeitschrift für Sozialforschung* 7, no. 1 (2010): 171–74.

Copp, David. "Rationality, Autonomy, and Basic Needs." In *Being Humans*, edited by Neil Roughley, 334–55. Berlin: de Gruyter, 2001.

Ferrarese, Estelle. " 'Gabba-Gabba We Accept You, One of Us': Vulnerability and Power in the Relationship of Recognition." *Constellations* 16 (2009): 604–15.

Fraser, Nancy. *Unruly Practices*. Minneapolis: University of Minnesota Press, 1989.

Fraser, Nancy, and Axel Honneth. *Redistribution or Recognition?* London: Verso, 2003.

Fricker, Miranda. *Epistemic Injustice*. Oxford: Oxford University Press, 2007.

Hamilton, Lawrence. *The Political Philosophy of Needs*. Cambridge: Cambridge University Press, 2003.

Hamilton, Lawrence. "Power, Domination and Human Needs." *Thesis Eleven* 119, no. 1 (2013): 47–62.

Honneth, Axel. "Brutalization of the Social Conflict: Struggles for Recognition in the Early Twenty-first Century." *Distinktion: Scandinavian Journal of Social Theory* 13, no. 1 (2012): 5–19.

Honneth, Axel. "Facets of the Presocial Self: A Rejoinder to Joel Whitebook." In *The I in We: Studies in the Theory of Recognition*, 217–31. Cambridge: Polity, 2012.

Honneth, Axel. *Freedom's Right: The Social Foundations of Democratic Life*. New York: Columbia University Press, 2014.

Honneth, Axel. "Grounding Recognition." *Inquiry* 45, no. 4 (2002): 499–519.

Honneth, Axel. *The Idea of Socialism*. Cambridge: Polity, 2017.

Honneth, Axel. "Invisibility: On the Epistemology of 'Recognition.' " *Proceedings of the Aristotelian Society* Supplementary Volume 75 (2001), 111–26.

Honneth, Axel. "Is there an Emancipatory Interest?" *European Journal of Philosophy* 25, no. 4 (2017): 908–20.

Honneth, Axel. "Moral Consciousness and Class Domination." *Praxis International* 2 (1982): 12–24.

Honneth, Axel. *The Struggle for Recognition: The Moral Grammar of Social Conflicts*. Cambridge: Polity, 1995.

Honneth, Axel, and Titus Stahl. "Wandel der Anerkennung: Überlegungen aus gerechtigkeitstheoretischer Perspektive." In *Strukturwandel der Anerkennung: Paradoxien sozialer Integration in der Gegenwart*, edited by Axel Honneth, Ophelia Lindemann, and Stephan Voswinkel, 275–300. Frankfurt: Campus, 2013.

Honneth, Axel, and Joel Whitebook. "Omnipotence or Fusion? A Conversation Between Axel Honneth and Joel Whitebook." *Constellations* 23, no. 2 (June 2016): 170–79.

Ikäheimo, Heikki. "A Vital Human Need." *European Journal of Political Theory* 8 (2009): 31–45.

Jaeggi, Rahel. "Anerkennung und Unterwerfung." Unpublished MS.

Jaeggi, Rahel. "What Is a (Good) Institution?" Unpublished MS.

Laitinen, Arto. "Recognition, Needs, and Wrongness." *European Journal of Political Theory* 8 (2009): 13–30.

Lepold, Kristina. "An Ideology Critique of Recognition: Judith Butler in the Context of the Contemporary Debate on Recognition." *Constellations* 25, no. 3 (2018): 474–84.

Markell, Patchen. "The Potential and the Actual: Mead, Honneth, and the 'I.'" In *Recognition and Power*, edited by Bert van den Brink and David Owen, 100–32. Cambridge: Cambridge University Press, 2007.

Rawls, John. *Political Liberalism*. New York: Columbia University Press, 1996.

Renault, Emmanuel. "A Critical Theory of Social Suffering." *Critical Horizons* 11 (2010): 221–41.

Renault, Emmanuel. *The Experience of Injustice: A Theory of Recognition*. New York: Columbia University Press, 2019.

Simmel, Georg. *Sociology: Inquiries Into the Construction of Social Forms*. Leiden: Brill, 2009. First published in 1908.

Taylor, Charles. "The Politics of Recognition." In *Multiculturalism: Examining the Politics of Recognition*, edited by A. Gutmann, 25–73. Princeton, NJ: Princeton University Press, 1994.

Tully, James. "Struggles Over Recognition and Distribution." *Constellations* 7 (2000): 469–82.

Waldron, Jeremy. "The Role of Rights in Practical Reasoning: 'Rights' Versus 'Needs.'" *Journal of Ethics* 4 (2000): 115–35.

Wiggins, David. *Needs, Values, Truth*. Oxford: Oxford University Press, 1998.

Wildt, Andreas. "Recognition in Psychoanalysis." In *The Philosophy of Recognition*, edited by H.-C. Schmidt am Busch and C. Zurn, 189–210. Lanham, MD: Lexington, 2010.

Zurn, Christopher F. *Axel Honneth: A Critical Theory of the Social*. Cambridge: Polity, 2015.

12

FREEDOM, EQUALITY, AND STRUGGLES OF RECOGNITION

Tully, Rancière, and the Agonistic Reorientation

DAVID OWEN

Within the broad field of philosophical reflections on recognition, we can distinguish two orientations to struggles of recognition: the teleological and the agonistic. The first, running from Rousseau through Hegel to Honneth, focuses on attempting to articulate philosophically the norms of recognition that are required to support and sustain the achievement of *social freedom*. Whether worked out through appeal to a philosophical anthropology, or by means of an immanent historical reconstruction, the role of the philosopher is to diagnose forms of social pathology that arise from nonrecognition and misrecognition, and to specify the forms of recognition requisite to a just and good society (thereby also distinguishing genuine claims to recognition from false or ideological claims). The second, running from Nietzsche through Foucault to Tully and Rancière, sees the role of philosophy not in terms of specifying principles of recognition, but rather in terms of redescribing the social and political practices in which participants are situated in order to enable them to free themselves from the grip of these current norms of recognition, which results in helping participants subject the norms to critical appraisal or contestation. The first of these orientations has received considerable attention in terms of the political philosophy of recognition, but my focus in this chapter will be on the second orientation. In terms of the thematic focus on this volume, we can draw the distinction between the two orientations thus: the teleological orientation acknowledges that historically situated practices of recognition may be ambivalent in the sense of enabling forms of domination as well as self-realization, but takes this to be a contingent feature of these practices and aims to articulate norms of recognition that transcend this ambivalence; whereas the agonistic orientation starts from the view that the ambivalence of recognition extends from practices to ideals, and that the idea of transcending this ambivalence (as opposed to transgressing a particular instantiation of it) is in itself a source of such ambivalence and that theoretically articulated ideals of recognition that claim to transcend this ambivalence simply reproduce it. In addressing the agonistic orientation to recognition through consideration of two contemporary exponents of agonistic political theory—James Tully and Jacques Rancière—I will be concerned to show how they enact this stance of acknowledging the ambivalence of recognition.

The most economical way to illustrate their commitment to agonism is to draw attention to their respective critical reflections on the project of political philosophy articulated in the teleological approach to recognition. In the case of Rancière, the project of political philosophy is seen as "*antipolitical* in the most total and fundamental sense: political philosophy is the name given for a philosophical project that tries to eliminate the political moment of dissensus, of disruption and disorder, so as to establish a stable (and sometimes timeless) social order."[1]

In the case of Tully, his adoption of the title "public philosophy" for his practice announces his rejection of "political philosophy" conceived as the orientation to a just, definitive, and final resolution of the struggle over recognition that eliminates the possibility of reason-based disagreement and dissensus.[2] Both thinkers are thus agonistic theorists, first, because they each reject any theory that seeks to render unthinkable the possibility of an agonistic relationship to the existing social order and, second, because they each stress the importance of the practice of such agonistic relationships. More particularly, each shares the worry that the teleological orientation of the Hegelian approach to recognition, in reconstructing norms of recognition from developing historical practice, legitimates forms of recognition that limit or undermine the subject's autonomy.[3] In this chapter, I show how the agonistic approach to recognition starts from an acknowledgment of recognition's ambivalence as practice and as ideal. However, I also take these two theorists as my focus in order to explore the relationship between equality and freedom in the agonistic orientation to struggles of recognition, since it is a notable feature of Rancière's work that it is motivated by a radical commitment to equality, while that of Tully's is fundamentally directed toward freedom. This raises the question of whether these two examples of an agonistic approach are in tension or conflict with one another, and it is part of the point of this chapter to dissolve this appearance of incompatibility.

RANCIÈRE: POLITICS, EQUALITY, AND DEMOCRACY

Rancière's work is oriented toward a radically egalitarian understanding of politics as the enactment of equality. The pivot around which Rancière's act of critical redescription turns is the distinction that he draws between politics and police, in which the former denotes the egalitarian disruption of the latter as a hierarchical order. Drawing on Foucault, he elucidates the concept of "police" as "an order of bodies that defines the allocation of ways of doing, ways of being, and ways of saying, and sees that those bodies are assigned by name to a particular place and task; it is an order of the visible and the sayable." This last phrase highlights the point that a police order is constitutive of, and constituted by, what Rancière calls "a distribution of the sensible," by which he means that the police order is an evaluative and normative ordering of what is apprehended by the senses—in the dual sense of what is visible/invisible, audible/inaudible, or sayable/unsayable, and what is visible as what or audible as what or sayable as what. The distribution of the sensible thus refers to what, following Wittgenstein, we may call "a regime of continuous aspect perception" (where "perception" stands for the senses more generally). It is this focus on seeing aspects that discloses the sense in which Rancière speaks of aesthetics as being at the core of politics.[4] Rancière defines "politics" as "whatever shifts a body from the place assigned to it or changes a place's destination. It makes visible what had no business being seen, and makes heard as discourse what was once only heard as noise."[5] Politics in this formal sense necessarily takes the form of "aspect change." Following the recent exchange between Rancière and Honneth (2016), we can put this point another way: *a police order is an order of recognition; politics is a struggle over recognition.*

We can reinforce this claim concerning police, politics, and seeing aspects by adducing two further points. The first is the distinction between "police" and "politics" as two forms of counting the parts of the community drawn by Rancière. "Police" is a way of counting that precludes the possibility of any remainder or supplement to the social realm. "Politics," by contrast, is the disruption of this count, the enactment of the claim that it is a miscount, through the making *visible* of a remainder or supplement that it occludes. Politics thus entails "aspect change." The second point is obtained by considering Rancière's insistence that politics is "primarily conflict over the existence of a common stage": "It must first be established that the stage exists for the use of an interlocutor who can't see it and who can't see it for good reason *because* it doesn't exist. Parties do not exist prior to the conflict they name and in which they are counted as parties."[6]

The staging of politics requires aspect change in order for what is seen as an issue of, say, misfortune, to appear as a claim of injustice and, in so doing, constitute the parties to this dispute as parties to a dispute. Aspect change is the necessary condition of the constitution of a common space of reasons within which the claim of injustice becomes intelligible as such a claim. Politics in this sense always appears to involve a double movement in eliciting aspect change—both (1) a disidentification of "the part of those with no part"[7] with the existing order of continuous aspect perception and (2) the exemplification of a world in which the distinction between those who have a part and those who have no part is erased.

To develop and ground these claims concerning the salience of the concepts of continuous aspect perception and aspect change for Rancière's police/politics distinction and, hence, the claim that Rancière provides one route for drawing out the import of these concepts for recognition theory, I will consider the case of the First Plebian Secession from the Roman Republic in 494 BCE. The plebian secession initially began as a protest by the plebs over their debts to the ruling class. When the Senate refused to listen to the plebian demands, one of the plebs, Lucius Sicinius Vellutus, recommended that the plebs secede from Rome by leaving the city en masse and camping on hills outside the city. The Senate attempted to resolve the crisis by dispatching a former consul, Agrippa Menenius Lanatus, to negotiate with the plebs. In Livy's account of the events, Menenius resolved the crisis by delivering an apologia to the plebs about how all the different parts of the body must work together in order for the body to survive. His implied message was that the plebs and patricians were separate parts of the same body (Rome), and in order for the Republic to survive, the two classes must work together. The agreement the patricians and plebs reached was to create a new class of magistrates called the Tribunes to represent the interests of the plebians. In *Disagreement*, Rancière analyzes not only Livy's account, but also a second account by the nineteenth century counterrevolutionary French historian Pierre-Simon Ballanche (1829). Rancière notes that in Ballanche's account the secession of the plebs is "a restaging of the conflict in which the entire issue at stake involves finding out whether there exists a common stage where plebians and patricians can debate anything."[8] Three features of Rancière's treatment of this exemplary confrontation are salient to our current concerns.

The first is the speech that Ballanche attributes to the Consul Appius Claudius (who favored using force to crush the plebians) concerning the report of Menenius that *words* were issuing from the mouths of the plebs when logically the only thing that could issue forth was noise:

> They have speech like us, they dared tell Menenius! Was it a god that shut Menenius's mouth, that dazzled his eyes, that made his ears ring? Did some holy daze take hold of him?. . . He was

> somehow unable to respond that they had only transitory speech, a speech that is fugitive sound, a sort of lowing, a sign of want and not an expression of intelligence. They were deprived of the eternal word which was in the past and would be in the future.[9]

This speech is the response of someone situated within an order of continuous aspect perception for whom the plebian is one kind of human being, namely, the kind of human being who lacks *logos* and whose individual existence leaves no trace other than instantiated through biological reproduction. Claudius's speech act is an immediate reaction to a report of an event to have occurred for which there is simply no logical space within the order of recognition that he inhabits. As Rancière observes: "This verdict does not simply reflect the obstinacy of the dominant or their ideological blindness; it strictly expresses the sensory order that organizes their domination, which is that domination itself."[10]

As a factual report, Menenius's account cannot *mean* anything determinate to the patricians. Hence Claudius felt it necessary to offer an explanation of this senselessness that is compatible with the existing logical space of reasons (e.g., sensory illusion).

The second salient feature of Rancière's example is the experience of aspect change of Menenius in relation to the plebs. It is this that drew Appius Claudius's response. The apologia that Menenius delivers to the plebs asserting the legitimacy of the rule of the patricians on the grounds that the plebs are "nameless" beings lacking "logos" involves a performative contradiction. The act of delivering the apologia necessarily attributes the capacities for logos that the content of the apologia denies: "The apologia implies an inegalitarian partition of the perceptible. The sense necessary to understand this division presupposes an egalitarian division that puts paid to the former, but only the deployment of a specific scene of revelation gives this equality any effectiveness."[11] This action thus serves to "light up" the relation between patricians and plebs pronounced in the apologia as an inequality between equals, as an inequality whose justification is undermined by the very act of offering a justification. The performative contradiction of the apologia is exposed by the plebian response to it: "they listen politely and thank him but only so they can then ask him for a treaty."[12] The important point here is that the plebs represent themselves to each other by conducting themselves "like beings with names." The plebs constitute themselves as an exemplar of *another* police order, they make *actual* another police order. This mode of action elicits aspect change in Menenius. When Menenius delivers his apologia, this act acknowledges the very thing that it purports to deny: the plebians are beings with names (that is beings of logos and not merely biological functioning). In performing this act, Menenius sees himself through their eyes and they see themselves through his eyes. Through his unintentional acknowledgment of the plebians as beings with names, Menenius recognizes the plebians as beings with names, as being just like him; a new world exemplified by the police order they enact becomes visible to him.

The third feature of the secession of the plebs is that the act of instituting an "other" police order is an act of politics (in Rancière's sense) only insofar as it succeeds in establishing a new order of continuous aspect perception for the plebians and creating the conditions of eliciting aspect change in the patricians. This matters for how we conceive of political action. We can distinguish between two forms of activity in that the police operate within a shared space of reasons, whereas politics has to constitute a shared space of reasons. Rancière's theory of political action may be that of "part taking" without legitimacy, without qualifications, and without expectations, but this characterization only underscores the point that political action cannot force aspect change. In enacting the improper egalitarian logic of taking a propriety (property of status, or mode of decorum) that does not belong to them, the political action of the plebians discloses a world in which the distinction marked by the propriety is erased and thus *may* elicit aspect change—there can be no security or guarantee of success for such "democratic takers."[13]

Having grounded my claim concerning the relationship of Rancière's discussion of police and politics to Wittgenstein on seeing aspects, we are now in a position to clarify an important point concerning Rancière's use of the concept of equality and his insistence that equality is the condition of politics. By equality, Rancière does not mean a substantive principle that can be stated independently and in advance of the particular disputes within which it is manifest (1999: 33). Instead, by equality Rancière means "the pure empty quality of equality between anyone and everyone."[14] Because Rancière conceives of equality in this sense, he speaks of it as "a mere 'assumption' that needs to be discerned within the practices implementing it." When Rancière speaks of democracy as the "improper" principle of politics marked by the absence of every title to govern, he means that to acknowledge one another as equals is to acknowledge that anyone at all can occupy the positions of governor and of governed. Conversely, any police order is characterized by criteria marking out those who have title to rule and those who do not.

This brief sketch of Rancière's theoretical position provides a basis for the comparison with Tully that will concern us, but before turning to that task we need to offer a similar sketch of Tully's approach.

TULLY: PUBLIC PHILOSOPHY, FREEDOM, AND RECOGNITION

Tully's approach to what he refers to as the agonistic activity of public philosophy can be seen as involving three steps.[15] The first is that, following Ludwig Wittgenstein, Quentin Skinner, and Michel Foucault, it grants a primacy to practice, that is, it focuses on the practices of governance and the exercise of freedom within and over the norms of these practices, norms that shape the forms of thought, conduct, and subjectivity characteristic of the present.[16] From Wittgenstein, Tully draws out the point that Hannah Arendt's understanding of the practice of freedom—of speaking and acting differently in the course of a language game and so modifying or transforming the game—is not a special feature of politics or a form of freedom restricted to certain modes of human interaction but, rather, is a general feature of human practices and relationships.[17] Tully takes Skinner and Foucault to be the primary inheritors of this outlook. In the case of Skinner, this involves tracing the intersubjective conventions that govern political reflection in a given context in order to show how political actors in that context have exercised their freedom in modifying those conventions.[18] In the case of Foucault, it involves providing a genealogy of the problematizations in the terms of which we understand ourselves as bound by certain limits; a genealogy which is, at the same time, a redescription of those limits. Foucault's approach shares both Arendt's understanding of the activity of freedom as modification, or transformation of games of governance, and the view of Wittgenstein and Skinner that such freedom is a feature of any and all human practices, even the most rule governed, but Foucault also develops Nietzsche's point that this activity of freedom is an *agonistic* relationship. He writes: "Rather than speaking of an essential freedom, it would be better to speak of an '*agonism*'—of a relationship which is at the same time reciprocal incitation and struggle; less of a face-to-face confrontation which paralyzes both sides than a permanent provocation."[19] As Tully points out:

> Foucault's unique contribution to this reorientation in the twentieth century is to link together the following elements: the practice of freedom, the modification of the rules governing the relationships among players in the course of a game and agonistic activity. He sees the modification of the rules of any game as itself an agonistic activity of freedom: precisely the freedom of speaking and acting differently. He asks us to regard human activities as games with rules and techniques of governance to be sure, and these are often agonistic games, but also, and more importantly, to look on the ways the players modify the rules by what they say and do as they carry on, and, in so doing, modify their identities as players: that is, the games of freedom within and against the rules of the games of governance.[20]

Public philosophy in Tully's sense begins with calling into question and concern a game of government to modify it, on the part of those subject to it. In this respect, it is best construed as an expression and enabling of the agonistic activity of freedom, where this freedom consists in, variously, endorsing, elaborating, contesting, and transforming practical norms of recognition.

The second step is that Tully does not attempt to develop a normative theory as a way of adjudicating or evaluating the calling into question of the game of government, and the recognitive relations through which it is articulated. Rather, public philosophy engages in what might be termed "redescription with critical intent." First, public philosophy focuses on disclosing the historically contingent conditions of possibility for the practices of governance and norms of recognition in question, and the form of problematization that it exhibits before; and second, offering a redescription that alters the self-understanding of those subject to it, and struggling within it, in ways that enable them to perceive "in what is given to us as universal, necessary, obligatory, what place is occupied by whatever is singular, contingent, and the product of arbitrary constraints."[21]

The final step in Tully's critical activity is that this "hard-won historical and critical relation to the present does not stop at calling a limit into question and engaging in a dialogue over its possible transformation" but also "seeks to establish an on-going mutual relation with the concrete struggles, negotiations and implementations of citizens who experiment with modifying the practices on the ground."[22] Public philosophy does not aim to speak for those subject to government, but rather aims to provide them with resources for speaking for themselves and, more fundamentally, to elicit the capacity to hear on the part of those who uphold the existing order of domination.

In terms of its implications for approaching the issue of recognition, Tully's public philosophy leads him to foreground and contest two limits on our political reflection on struggles of recognition that he finds to be embedded in our theoretical responses to such struggles. The first relates to the use of the term "recognition" and emerges from Tully's reflection on Foucault's point that practices of governance are norm-governed activities in which the norms articulate the terms in which participants in the practice come to recognize each other as governors and governed, as standing in certain relationships, and form their practical identities on the basis of these practical relations of recognition. As Tully notes, "Norms of mutual recognition are a constitutive feature of any system of rule-governed cooperation, not just of formal political systems."[23] The crucial point being made here is that the scope of the notion of recognition is coextensive with practices of governance. The second point is that the approach taken here to struggles of recognition is not that of providing a theory of recognition. A key difference between theoretical and public philosophical approaches with respect to the working out of the form and content of recognition can be articulated as follows. For advocates of a theoretical approach, struggles by individuals or groups are seen as struggles for recognition in which the form and content of recognition is spelled out in terms of a theory of justice or, for critics of liberalism such as Taylor and Honneth, a theory of ethical life—and such theories will include some accounts of how the goods specified by the favored metric of equality (e.g., primary and secondary goods, resources, opportunity for welfare, etc.) are to be distributed. By contrast, for proponents of a public philosophical approach, struggles by individuals or groups are seen as struggles over recognition in which the form and content of recognition is governed by the actual processes of deliberation and contestation in which citizens engage. The point here is not to deny that struggles for recognition involve the contestation of intersubjective norms (for example, norms of recognition that exclude women from the public sphere); it is rather to reorient our perspective toward struggles of recognition from a conceptualization of them as struggles *for* recognition to one as struggles *over* recognition. Thus Tully holds that we should focus on the field of interaction in which the conflict arises and needs to be resolved. A conflict is not a struggle of one minority for recognition in relation to other actors who are independent of, unaffected by, and neutral with respect to the form of recognition that the minority seeks. Rather, a struggle for recognition of a "minority" always calls into question, and (if successful) modifies, often in complex ways, the existing forms of reciprocal recognition of the other members of the larger system of government of which the minority is a member. The most perspicuous way of putting this is to say that struggles over recognition are struggles over the intersubjective "norms" (laws, rules, conventions, or customs) under which the members of any system of government recognize each other as members and coordinate their interaction. Hence, struggles over recognition are always struggles over the prevailing intersubjective norms of mutual recognition through which the members (individuals and groups under various descriptions) of any system of action coordination (or practice of governance) are recognized and governed.

RANCIÈRE AND TULLY: STRUGGLES OVER RECOGNITION

To begin the comparative analysis of Rancière and Tully, it may be helpful to start by considering Tully's work in relation to the struggles over recognition of indigenous peoples in settler-colonial societies such as Canada.[24] In *Strange Multiplicity* (1995), Tully addresses the question of the spirit or critical attitude that contemporary constitutionalism should adopt to the struggles of indigenous people in order to focus on whether the language in which such enquiries proceed is capable of giving each speaker his or her due. Another way to put Tully's question is this: Can contemporary constitutionalism construct a common stage between the settler-colonial state and indigenous peoples? His argument is that the current "modern constitutionalist" order of recognition—what, following Rancière, we might call the police order—is an order of domination precisely because it obstructs the construction of such a common stage:

> How can the proponents of recognition bring forth their claims in a public forum in which their cultures have been excluded or demeaned for centuries? They can accept the authoritative language and institutions, in which case their claims are rejected by conservatives or comprehended by progressives within the very languages and institutions whose sovereignty and impartiality they question. Or they can refuse to play the game, in which case they become marginal and reluctant conscripts or they take up arms.[25]

We can put Tully's point in Rancierian terms by saying that the struggles of indigenous peoples are seen as struggles internal to the police order, visible to the settler colonial state only within the terms of the order of recognition that it instantiates. Integral to this police order is the view that "modern constitutionalism" is the rational form of constitutionalism, a universalist framework for the just conciliation of groups with diverse outlooks and interests; alternative approaches, such as the traditional practices of indigenous peoples, are premodern and hence lack rational standing. Much of the work of Tully's analysis in *Strange Multiplicity* is concerned with showing that the emergence and development of the language and practices of modern constitutionalism is forged within, and intimately bound up with, European imperial and colonial practice and Tully concludes his genealogical investigation thus:

> While masquerading as universal [modern constitutionalism] is imperial in three respects: in serving to justify European imperialism, imperial rule of former colonies over indigenous peoples,

> and cultural imperialism over the diverse citizens of contemporary societies. When members of the authoritative schools today write about constitutionalism, whether they claim to be universal, historical or transcendental, they do so with the conventions of universality, history and transcendence of this captivating map of mankind. They . . . think that they are tracing the contours of humanity's constitutions, yet they are merely tracing round the "splendorous" frame through which they look at them.[26]

"Modern constitutionalism" is thus presented by Tully as a regime of continuous aspect perception, and the possibility of constructing a common stage requires getting free of the grip of this regime. Having weakened its grip by undermining our grounds for rational confidence in the authority of modern constitutionalism, Tully also reconstructs an alternative form of constitutionalism—"common constitutionalism"—and attends to historical exemplars of this practice that have been rendered invisible by the hegemony of modern constitutionalism.

Now one way of bringing what Tully is doing into focus in relation to Rancière's account of politics is to see Tully's role in *Strange Multiplicity* as occupying a position akin to that of a Menenius, *after* his acknowledgment of the plebians, who is attempting to bring the Senators to see the plebians as beings with *logos*. The problem confronted by indigenous peoples is not that they are not engaged in political struggles, that they disidentify with the existing police order and that, in their daily practices, they seek to exemplify an "other" police order in which the distinction that expresses their domination is erased. It is, rather, that, despite this, their struggle is seen as a struggle *for* recognition within the terms of the existing police order rather than a struggle *over* the very terms of recognition that constitute this order. When Rancière considers the example of the plebian revolt in ancient Rome, the importance of this moment is registered but underplayed in *this* example since, on Rancière's reading, aspect change appears to be easily elicited;[27] however, that is a specific feature of this example that does not generalize. Rancière's view that "politics is both argument and opening up the world where argument can be received and have an impact"[28] acknowledges that this eliciting of aspect change is integral to the successful performance of political action. In Tully's terms, struggles over recognition are always struggles over the prevailing intersubjective norms of mutual recognition through which the members (individuals and groups under various descriptions) of any system of action coordination (or practice of governance) are recognized and governed, and hence such a struggle is successful only insofar as it changes the norms of *mutual* recognition by eliciting aspect change in both parties, and thus (re)constituting them as parties to a dispute in which the wrong that constitutes the dispute is made visible. Tully's central aim in *Strange Multiplicity* is to elicit such aspect change on the part of the nonindigenous citizenry of the settler-colonial state and, at the same time, to disclose a world to indigenous peoples in which their claims can be comprehended by the settler-colonial state, and thus to sustain the nonviolent struggles in which they are engaged.

RANCIÈRE AND TULLY: EQUALITY AND FREEDOM

If the preceding section is cogent, we may suspect that the difference that emerges between Rancière and Tully expresses the distinction between the stances that they occupy as theorists. Put briefly, the point could be put thus: in stepping back from general or specific struggles with the current police order, Rancière aims to reorient our relationship to the terrain of political struggle as such by identifying democracy with the agonistic contestation of hierarchy and differential entitlements to rule in the name of an equality that cannot be codified, whereas in engaging in general or specific struggles, Tully aims to enable and enact "civic freedom," that is, agonistic contestation of the contemporary police order. To substantiate this claim, I want to consider two issues. The first is the understanding of "democratic citizenship" in the contemporary police order. The second concerns the normative or evaluative differentiation of police orders with respect to equality.

The dominant picture of "democratic citizenship" can be cashed out in terms of a "mode of citizenship"—where this phrase refers to both "a distinctive language of citizenship and its traditions of interpretation" and "the corresponding practices and institutions to which it refers and in which it used"[29]—which sees citizenship as "a universalisable legal status underpinned by institutions and processes of rationalisation that enable and constrain the possibility of civil activity."[30] On this view, civil action necessarily presupposes an institutional structure of legal rules, and civil citizens' stand toward themselves as persons who are *at liberty* (i.e., free from subjection to the will of another) in virtue of their enjoyment of the civil rights and duties that compose the office of citizenship under law, to take up opportunities to participate as political equals in determining the law to which they are subject as subjects of a given political institution of governance. The citizen/governor relationship is pictured as an hierarchical institutional relationship which specifies, in broadly contractual fashion, a set of rights and obligations between the parties to the relationship (as well as procedures for adjudicating disputes between them) and is structured in terms of the authority of command. Governors who meet the relevant legitimacy conditions are entitled, within a contractually specified range of rule, to issue imperatives (in the form of law) which citizens are obliged to obey. Not the least of the implications of this picture is that the question of what qualities and competences are required to assume the respective offices of "citizen" and "governor" becomes a central problematic for this structure of recognition.

This is, broadly, the picture of democratic citizenship that both Rancière and Tully reject. For Rancière, democracy is not a structure of rule and citizenship is not a legal status; rather, democracy is the egalitarian disruption of police and democratic citizenship is this civic activity of egalitarian disruption exemplified, for example, by the plebian revolt or by Blanqui declaring his profession to be "proletariat,"[31] or by Jeanne Deroin "when, in 1849, she presents herself as a candidate for a legislative election in which she cannot run."[32] Rancière's multiplication of exemplars of such "democratic takers"[33] points to an "other" mode of democratic citizenship, but does so in a way that abstracts from the historical specificity of modern civil citizenship and of contemporary political struggles. While Tully shares Rancière's rejection of this civil picture of democratic citizenship, his focus is on the articulation of the conditions that gave rise to modern civil citizenship in its historical specificity.[34] Thus he argues that "modern citizenship" became dominant with the "civil thesis of the superiority of institutional rule" that was developed in the aftermath of the Thirty Years War and which provided ideological support to the imperialist projects of European states in the non-European world. The development of the institutionalization thesis, on Tully's account, is accomplished in the early modern period:

> The civil theorists argued that the existing practices of governance and citizenship constituted an informal, haphazard, conflict-ridden, uncertain and insecure crazy quilt of overlapping jurisdictions that gave rise to the Thirty Years War. Civil philosophers, lawyers and administrators explained that only centralisation and institutionalisation would resolve these problems of informal (under-institutionalised and under-rationalised) practices of law, governance and citizenship.[35]

Like Rancière, Tully points to an "other" mode of democratic citizenship which he terms "civic" or "diverse" citizenship:

> diverse citizenship focuses on the singular civic activities and diverse ways that these are more or less institutionalised or blocked in different contexts (a civic activity/contextual orientation). Citizenship is not a status given by the institutions of the modern constitutional state and international law, but negotiated practices in which one becomes a citizen through participation.[36]

In general terms, then, "modern citizenship" as a mode of citizenship is conceived of "as a [legal] status within an institutional framework," whereas "diverse citizenship" is understood "as *negotiated practices*, as praxis—as actors and activities in contexts."[37] On the latter view, primacy is accorded to "the concrete games of citizenship and the ways that they are played."[38] Thus, in relation to diverse citizenship, Tully stresses: "Civic activities—what citizens do and the ways they do them—can be more or less institutionalised and rationalised (in countless forms), but this is secondary."[39] Notice that this general contrast already constructs a fundamental difference in the mode of self-relation of individuals to themselves as citizens. The mode of citizenship formation characteristic of the modern civil stance is of the individual standing to him- or herself as occupant of an "office" specified by a range of rights and duties, whereas that of the diverse civic stance is of the individual standing to him- or herself as an agent with a (nonfixed) range of powers. One way in which this contrast discloses itself is in the contrast between these practical attitudes as attitudes toward autonomy. As Tully notes, the contrast can be cast in terms of the grammatical distinction between liberty and freedom in which the latter but not the former can be predicated of actions .[40] Civil citizens stand toward themselves as persons who are *at liberty*. By contrast, civic citizens "manifest the freedom *of* participation":

> Civic freedom is not an opportunity [to participate] but a manifestation: neither freedom *from* nor freedom *to* . . . , but freedoms *of* and *in* participation, and *with* fellow citizens. The civic citizen is not the citizen of an institution (a nation-state or an international law) but the free citizen of the "free city": that is, *any* kind of civic world or democratic "sphere" that comes into being and is reciprocally held aloft by the civic freedom of its citizens, from the smallest *deme* or commune to glocal federations.[41]

This practical idea of freedom of participation is precisely that of freedom as engaging norms of interaction. Tully's articulation of this mode of citizenship and the agonistic relation in which it stands to the mode of citizenship characteristic of the current police order is consonant with Rancière's abstract understanding. It is, however, explicitly articulated in order to provide a civic self-understanding that can link a diverse range of contemporary struggles over recognition, and a plurality of contestations of the current police order that are already in process, in a common understanding of democratic citizenship as the free activity of "civicizing" relations of governance.

We can develop this discussion further by turning to the question of the differentiation of police orders. It is an important point for Rancière that in drawing the distinction between politics and police, he is not equating different police orders: "one kind of police order may be infinitely preferable to another."[42] But this raises the question of what criteria differentiate police orders such that one is "preferable" to another? Rancière is unclear on these issues; however, any plausible response to this question must be constructed in terms of the relationship of politics and police such that one police order is preferable to another in the normatively salient sense if it better enables the egalitarian activity of politics. It is not simply a matter of capacity to contest the police order—or engage in struggles over recognition—but also the disposition to do so. Tully's concept of "civic freedom," as the ability and disposition to engage in struggles over recognition, may then be understood as specifying the criterion in terms of which we can differentiate police orders; one police order is preferable to another to the extent to which it is characterized by a greater degree of civic freedom.

If this is cogent, we can indeed see Rancière's focus on equality and Tully's emphasis on freedom as expressing the distinct positions from which they engage in their theoretical activity rather than in any significant conflict between their respective attempts to articulate an agonistic approach to recognition. Both share a general orientation to an equality that cannot be specified independently and in advance of this struggle, but is given expression in and through the process of struggle, and it is for this reason that an agonistic understanding of freedom that gives exemplary expression to this egalitarian ethos can also be seen as central to both of these thinkers, despite the relative absence of the term from Rancière's approach. However, whereas Rancière's standpoint (at least in *Disagreement*) abstracts from contemporary political struggles to attempt to articulate this reorientation against the project of political philosophy, Tully's standpoint is explicitly located at the activist level of engaging in genealogical investigations designed to support general and specific struggles against the contemporary police order: to enact and incite the practice of politics in Rancière's sense.

Does the ambivalence of recognition extend from the contingent practice of recognition to the ideal of recognition itself? The agonistic approach to recognition that I have addressed in this chapter wagers that this is the case. It articulates the sense in which a police order is an order of recognition, and hence that politics is the disruption of recognitive order. By drawing Rancière and Tully into a relationship of reciprocal elucidation, it proposes that political action as an egalitarian logic may be understood as the agonistic exercise of civic freedom. By shifting our stance from seeing struggles *of* recognition as struggles *for* recognition, and hence an orientation that calls for an account of what just or good recognition requires, to that of regarding struggles *of* recognition as struggles *over* recognition and hence an orientation that is focused on the construction of the parties to the dispute and the ability to contest existing terms of recognition, the agonistic orientation acknowledges the centrality of recognition to human agency, but also takes its ambivalence as a constitutive feature of practices of recognition, one that is disguised by approaches that imagine that this ambivalence may be transcended. The history of ideals of recognition, as Tully's account of modern constitutionalism exemplifies, is one in which the claim to transcend ambivalence legitimates ideals which enable and disguise forms of domination for some, even as they support the self-realization of others.

NOTES

I am grateful to the editors for their invitation, encouragement, comments, and patience in respect of this chapter. I owe a particular debt to Clif Mark, who gave me very acute and detailed comments on the whole chapter, which I have tried to accommodate as far as possible.

1. Samuel A. Chambers, *The Lessons of Rancière* (Oxford: Oxford University Press, 2014), 136.
2. James Tully, *Public Philosophy in a New Key* (Cambridge: Cambridge University Press, 2008), 306. For a clear articulation of this rejection of finality orientations, see David Owen and James Tully, "Recognition and Redistribution," in *Multiculturalism and Political Theory*, ed. A. Laden and D. Owen (New York: Columbia University Press, 2007).
3. Honneth partially recognizes this concern in his discussion of ideological forms of recognition. However, I don't think that the account that he provides is compelling (Axel Honneth, "Recognition as Ideology," in Bert van den Brink and David Owen, eds., *Recognition and Power: Axel Honneth and the Tradition of Critical Social Theory* (Cambridge: Cambridge University Press), 323–47; David Owen, "Reification, Ideology and Power: Expression and Agency in Honneth's Theory of Recognition," *Journal of Power* (now *Journal of Political Power*) 3, no. 1 (2010): 97–109. The wider issue is also pointedly raised in Amy Allen, *The End of Progress?* (New York: Columbia University Press, 2016).
4. For a fuller account of the way in which Wittgenstein's analysis of seeing aspects shed light on Rancière's theory, see Jonathan Havercroft and David Owen, "Soul-Blindness, Police Orders and Black Lives

Matter," *Political Theory* 44, no. 6 (December 2016): 739–63, doi: 10.1177/0090591716657857, on which I draw in part in this section.

5. Rancière, *Disagreement*, 30.
6. Rancière, *Disagreement*, 27.
7. Rancière, *Disagreement*, 30.
8. Rancière, *Disagreement*, 23.
9. Ballanche, 1829, 94; cited in Rancière, *Disagreement*, 24.
10. Rancière, *Disagreement*, 24.
11. Rancière, *Disagreement*, 25.
12. Rancière, *Disagreement*, 25.
13. Bonnie Honig, *Democracy and the Foreigner* (Princeton, NJ: Princeton University Press, 2003), 79.
14. Rancière, *Disagreement*, 35.
15. For a fuller account of Tully's approach and its development over time, see David Owen, "Foucault, Tully and Agonistic Struggles Over Recognition," in *Recognition Theory and Contemporary French Moral and Political Philosophy*, ed. M. Bankovsky and A. Le Goff (Manchester: Manchester University Press, 2012), 88–108.
16. Tully, *Public Philosophy*, 16.
17. Tully, *Public Philosophy*, 139–41.
18. Tully, *Public Philosophy*, 141.
19. Michel Foucault, "The Subject and Power," *Critical Inquiry* 8, no. 4 (1982): 790.
20. Tully, *Public Philosophy*, 143.
21. Michel Foucault, "What Is Enlightenment?," in *The Foucault Reader*, ed. P. Rabinow (London: Penguin, 1984), 45.
22. Tully, *Public Philosophy*, 17.
23. Tully, *Public Philosophy*, 293.
24. For a much more detailed analysis of Tully's work in *Strange Multiplicity*, see David Owen, "Political Philosophy in a Post-Imperial Voice," *Economy and Society* 28, no .4 (1999): 520–49.
25. James Tully, *Strange Multiplicity* (Cambridge: Cambridge University Press, 1995), 56.
26. Tully, *Strange Multiplicity*, 96.
27. Rancière, *Disagreement*, 25–6.
28. Rancière, *Disagreement*, 56.

29. Tully, *Public Philosophy*, 246.
30. Tully, *Public Philosophy*, 248.
31. Rancière, *Disagreement*, 37.
32. Rancière, *Disagreement*, 41.
33. Honig, *Democracy and the Foreigner*, 79.
34. For a fuller discussion of Tully on citizenship, see Adam Dunn and David Owen, "Instituting Civic Citizenship," in *On Global Citizenship: James Tully in Dialogue*, ed. James Tully (London: Bloomsbury, 2014).
35. Tully, *Public Philosophy*, 288.
36. Tully, *Public Philosophy*, 248.
37. Tully, *Public Philosophy*, 269, my insertion.
38. Tully, *Public Philosophy*, 269.
39. Tully, *Public Philosophy*, 269.
40. Tully, *Public Philosophy*, 272.
41. Tully, *Public Philosophy*, 272.
42. Rancière, *Disagreement*, 31.

BIBLIOGRAPHY

Allen, Amy. *The End of Progress?* New York: Columbia University Press, 2016.

Chambers, Samuel A. *The Lessons of Rancière*. Oxford: Oxford University Press, 2014.

Dunn, Adam, and David Owen. "Instituting Civic Citizenship." In *On Global Citizenship: James Tully in Dialogue*, edited by James Tully. London: Bloomsbury, 2014.

Foucault, Michel. "The Subject and Power." *Critical Inquiry* 8, no. 4 (1982): 777–95.

Foucault, Michel. "What Is Enlightenment?" In *The Foucault Reader*, edited by P. Rabinow, 32–50. London: Penguin, 1984.

Havercroft, Jonathan, and David Owen. "Soul-Blindness, Police Orders and Black Lives Matter: Wittgenstein, Cavell, and Rancière." *Political Theory* 44, no. 6 (December 2016): 739–63. doi: 10.1177/0090591716657857.

Honig, Bonnie. *Democracy and the Foreigner*. Princeton, NJ: Princeton University Press, 2003.

Honneth, Axel. "Recognition as Ideology." In Bert van den Brink and David Owen, eds., *Recognition and Power: Axel Honneth and the Tradition of Critical Social Theory* (Cambridge: Cambridge University Press), 323–47.

Owen, David. "Political Philosophy in a Post-Imperial Voice." *Economy and Society* 28, no. 4 (1999): 520–49.

Owen, David. "Tully, Foucault and Struggles of Recognition." In *Recognition Theory and Contemporary French Moral and Political Philosophy*, edited by M. Bankovsky and A. Le Goff, 88–108. Manchester: Manchester University Press, 2012.

Owen, David, and James Tully. "Recognition and Redistribution." In *Multiculturalism and Political Theory*, edited by A. Laden and D. Owen. New York: Columbia University Press, 2007.

Rancière, Jacques. *Disagreement: Politics and Philosophy*. Translated by Julie Rose. Minneapolis: University of Minnesota Press, 1999.

Tully, James. *Public Philosophy in a New Key*. Cambridge: Cambridge University Press, 2008.

Tully, James. *Strange Multiplicity*. Cambridge: Cambridge University Press, 1995.

CONTRIBUTORS

Amy Allen is Liberal Arts Professor of Philosophy and Women's, Gender, and Sexuality Studies in the Department of Philosophy of Pennsylvania State University. Her main research areas are critical theory, Foucault and post-structuralism, and feminist theory. She is the author of *The Power of Feminist Theory: Domination, Resistance, Solidarity* (Perseus, 1999), *The Politics of Our Selves: Power, Autonomy, and Gender in Contemporary Critical Theory* (Columbia University Press, 2008), *The End of Progress* (Columbia University Press, 2015) and *Critical Theory Between Klein and Lacan: A Dialogue*, coauthored with Mari Ruti (Bloomsbury, 2019). She is currently working on a monograph on the role of psychoanalysis in critical theory.

Judith Butler is Maxine Elliot Professor in the Departments of Rhetoric and Comparative Literature at the University of California, Berkeley. Her work on gender, power, and recognition plays a central role in the contemporary debate on recognition. Her many publications include *Senses of the Subject and Notes Toward a Performative Theory of Assembly* (2015), *Frames of War: When is Life Grievable?* (2009), *Precarious Life: The Powers of Mourning and Violence* (2004), *The Psychic Life of Power: Theories of Subjection* (1997), *Gender Trouble: Feminism and the Subversion of Identity* (1989), *Subjects of Desire: Hegelian Reflections in Twentieth-Century France* (1987). Her most recent book is *The Force of Nonviolence: An Ethico-Political Bind* which appeared with Verso in 2020.

Robin Celikates is professor of practical philosophy at Free University Berlin. His areas of research include civil disobedience, collective action, recognition, and methodological questions in political and social philosophy. Among his publications are *Critique as Social Practice* (2018), *Sozialphilosophie: Eine Einführung* [Social philosophy: An introduction], coauthored with Rahel Jaeggi (2017), *Einführung in die Politische Philosophie* [Introduction to political philosophy], coauthored with Stefan Gosepath (2013), and the edited collections *Handbuch der Politischen Philosophie und Sozialphilosophie* [Handbook of political philosophy and social philosophy], 2 vols. (2008), and *Socialité et Reconnaissance* [Sociality and recognition] (2007).

Jean-Philippe Deranty is professor of philosophy at Macquarie University in Sydney. He works on French and German critical theory, theories of recognition, and the philosophy of work. He is, amongst other books, the author of *Beyond Communication: A Critical Study of Axel Honneth's Social Philosophy*, as well as coauthor of *The Return of Work in Critical Theory*, which he published together with Christophe Dejours, Emmanuel Renault, and Nicholas H. Smith (Columbia University Press, 2018). Together with Katia Genel, he edited the exchange between Jacques Rancière and Axel Honneth, titled *Recognition or Disagreement?*, which also appeared with Columbia University Press in 2016.

Axel Honneth is Jack Weinstein Professor of the Humanities at Columbia University. Until 2019, he was the Director of the Institute for Social Research in Frankfurt. His many book publications include *The Idea of Socialism: Towards a Renewal* (2017), *Freedom's Right: The Social Foundations of Democratic Life* (2014), *Reification: A New Look at an Old Idea* (2007), *Redistribution or Recognition? A Political-Philosophical Exchange*, coauthored with Nancy Fraser (2003), *The Struggle for Recognition: The Moral Grammar of Social Conflicts* (1995), *The Critique of Power: Reflective Stages in a Critical Social Theory* (1991). His most recent monograph is *Recognition: A Chapter in the History of European Ideas*.

Heikki Ikäheimo is senior lecturer in philosophy at UNSW Sydney, Australia. His work focuses on Hegel, recognition, personhood, social ontology, and critical social philosophy. His publications include the monograph

Anerkennung (2014), the edited collections *Handbuch Anerkennung* (forthcoming), *Recognition and Social Ontology* (2011), and *Dimensions of Personhood* (2007), as well as numerous articles and book chapters.

Kristina Lepold is junior professor of social philosophy/critical theory at Humboldt University Berlin. Prior to this, she taught philosophy as a postdoctoral research associate at Goethe University Frankfurt. Her main research areas are social philosophy, critical theory, critical philosophy of race, and feminist theory. Her German-language monograph on ambivalent recognition will appear in the book series of the Institute for Social Research in 2021. Together with Marina Martinez Mateo, she is also currently working on a German-language reader on critical philosophy of race for Suhrkamp. In 2020, the collection *Debating Critical Theory: Engagements with Axel Honneth*, coedited with Julia Christ, Daniel Loick, and Titus Stahl, appeared with Rowman and Littlefield.

Lois McNay is professor of theory of politics and fellow at Somerville College at Oxford University. She has worked and published extensively on gender and feminist theory, subjectivity and agency, critical theory, and political theory. Her most recent book, *The Misguided Search for the Political: Social Weightlessness in Democratic Theory*, published with Polity in 2014, provides a critique of the abstractions of theories of radical democracy. Other publications of hers include, most notably, *Against Recognition* (Polity, 2008), *Gender and Agency: Reconfiguring the Subject in Feminist and Social Theory* (Blackwell, 2000) and *Foucault and Feminism: Power, Gender and the Self* (Polity, 1992).

David Owen is professor of social and political philosophy within the School of Economic, Social and Political Sciences at the University of Southampton. He has published widely on Nietzsche and post-structuralism, multiculturalism and migration, and democratic theory. He is the author of *What Do We Owe Refugees?* (Polity, 2020), *Nietzsche's Genealogy of Morality* (Acumen, 2007), *Nietzsche, Politics and Modernity* (1995), and *Maturity and Modernity* (1994). He is the coauthor of *Prospects for Citizenship* (Bloomsbury, 2011), with Gerry Stoker and others. He has coedited, amongst others, the collections *Multiculturalism and Political Theory* (Cambridge University Press,

2007), together with Anthony Laden, as well as *Recognition and Power* (2007), together with Bert van den Brink.

Titus Stahl is assistant professor of social and political philosophy (tenured) at the University of Groningen, the Netherlands. His work focuses on systematic and historical issues in critical theory, the conceptual foundations of social philosophy, power, oppression, the politics of privacy, and the politics of hope. He is the author of *Immanente Kritik* (2013) and numerous articles on these topics.

INDEX

NEW DIRECTIONS IN CRITICAL THEORY

Narrating Evil: A Postmetaphysical Theory of Reflective Judgment, María Pía Lara

The Politics of Our Selves: Power, Autonomy, and Gender in Contemporary Critical Theory, Amy Allen

Democracy and the Political Unconscious, Noëlle McAfee

The Force of the Example: Explorations in the Paradigm of Judgment, Alessandro Ferrara

Horrorism: Naming Contemporary Violence, Adriana Cavarero

Scales of Justice: Reimagining Political Space in a Globalizing World, Nancy Fraser

Pathologies of Reason: On the Legacy of Critical Theory, Axel Honneth

States Without Nations: Citizenship for Mortals, Jacqueline Stevens

The Racial Discourses of Life Philosophy: Négritude, Vitalism, and Modernity, Donna V. Jones

Democracy in What State?, Giorgio Agamben, Alain Badiou, Daniel Bensaïd, Wendy Brown, Jean-Luc Nancy, Jacques Rancière, Kristin Ross, Slavoj Žižek

Politics of Culture and the Spirit of Critique: Dialogues, edited by Gabriel Rockhill and Alfredo Gomez-Muller

Mute Speech: Literature, Critical Theory, and Politics, Jacques Rancière

The Right to Justification: Elements of Constructivist Theory of Justice, Rainer Forst

The Scandal of Reason: A Critical Theory of Political Judgment, Albena Azmanova

The Wrath of Capital: Neoliberalism and Climate Change Politics, Adrian Parr

Media of Reason: A Theory of Rationality, Matthias Vogel

Social Acceleration: A New Theory of Modernity, Hartmut Rosa

The Disclosure of Politics: Struggles Over the Semantics of Secularization, María Pía Lara

Radical Cosmopolitics: The Ethics and Politics of Democratic Universalism, James Ingram

Freedom's Right: The Social Foundations of Democratic Life,
Axel Honneth

Imaginal Politics: Images Beyond Imagination and the Imaginary,
Chiara Bottici

Alienation, Rahel Jaeggi

The Power of Tolerance: A Debate, Wendy Brown and Rainer Forst, edited by Luca Di Blasi and Christoph F. E. Holzhey

Radical History and the Politics of Art, Gabriel Rockhill

Starve and Immolate: The Politics of Human Weapons, Banu Bargu

The Highway of Despair: Critical Theory After Hegel, Robyn Marasco

A Political Economy of the Senses: Neoliberalism, Reification, Critique,
Anita Chari

The End of Progress: Decolonizing the Normative Foundations of Critical Theory, Amy Allen

Recognition or Disagreement: A Critical Encounter on the Politics of Freedom, Equality, and Identity, Axel Honneth and Jacques Rancière, edited by Katia Genel and Jean-Philippe Deranty

What Is a People?, Alain Badiou, Pierre Bourdieu, Judith Butler, Georges Didi-Huberman, Sadri Khiari, and Jacques Rancière

Death and Mastery: Psychoanalytic Drive Theory and the Subject of Late Capitalism, Benjamin Y. Fong

Left-Wing Melancholia: Marxism, History, and Memory, Enzo Traverso

Foucault/Derrida Fifty Years Later: The Futures of Genealogy, Deconstruction, and Politics, edited by Olivia Custer, Penelope Deutscher, and Samir Haddad

The Habermas Handbook, edited by Hauke Brunkhorst, Regina Kreide, and Cristina Lafont

Birth of a New Earth: The Radical Politics of Environmentalism,
Adrian Parr

Genealogies of Terrorism: Revolution, State Violence, Empire,
Verena Erlenbusch-Anderson

The Practice of Political Theory: Rorty and Continental Thought,
Clayton Chin

Queer Terror: Life, Death, and Desire in the Settler Colony,
C. Heike Schotten

Naming Violence: A Critical Theory of Genocide, Torture, and Terrorism,
Mathias Thaler

Avicenna and the Aristotelian Left, Ernst Bloch

The Experience of Injustice: A Theory of Recognition, Emmanuel Renault

Fear of Breakdown: Politics and the Work of Psychoanalysis,
Noëlle McAfee

Transitional Subjects: Critical Theory and Object Relations,
edited by Amy Allen and Brian O'Connor

Capitalism on Edge: How Fighting Precarity Can Achieve Radical Change Without Crisis or Utopia, Albena Azmanova

Hermeneutics as Critique: Science, Politics, Race and Culture,
Lorenzo C. Simpson

Critique on the Couch: Why Critical Theory Needs Psychoanalysis,
Amy Allen

CPSIA information can be obtained
at www.ICGtesting.com
Printed in the USA
LVHW010058210921
698253LV00001BA/3

9 780231 177610